THE POLITICS OF COMMAND

in the American Revolution

THE POLITICS
in the

OF COMMAND
American Revolution

JONATHAN GREGORY ROSSIE

SYRACUSE UNIVERSITY PRESS 1975

E 259
R 67
cop. 2

Library of Congress Cataloging in Publication Data

Rossie, Jonathan Gregory.
    The politics of command in the American Revolution.

    Bibliography: p.
    Includes index.
    1. United States. Army. Continental Army. 2. United
States—Politics and government—Revolution, 1775–1783.
3. United States—History—Revolution, 1775–1783—Campaigns
and battles. I. Title.
E259.R67   973.3'1   75–30712
ISBN 0-8156-0112-3

Manufactured in the United States of America

For my Mother and Father

Jonathan Gregory Rossie is professor of history and Chairman of the Department of History at St. Lawrence University, Canton, New York. He has written extensively on the Revolutionary period, and is the author of the *New York Times* special supplements, "The Oncoming Revolution, 1774–1775," and "The Revolution Breaks, 1776," "contemporary" reports of the war. Rossie received the B.A. from Harpur College and the M.S. and Ph.D. from the University of Wisconsin, Madison.

Contents

Preface

ALTHOUGH many volumes have been written about the American Revolution, none have dealt specifically with one of the most significant aspects of that conflict—the role played by factionalism within both Congress and the army in shaping political and military decisions affecting the course of the war. This is a serious omission. At times, especially during the first three years of the war, political conflict within both the army and Congress threatened the unity of the states and endangered the American cause.

One historian who did take a look at certain aspects of the political conflict within the Continental army and between the army and Congress, was Bernard Knollenberg. Thirty-five years ago, his *Washington and the Revolution: A Reappraisal* challenged some long-held assumptions concerning the American Revolution. Knollenberg presented evidence which brought into question the traditional view of George Washington's relationship with his chief subordinates and members of Congress. Among other things, he asserted that Horatio Gates was probably a far better general than he is usually credited with having been, and that his reputation has been denigrated by historians, largely because of his alleged involvement in a plot to remove Washington as commander in chief. Knollenberg not only doubted that Gates played a role in the plot, but indicated that the plot—the infamous Conway Cabal—may never have existed except in the minds of Washington and his close associates. In the end, Knollenberg concluded that the aura of infallibility which came to surround the figure of George Washington has seriously distorted historical assessment of those men who, for various reasons, found themselves in conflict with him.

My interest was aroused by Knollenberg's work, and I set out to investigate the causes of discord among the high-ranking officers of the Continental army, and between those officers and the Continental Congress. In so doing I discovered that recent biographies of Washington have adequately dealt with many of the qustions raised by Knollenberg concerning the commander in chief's personal relations with officers and politicians. To retell that story would be redundant.

However, I also found that there were other aspects of civil–military relations during the American Revolution that were of equal or greater importance than those involving Washington. The jockeying for advancement in rank by a host of colonels and generals, all with their spokesmen in Congress, often led to serious command problems within the army and bitter battles in Congress. Without doubt, the most significant of these factional command disputes swirled around two of the highest ranking officers in the American army—Philip Schuyler and Horatio Gates.

I am now convinced that the most serious divisive force within both the army and Congress during the first three years of the war was the result of the rivalry between these two men over command of the Northern department. Each had powerful friends in Congress determined to see the man they favored confirmed in that important command. Furthermore, the congressional division on the Schuyler–Gates controversy tended to reinforce the factionalism stemming from the major political issues of whether the colonies should seek independence, and, if they did, the new form of government that should be created.

Specific circumstances made this rivalry for the Northern command a matter of the greatest consequence. Charged with the responsibility of thwarting British attempts to invade the colonies from Canada, the Northern army often played a role that was more important than that played by the main army under Washington. In addition, the difficulties that would have attended any attempt by George Washington to maintain close control of an army operating many hundreds of miles to the northward led the commander in chief to shift most of the responsibility for regulating that army to the Continental Congress. The commander of the Northern department, then, while technically still subordinate to Washington, in fact enjoyed an independent command, answerable directly to Congress. Consequently, when it appeared that the Northern army could not meet the challenge of a major British invasion in 1777, Congress felt free to intervene, to replace the commander of that army, and thereby to precipitate a political and military crisis of major proportions. It is the antecedents and consequences of this crisis that constitutes the central focus of this book.

In the course of writing this book I received valuable assistance from numerous people. I am particularly indebted to Merrill Jensen and Edward M. Coffman who read the manuscript and gave helpful suggestions. Successive drafts of the manuscript were diligently typed by Esther Luedtke and Jean Deese. I also wish to thank the librarians at the various libraries and archives where I worked for their kind assistance. I have appreciated the advice and assistance offered by my colleagues Joseph A. Ernst, Richard H. Kohn, Ronald Hoffman, and Robert B. Carlisle.

Of great importance to this project has been the continual participation of my wife, Ann Hanson Rossie. She typed the first draft and helped me to prepare the index. She has read and edited every draft. Her aid and comfort have been invaluable.

I offer special thanks to Frank P. Piskor for the encouragement and support I have received from St. Lawrence University.

Jonathan Gregory Rossie

Canton, New York
Spring 1975

Congress Adopts an Army

The RATTLE of musket fire which broke the early morning calm at Lexington on April 19, 1775, ended long months of tension. The peaceful petitions of the First Continental Congress finally had been answered by the ministry of Frederick Lord North. Specific directions to General Thomas Gage to reassert forcefully Britain's authority in rebellious Massachusetts resulted in the long-dreaded clash between British regulars and Yankee militiamen. The regulars sustained heavy casualties in their withdrawal from Concord, and to their chagrin, once back in Boston, they found themselves besieged by a host of ill-equipped, indifferently trained provincials.

News of Lexington and Concord spread swiftly through the American colonies and elicited a rare show of military spirit. In the other New England colonies, companies of militia were soon on the march to join their Massachusetts brethren. When the news arrived in New York City, turmoil ensued. Magistrates stood helplessly by while popular leaders seized arms from the armory, distributed them to the citizenry, and urged them to "learn the manual exercise."[1] Similar scenes were enacted in the other colonies as weary express riders spread the alarm southward.

Thus a martial spirit pervaded the colonies when the Second Continental Congress convened on May 10 to seek a solution to the two crucial questions of the hour: Was New England's resort to arms to be sanctioned by Congress, and, if it was, would the Continental Congress assume responsibility for the support and direction of the army gathered before Boston?

The New England delegates to Congress were determined to secure an affirmative answer to both of these questions. In doing so they could

1

turn the still local conflict into the cause of all America—something which was essential if the New England colonies were to survive the inevitable British retaliation. To bolster her request for Continental assistance, the extralegal Massachusetts Provincial Congress pointed out that British retaliation might not be confined to New England. The capital cities of America were, for the most part, deep sea ports and could easily fall prey to the retributive guns of the Royal Navy. If the colonies as a whole were to escape Britain's "relentless fury," then they must stand united in support of a continental military force.[2]

For some delegates—including those whom Joseph Galloway had derogated as "republicans" in the First Congress—Britain's resort to force severed the last tenuous ties between the colonies and England. As a result, secretly at first, but more openly as months passed, these men became advocates of American independence.

But for most of the delegates to the Second Congress, Massachusetts' request for aid created a dilemma. They still hoped that a reconciliation with the mother country could be effected and they wished to avoid any action which might jeopardize that longed-for event. On the other hand, meek submission to the use of force was out of the question. Nearly all eventually agreed that force should be met with force, and to this end even the creation of an American army was justifiable. In this manner Congress could firmly resist coercion while at the same time continuing to seek, through petitions to Crown and Parliament, a reconciliation on constitutional grounds.

Had the conflict been confined to the Boston area, the moderate position favored by those who still sought reconciliation might have been tenable. Conceivably, with the provincial force becoming more powerful, General Gage might refrain from any further excursions into the Massachusetts countryside. Further effusion of blood might then be prevented and a peaceful political solution obtained from a ministry sobered by the events of April 19. Those who cherished such hopes were disappointed when, shortly after Congress convened, reports indicated that actions by both the British and Americans would soon spread the war into New York.

By the middle of April, the British ministry had decided that four regiments of foot—the 22nd, 40th, 44th, and 45th—ordered to reinforce Gage in Boston, would instead proceed to New York to support the friends of Government, secure control of the Hudson River, and "defeat . . . any attempt to send succor to the New England people from the middle Colonies."[3] The colonists were warned of this plan in the *New York Journal,* May 11, 1775, by Benjamin Franklin, who returned from England on May 5.

Popular leaders in New York City were naturally alarmed, and instructed their delegates to ask Congress for advice as to how New York should react when the troops arrived. In conjunction with this request, the defenseless position and strategic importance of New York was ably pointed out to Congress by James Duane. The insular location of the city of New York put it at the mercy of the British fleet, and ships of war could penetrate by way of the Hudson River, nearly 100 miles into the interior of the province. Its western frontier was exposed to the ravages of the western Indian nations, and the northern and eastern frontiers were threatened by those traditional enemies—the Canadians and their savage allies.

Duane further observed that the British, by controlling Lakes George and Champlain to the north, and the Hudson River to the south, could effectively isolate New England from the rest of the colonies. Consequently, Duane believed that "the force of America must . . . be divided into two bodies—one to defend the Massachusetts, the other to secure New York. . . . The army which is to defend New York must again be subdivided—a sufficient number to overawe and confine the troops which may be landed in the city of New York; and the rest to oppose the attempts of the Indians and Canadians."

In this disquisition, Duane, one of the leaders of the conciliation faction, made it clear that the troops raised for the defense of New York shoud be used only defensively. They were to "overawe and confine" the British, but not to contest their landing—nor, presumably, their occupation of the city. Further, he rejected the idea of raising batteries or fortifications. Although clearly defensive measures, Duane believed they would be provocative and lead to "opposing inexperience with discipline and meeting regular troops in their own way and on their own guard." It would be sufficient to maintain an army outside of the city, strong enough to check any British foray into the interior, but otherwise to offer no provocation.[4]

Congress heeded Duane's counsel and advised New York not to oppose the landing of British troops, and thereafter to leave them in peace unless they committed hostile acts or erected fortifications.[5] Congress did not indicate what was to be construed as a hostile act. Could not the occupation of New York by a sizable force, in itself, be interpreted as a hostile act? Also, New York already had some fortifications. Was the occupation and/or improvement of these less hostile than the erection of new works? In effect, Congress begged the question, and the problem of determining the nature and extent of opposition to the British in New York was left to the discretion of the local authorities.

Only two days after Congress urged restraint upon the inhabitants of New York, news arrived in Philadelphia which severely compromised the defensive war policy. In the predawn hours of May 10, a small band of armed men crossed Lake Champlain and landed a half mile below Fort Ticonderoga. Eighty-three men, led by Colonels Ethan Allen and Benedict Arnold, made the crossing in two old scows, and, as the sun rose, they approached the main entrance in the south wall of the fort. This, like much of the rest of the once formidable works, was in a ruinous condition, and the provincials, scrambling over the rubble, easily surprised the solitary sentry. Within minutes the futility of resistance was apparent, and a disheveled Captain William Delaplace surrendered the fort, its valuable store of cannon and munitions, and the small detachment of the 26th Regiment under his command.

Coming less than a month after Lexington and Concord, the capture of Ticonderoga was a significant strategic coup. For a half century the portage between Lake Champlain and Lake George guarded by this fort had been the key to the northern invasion route to or from Canada. With the British holding that key, the back door to New York and New England was open to invasion. However, the door swung both ways. American control would open the way for colonial armies to strike at the heart of British Canada.

An express rider, carrying news of the fort's capture, reached Philadelphia on the night of May 17, and the next morning congressional president Peyton Randolph read the dispatches to Congress. The news evoked mixed feelings. The New Englanders, having paid dearly because of enemy control of the post during the French Wars, readily appreciated the strategic importance of its capture. They were also pleased with the political significance of the move. It was the first offensive operation by colonial forces. Others, including those who adhered to the policy of conciliation and its concommitant proposition of a defensive war, were not so pleased.

The bearer of the news, John Brown, was called before Congress and questioned concerning the value of Ticonderoga and the disposition of the Canadians toward the American cause. Brown, a Yale graduate and former King's attorney in New York, had been sent into Canada the previous February by the Massachusetts Provincial Congress. In his report he had recommended the seizure of Ticonderoga and the invasion of Canada, but had warned not to expect too much cooperation from the Canadians. He reiterated his doubts about the Canadians to Congress, but at the same time stressed the value of Ticonderoga.[6]

In the debate that ensued, the conciliation faction joined with those who failed to grasp the strategic importance of Ticonderoga to pass a resolution which, had it been carried out, would have returned the post to the British. In an attempt to make the capture appear a purely defensive action, the resolution claimed that there was "indubitable evidence that a design is formed by the British ministry to make a cruel invasion from the Province of Quebec . . . for the purpose of destroying our lives and liberties, and some steps have actually been taken to carry the said design into execution." To thwart this scheme, "several inhabitants . . . residing in the vicinity of Ticonderoga . . . impelled by a just regard for the defense and preservation of themselves and their countrymen from such imminent dangers and calamities have taken possession of that post."[7]

Since there were fewer than 700 British regulars in all of Canada, Congress was exaggerating the danger of "a cruel invasion from the Province of Quebec." However there was some basis for rumors that British troops would be sent to that area. Several months before, during March, disgruntled settlers seized control of New York's Cumberland County—deep inside the disputed New Hampshire Grants region east of Lake Champlain. Convinced that local forces could not quell this insurrection, Lieutenant Governor Cadwallader Colden of New York requested assistance from General Gage. If a considerable force of regulars marched into Cumberland from Crown Point and Ticonderoga, Colden believed the rebellion would quickly collapse. As a further inducement to Gage, the governor pointed out that "a body of troops so near the borders of Massachusetts Bay may be very effectually employed in executing the coercive measures which seem unavoidable for bringing the Eastern colonies under submission to Great Britain."[8]

With the prospect of armed rebellion in Massachusetts increasingly imminent, the idea of a force capable of threatening the western counties of that colony appealed to Gage. So, instead of turning down Colden's request (as he had all previous ones), the British commander in chief ordered the 7th Regiment from Quebec to Crown Point to lend assistance to the New York authorities.[9] Hard pressed after Lexington and Concord, Gage rescinded these orders; but this was not known to the alarmed inhabitants in northern New York.

To further strengthen its contention that the seizure of Ticonderoga was a purely defensive act, Congress claimed that it was the work of "several inhabitants . . . residing in the vicinity." This lent an air of spontaneity to the whole affair which was quite misleading. While the bulk of the men were "Green Mountain Boys" from the nearby New Hampshire Grants, plans to capture the fort had been concocted by John Brown and Ethan Allen the previous February when Brown was on his mission for the Massachusetts Congress. In addition, Allen received the blessings as well as considerable financial support for his expedition from the government of Connecticut, while Benedict Arnold was similarly authorized by the Massachusetts Committee of Safety to secure the fort in the name of Massachusetts Bay.

In a final attempt to wash its hands of a troublesome doctrinal problem, Congress decided to demolish the works at Ticonderoga and Crown Point, and to remove the military stores to the south end of Lake George. Although these stores were sorely needed, Congress balked at simply confiscating them as spoils of war. To do so would acknowledge the existence of a state of war, and the more conservative members were not yet ready for this step. Instead, Congress resolved "that an exact inventory be taken of all such cannon and stores in order that they may be safely returned when the restoration of the former harmony between Great Britain and these colonies so ardently wished for by the latter shall render it prudent and consistent with the overruling law of self-preservation."

This resolution was a marked victory for those in Congress who favored conciliatory policies. A number of factors combined to make this success possible. It would have been difficult to convince a majority of delegates that Congress should undertake a northern adventure while its policy toward the British in Boston was as yet undefined. Even under the most favorable of conditions, to do so would mean the enlargement of the conflict, and, almost certainly, the precipitation of a war whose outcome was anything but certain. However, conditions appeared to be quite unfavorable, for the British still held a post at St. Johns commanding the northern outlet of Lake Champlain, and, most important, they possessed the only war vessel on the lake. Thus, the conciliators were able to convince a majority of the delegates of the wisdom of the resolution.

Their victory was short-lived. A few days after passing the above resolve, Congress learned that the American forces had gained undisputed supremacy of the northern lakes. On May 13, Colonel Arnold had led 35 men in a raid at St. Johns, captured the small garrison, and taken possession of the 70-ton sloop of war in the harbor. Until the British could construct new war vessels, Ticonderoga was secure, the lakes under American control, and the way open for the invasion of Canada.

With the major objection to holding the northern post removed, Congress rescinded its previous orders, requested Governor Jonathan Trumbull of Connecticut to send a strong reinforcement to Ticonderoga, and directed that the cannon and stores necessary for its defense should be retained at that post. For the present, the Connecticut delegates informed Trumbull, it was believed that 1,000 men would suffice for the task. In addition, the New York Provincial Congress was asked to supply the Connecticut troops with all necessary provisions and stores.[10]

Faced as they were with a fluid situation in northern New York and Canada, it is not surprising that the delegates found little time to spare for decisions affecting the relatively static siege of Boston. The multitude of problems referred to Congress by the individual colonies imposed an additional burden. Some delegates believed that a solution to this problem would be the adjournment of Congress to a place nearer the army in Massachusetts. They reasoned that if Congress were closer to the army, it could act more expeditiously in adopting measures to regulate operations in that quarter. They may also have believed that proximity to the field of battle would goad Congress into adopting a more decisive and militant policy.

On May 21, one of the delegates from Connecticut, Silas Deane, hinted that Congress might remove to Hartford, but, he added, "no motion has as yet been stirred or made public on the subject, and all is uncertainty." Titus Hosmer, one of Deane's correspondents, warned that such a move might actually defeat its intended purpose: "The removal of the Congress northward is, as you observe, a very delicate point. The union of the colonies is our safety; should it endanger that, although remotely, it would countervail any proposed advantage. I own, I *fear,* were you as near you would have too many questions referred to you, and too much business cast upon you by the New England colonies, to leave you the leisure you ought to have to digest and perfect matters of greater importance."

If Congress was determined to move nearer the scene of action, Hosmer suggested it adjourn to New York. That city was already notorious as a hotbed of Toryism, and many New Englanders believed that the conservative New York Provincial Congress was tainted with the same loathesome disease. Hosmer thought the presence of Congress would have a salutary effect, for "wherever the Congress is, there will be the spirit of liberty."

Joseph Hewes, a delegate from North Carolina, felt that sectional jealousy would prevent any such move. Although he and his fellow delegate, William Hooper, were willing, many of the Southern delegates had not consented, nor did he think they ever would.[11] Nor did they. While the question of an adjournment to New England continued to be agitated "out of doors," for the remainder of the session, Congress never officially debated such a move. Eventually, the problem raised by the press of business was partially solved by the creation of standing committees and special boards, but for now, the delegates struggled on as best they could.

Meanwhile, the members of the Massachusetts Congress grew impatient. Receiving no answer to their earlier plea for congressional assistance, they drafted a second letter on May 16. In it they posed two crucial questions: should Massachusetts assume and exercise full powers of civil government, and would Congress assume responsibility for the army besieging Boston?[12]

For all practical purposes, the provincial congress already had assumed the powers of civil government. However, it was a convention type of government, and, therefore, extralegal. What they now asked for was congressional sanction to establish a "legal" government which would contravene the Massachusetts Government Act of 1774. Such an act on the part of Massachusetts would constitute a *de facto* declaration of independence, and, if Congress approved, it would establish a precedent for other colonies to follow.

To lend weight to their request, the provincial congress claimed that the growing military power in Massachusetts necessitated the creation of a strong civil government to hold it in check. This, it was hoped, would stir Congress to action, for there was nothing so fearsome to the eighteenth-century Englishman, Whig or Tory, as the specter of unchecked militarism. The Massachusetts delegates were given a more explicit account of this danger:

> . . . [The people] now feel rather too much their own importance, and it required great skill in gradually checking them to such a subordination as is necessary to good government. This principally takes place in the army and there being many officers (good men in their station) that have but little connection in government, they have affected to hold the military too high. But the civil must at all events be supported, and unless an established form of government takes place, it will be impossible to effect it. Every day's delay in this matter will make the task more arduous of those who shall fill the places of civil power.[13]

Nevertheless, the army besieging Boston was necessary and some means had to be found to maintain it. Since it was composed of troops from several colonies and was acting in the defense of the rights of all America, the provincial congress urged Congress to assume responsibility for its direction and support.

The arrival of this letter on June 2 at last forced Congress to act. The time for equivocation and half-measure was over, and it now had to decide how far the Continent would be committed to the war in Massachusetts. A committee was appointed to consider the Massachusetts letter and make recommendations. Three of the committeemen (John Rutledge, Thomas Johnson, and John Jay) favored a conciliatory policy, while one (Richard Henry Lee) did not, and the final member (James Wilson) vacillated between the two factions. After a full week of deliberation, the committee submitted its report to Congress, and that part of it which dealt with the establishment of civil government in Massachusetts was immediately accepted.

Clearly a victory for the moderate, conciliatory faction in Congress, the resolution advised Massachusetts to ignore the Massachusetts Government Act and proceed immediately to establish the form of government sanctioned by the Charter of 1691. Of course Gage's position as governor of the province and his orders to implement the provisions of the Massachusetts Act presented problems which could be finally solved only when "a governor, of his Majesty's appointment, will consent to govern the colony according to its charter." In the meantime, Congress recommended that the assembly and council should exercise the full powers of government.

Congress took no direct action on the portion of the committee's report dealing with the assumption of responsibility for the army. From circumstantial evidence, however, it appears the committee favored its adoption. On the same day, June 9, Congress requested the New York Provincial Congress to send 5,000 barrels of flour to Massachusetts for the use of the "Continental army," and pledged itself to reimburse all expenses. And the following day, it recommended that the New England colonies supply the army with all the powder they could spare—again, at the Continental expense.[14]

For many New Englanders, these gestures toward the support of the army were inadequate. John Adams, for one, thought the failure to adopt stronger measures was due to the appeal of the conciliators' doctrine "to hold the sword in one hand and the olive branch in the other— to proceed with warlike measures, and conciliatory measures *pari passu*." Such a policy, he feared, would have an adverse effect, for "petitions, negotiations, everything which hold out to the people hopes of reconciliation without bloodshed is greedily grasped at and relied on,—and they cannot be persuaded to think that it is so necessary to prepare for war as it really is." The opponents of this policy must be patient, Adams observed, for "this continent is a vast, unwieldy machine. We cannot force events. We must suffer people to take their own way in many cases, when we think it leads wrong, hoping however and believing that our liberty and fidelity will be preserved in the end, tho' not in the speediest and surest manner."[15]

John Adams, however, did not heed his own advice. Instead, during the first two weeks of June he strove to "force events" by pressing upon a hesitant Congress the necessity of adopting the New England army. In this he was blocked not only by those who thought petitions the only weapons Congress should employ, but also by a "Southern party" which harbored dark suspicions of a New England army commanded by New England generals. The ultraconservatives, few in number and lacking substantial influence, could be ignored. But the "Southern party" found support in every colony outside of New England, and it was soon apparent that unless a Southerner was chosen commander in chief, this party would block permanently the adoption of the army.[16]

As one contemporary observer remarked, "A common danger has united the colonies; but has not eradicated all the jealousies that before existed among them." The delegates from New York, Pennsylvania, and the Southern colonies were particularly wary of entrusting the direction of a Continental military force to New Englanders. And with good reason, for, while "the other colonists were in the pursuit of an honorable accommodation, . . . they could not be certain, whatever was the case at the present, that the Massachusetts would not shortly aim at separation: it was then a matter of consequence who headed the army."[17]

While striving to overcome this opposition, Adams found himself thwarted by a division in the Massachusetts delegation. John Hancock and Thomas Cushing would not commit themselves, nor would Robert Treat Paine. Even the redoubtable Samuel Adams seemed to lack resolution. Hancock's reticence was at least understandable—he wanted to be the commander in chief!

John Adams later recalled that while walking the State House yard, he confided to Samuel Adams his fear for the fate of the army and the American cause in general. His cousin agreed that the situation was critical, but what could they do? John responded that he had made every effort to get his colleagues to agree upon some plan, but to no avail. He was now determined that they would declare for or against something! Since the appointment of George Washington as commander in chief was the price the "Southern party" placed on its acquiescence, he would introduce a motion to that effect and then move that Congress adopt the army at Boston.

Accordingly, when Congress assembled, John Adams rose and delivered a speech presenting the state of the colonies, the expectations and anxieties of the people, and the distress of the army. He concluded with a motion that Congress adopt the army and appoint a general to command it. While it was not the proper time to nominate a general, he declared he had but one man in mind, "and that was a gentleman from Virginia who was among us and very well known to all of us, a gentleman whose skill and experience as an officer, whose independent fortune, great talents and excellent universal character, would command the approbation of all America, and unite the cordial exertions of all the colonies better than any other person in the Union." As soon as Adams alluded to him, Washington left the room, overcome with embarrassment.

Another person visibly affected by the speech was John Hancock, president of the Congress. While Adams was describing the state of the colonies and the needs of the army, Hancock appeared pleased. But when he came to describe Washington as the man best suited to be commander in chief, Adams "never remarked a more sudden and sinking change of countenance. Mortification and resentment were expressed as forcibly as his face could exhibit them. Mr. Samuel Adams seconded the motion, and that did not soften the president's physiognomy at all."

Although the Journals of Congress show that George Washington was unanimously elected commander in chief on June 15, there were some objections. Several of the New England delegates maintained that since the army was all from New England, the commanding general ought to be as well. Besides, they already had a general, Artemas Ward, and he had thus far proved himself able to confine the British to Boston—what more could Congress desire? Edmund Pendleton of Virginia and Roger Sherman of Connecticut were the most outspoken opponents of the choice of a non-New Englander. Thomas Cushing and Robert Treat Paine also expressed their fear that the choice would cause discontent in New England, and in the army in particular. Paine even rose and delivered an oration on the abilities of General Ward. Consequently, the subject was postponed to a future day. "In the meantime," Adams recalled, "pains were taken out of doors to obtain a unanimity, and the voices were generally so clearly in favor of Washington that the dissentient members were persuaded to withdraw their opposition, and Mr. Washington was nominated, I believe by Mr. Thomas Johnson of Maryland, unanimously elected, and the army adopted."[18]

If concern over the consequences of Washington's election was genuine, it was ill founded. Elbridge Gerry had informed the Massachusetts delegates on June 4, 1775, that he and Joseph Warren would "heartily rejoice to see this way, the renowned and beloved General Washington, with forces, and doubt not that the New England generals would acquiesce in having shown to our sister colony of Virginia, which ranks highest in numbers, the respect which it has before experienced from the Continent, by making him their generalissimo."

Nevertheless, some of the New England delegates were still apprehensive. One of these, Eliphalet Dyer of Connecticut, took pains to explain the choice of Washington to General Spencer and Joseph Trumbull, Commander and Commissary, respectively, of the Connecticut contingent in the Army of Observation. "He is a gentleman," Dyer informed them, "highly esteemed by those acquainted with him tho' I don't believe as to his military and for real service he knows more than some of ours." However, his election was "absolutely necessary in point of prudence," for "it removes all jealousies, more firmly cements the Southern to the Northern, and takes away the fear of the former lest an enterprising eastern New England general proving successful, might with his victorious army give the law to the Southern and Western gentry." All things considered, Dyer thought that Washington should be popular with the New Englanders, for "he is clever, and if anything too modest." Also, he was far from the stereotyped, frivolous Southern gentleman, but instead "discreet and virtuous, no harum skarum ranting swearing fellow but sober, steady and calm."[19]

Most of the concern expressed about Washington's compatibility with the New Englanders was unjustified, and all of it was misdirected. They were to find him much more acceptable than he found them.

In addition to electing a commander in chief, Congress also pledged itself to maintain an army of 15,000 men in Massachusetts, and another of 5,000 men in New York. It then turned to the difficult business of choosing the Continental general officers who would serve under Washington. According to the plan of organization, adopted on June 16, there were to be two major generals, five brigadier generals, and an adjutant general.[20] If the election of Washington was attended by some display of provincial jealousies, it was nothing compared with what now ensued. When the appointments had finally been made, John Adams wearily reported that "nothing has given . . . more torment, than the scuffle we have had in appointing the general officers.[21]

It seemed reasonable to assume that General Ward, who had enjoyed the chief command until the election of Washington, would be chosen second in command of the new Continental army. He was highly esteemed by most New Englanders, and, although rather on the portly side, he was relatively young and in good health. Moreover, he had served with some distinction during the French and Indian War, and, thus far, had acquitted himself well in directing the operations in Massachusetts. However, there were some doubts concerning his ability to command an army. Thus, while he was chosen "first major general," he was not designated second in command.[22]

The next position to be filled, that of adjutant general, caused no difficulty, and Horatio Gates was quickly appointed and given the rank of brigadier general. Major Gates was a half-pay officer in the British army, and had served with meritorious distinction during the late war with France. Washington had a high opinion of this former comrade in arms, who was now a neighboring plantation owner, and it is probable that he had much to do with Gates's appointment.[23]

Washington also recommended another new Virginia planter, Charles Lee, to be second major general. Lee was also a half-pay British officer with the rank of lieutenant colonel. However, he had also been a mercenary, and attained the rank of major general in the Polish service before retiring to Virginia in 1773. Because of his high opinion of his own abilities, Lee was miffed at having a man of Ward's caliber placed over him, but finally accepted Ward's seniority as a piece of unavoidable political expediency.[24]

Aware of Lee's conceit, John Adams did not let it blind him to the man's real abilities. Although a number of the delegates opposed Lee's appointment, John, and his cousin Samuel, "fought for him . . . through all the weapons." As John reported to his friend James Warren, "dismal bugbears were raised. There were prejudices enough among the weak and fears enough among the timid, as well as other obstacles from the cunning: but the great necessity for officers of skill and experience, prevailed." To make certain that Warren understood his motives in fighting for Lee's appointment, Adams assured him that it was not from "any friendship or particular connection," but rather, because "upon the most mature deliberation," he regarded Lee as the man best qualified for the post. If he was mistaken, he was "willing to abide the consequences."[25]

These three appointments on June 17 served to intensify provincial jealousies. The commander in chief, one of the two major generals, and the adjutant general were all from Virginia! This rankled the New Englanders. It was one thing to name a Virginian to the top post for the sake of colonial unity, but it was carrying things too far to give that colony three generals before she had enlisted a single man for the Continental service.

The New York delegates were also unhappy. Although that province had yet to field an armed force, it was in the process of raising one, and it was the consensus that New York would become a theater of war. Since Congress had voted to maintain an army of 5,000 men in that province, it was only natural that the New York delegates should press for the appointment of a compatriot to command it.

As early as June 3, the delegates from New York had informed their provincial congress that "as general officers will, in all probability, be shortly appointed by this Congress, your express should return immediately, with a warm recommendation of those persons in our province whom you think may safely be trusted with the first and second commands, as major and brigadier generals."[26]

The provincial congress promptly replied, enclosing two letters. It was left to the delegates to decide which of these letters should be presented to Congress. Both letters recommended Philip Schuyler, a rich, landed proprietor from Albany County, and Richard Montgomery, a British half-pay officer, now living in New York, for the first and second commands, respectively. The only difference between the two letters was that one, predicated on the assumption that Congress would allow the appointments already made by the New England colonies to stand unchanged, merely asked Congress to confirm New York's appointment of Schuyler and Montgomery. But, in the event that Congress took upon itself the sole responsibility for appointing the general officers of the new army—which it did—then New York respectfully submitted, in the second letter, its recommendation of the two men, and hoped Congress would see fit to appoint them.[27]

It was tactful of the provincial congress to pen these two letters, but, as of June 17, it appeared that neither would be of value since New York had not been allotted a major generalcy.

Connecticut, whose contribution to the war thus far was exceeded only by that of Massachusetts, was also considerably annoyed that one of her sons had not been made a major general. Consequently, a compromise was worked out over the weekend to pacify these two colonies. The results of this compromise were as unfortunate as they were unforeseen.

When Congress reconvened on Monday, June 19, it increased the number of major generals by two, and the proposed number of brigadiers by three. This was done solely as a matter of political expediency to soothe the pride of Connecticut and New York. The way thus cleared, Philip Schuyler was promptly elected the third major general in the Continental establishment.[28]

Wealthy, influential, and a delegate to Congress, Schuyler was New York's counterpart to Washington. He too had seen service in the last French and Indian War, and had been an active leader of the popular faction in the New York Assembly. Nevertheless, his qualifications for high command were questionable. Even his future subordinate, Richard Montgomery, expressed doubt on this point in a letter to his brother-in-law, Robert R Livingston. While admitting that Schuyler's "consequence in the province makes him a fit subject for an important trust," he questioned whether he had the *"strong nerves"* so necessary for a military command. Montgomery concluded that he "could wish to have that point well assured with regard to any man so employed."[29]

Whatever his merits, political considerations dictated Schuyler's appointment. For one thing, with New Yorkers still viewed by most New Englanders as reluctant rebels at best, granting Schuyler high rank would "sweeten and keep up the spirit in that province."[30]

Connecticut's "sweetener" was Israel Putnam's election as the fourth major general. At 57, Putnam was the oldest of the major generals. His many exploits during the late war with France were known throughout New England. Most of these were grossly exaggerated, as were most of the tales told about Putnam's activities. As a young man, Putnam had killed a wolf which had been raiding the stock on his and neighboring farms. Within a short period of time this incident was embellished until it appeared that Putnam had slain a werewolf! Colorful, energetic, and popular, Putnam would have made a good regimental commander—or, at most, a brigadier—but not a major general.

The immediate cause of Putnam's sudden promotion was the news of the "battle" of Noddle's Island which, reaching Congress on the 19th, had the delegates all agog. So impressed were they with the highly colored account of this action that they confirmed Putnam's appointment unanimously—a distinction hitherto accorded only to Washington.

Actually, the engagement on Noddle's Island was a dismal little affair. An American foraging party had landed on this island in Boston harbor to confiscate the livestock. While in the process of "liberating" the cattle, the Americans were attacked by 40 of His Majesty's marines. Brigadier General Putnam, with 1,000 Connecticut troops and two field pieces, arrived in time to beat off the marines before they could do much damage. Indeed, the total casualties were four Americans slightly wounded, two marines killed and several wounded, and an undetermined number of punctured cows. For this glorious feat of arms, Israel Putnam was given the rank of major general in the Continental army.[31]

The election of major generals finally dispensed with, Congress proceeded to draw up instructions for George Washington. These covered the steps the commander in chief should take in organizing, recruiting, and supplying the army. He was to make a report of the forces he found at Boston, and the military stores and provisions on hand in the camp; recruit the army to a strength he thought sufficient, provided it did not exceed twice that of the enemy; make brevet appointments of colonels and all officers below that rank, until such vacancies were filled by the colonial convention or assembly which had raised the regiments involved; take every measure within his power, consistent with prudence, to destroy the enemy; and, finally, since all contingencies could not be foreseen, he was, in all cases not covered by his instructions, to act according to his best judgment and the advice of his council of war in directing the army under his command.[32]

Next, Congress turned to the selection of brigadier generals. To avoid the difficulties experienced in the appointment of major generals, these appointments were carefully prearranged before they reached the floor of the house.[33] Consequently, Massachusetts received three brigadiers, Connecticut two, and New York, New Hampshire, and Rhode Island one each. In order of their rank there were: Seth Pomeroy (Mass.), Richard Montgomery (N.Y.), David Wooster (Conn.), William Heath (Mass.), Joseph Spencer (Conn.), John Thomas (Mass.), John Sullivan (N.H.), and Nathanael Greene (R.I.).[34]

With the possible exception of Artemas Ward's appointment, Congress paid no regard to the seniority that the general officers it chose had enjoyed in their respective colonial establishments. This quickly proved an unfortunate oversight.

The rearrangement of the Connecticut generals was particularly serious. In April, David Wooster had been made major general of the Connecticut forces, while Joseph Spencer and Israel Putnam had been selected his first and second brigadiers, respectively. Now, both Wooster and Spencer found themselves junior in the Continental service to their former subordinate. In an attempt to soothe Wooster's pride and forestall his resignation, Roger Sherman explained the circumstances of Putnam's appointment. "I informed [Congress] of the arrangement made by [the] Assembly, which I thought would be satisfactory, to have them continue in the same order," he asserted, "but as General Putnam's fame was spread abroad and especially his successful enterprise at Noodle's [sic] Island, the account of which had just arrived, it gave him a preference in the opinion of the delegates in general." In conclusion, Sherman pleaded with Wooster to remain in the army and to "accept the appointment made by Congress."[35]

Despite this, and similar attempts to allay resentment, when news of the Continental appointments reached the camp before Boston, it threatened to disrupt the army. To make matters worse, no one saw fit to explain this delicate situation to Washington. Thus, the new commander in chief left Philadelphia on June 23, unprepared for the bitterness that would greet him at Cambridge.

Provincial Jealousy
vs. Continental Unity
The Impact of Congressional Appointments

WHILE Congress was engaged in selecting general officers, the army for which they were intended was fighting the first major engagement of the war. Fought on the low hills of the Charlestown peninsula, it was, in a number of respects, a crucial battle.

By early June the British command concluded that some blow must be struck at the encircling American army. Tactically, their position in Boston was untenable if the Americans erected batteries on either Dorchester Heights or the hills of the Charlestown peninsula. Also, for morale purposes, the British army could not long endure the humiliation of appearing to be at the mercy of a mob of provincials. Finally, in modern terminology, the rebellion was "escalating." General Gage realized that if it were not nipped in the bud, England faced the prospect of a long and costly war.[1]

The long-awaited British reinforcements finally arrived at Boston accompanied by three major generals—William Howe, Henry Clinton, and John Burgoyne. This trio was destined to play a decisive role in shaping military policy in the years ahead. Even with the new arrivals, the entire British force in Boston numbered barely 6,500 rank and file as opposed to the American army of approximately 16,000 men.[2] This disparity in numbers did not worry "Gentleman Johnny" Burgoyne. He referred to the Americans contemptuously as "peasants" and vowed that, given the opportunity, he would "soon find elbow-room."[3]

This was not the idle boast it sounded. The American army, for all its size, was spread thinly in a wide arc around Boston. The British, on the other hand, were concentrated in the center. Thus, at any time they could bring overwhelming force to bear on any particular segment

17

of the American lines. In addition, the guns of the British ships of war could support any such move. With this in mind, the British high command planned to occupy and secure Dorchester Heights on June 18. The New Englanders learned of this plan, and, on June 15, it was decided to forestall the British move by occupying the hills on the Charlestown peninsula.[4]

The American countermove was unwise for a number of reasons. Charlestown Neck, connecting the peninsula to the mainland, was extremely narrow and nearly submerged at high tide. This fact, coupled with the British naval command of the harbor, could result in the isolation of any American force deployed on the peninsula. In addition, such a force would be inadequately supplied with powder since there were but 11 barrels in camp.

In view of these circumstances, both Artemas Ward and Joseph Warren opposed the move, but the insistence of Israel Putnam, Seth Pomeroy, and William Prescott finally forced them to give in.[5] Thus, on the night of June 16–17 the Americans threw up breastworks and a redoubt on Breed's Hill at the end of the peninsula.

When dawn revealed the new American position, General Gage immediately called a council of war. The presence of the Royal Navy gave the British generals a choice of several tactical moves to counter this latest piece of American effrontery. Typically, they chose the worst. Clinton, it is said, realized that the Americans had obligingly placed themselves in a trap. To spring it, the British had only to place a force of several hundred men on the Neck and deploy the ships of war in such a way as to discourage American reinforcements from attempting to reach the peninsula. The American force already on the peninsula could then be reduced at leisure. Had this plan been adopted, the British could have secured the peninsula with few casualties. Clinton's colleagues, however, insisted upon doing it the hard way—a frontal bayonet assault on the American works.

Still, the assault might have been successful had not the British been forced to wait for high tide at two o'clock in the afternoon. Only then could the troops be ferried across to the peninsula. This delay gave the Americans six more hours to strengthen their position and to increase the size of their force on the peninsula to about 1,500 men. On Breed's Hill, Colonel William Prescott commanded the main position, although two volunteers—Joseph Warren and Seth Pomeroy—outranked him.[6]

In the battle that ensued, the 2,400 British troops under the command of General Howe suffered two bloody repulses before the American defenders, their ammunition exhausted, were finally driven from their works.

William Howe learned a hard lesson that June day—one he never forgot while he commanded His Majesty's army in America. Never again would he underestimate his adversaries. Even if they were not smartly uniformed or well disciplined by parade-ground standards, they could be a dangerous and courageous enemy. Nor, for the remainder of the war, could he bring himself to assault an entrenched position. Of the 2,400 men he had led to the peninsula, 1,054 were now casualties—including 92 officers. Of the 12 staff officers that accompanied him, all were either dead or wounded before the day ended. How apt was General Clinton's remark: "A few more such victories would have shortly put an end to British dominion in America."[7]

By comparison, the American losses were light. Of the 1,500 men on the peninsula, 140 were killed and 271 wounded. Most of these casualties were suffered at the end of the engagement when the Americans were forced from their earthworks. One of these was Joseph Warren, whose death was a grievous loss to the American cause.

The battle forced the British leadership to recognize the seriousness of the American rebellion. As General Gage informed Lord Dartmouth, the American army was "not the despicable rabble too many have supposed them to be." This, he found, was due to "a military spirit encouraged amongst them for a few years past, joined with an uncommon degree of zeal and enthusiasm," and "whenever they find cover they make a good stand, and the country, naturally strong, affords it them." He also observed, with some irony, that "in all the wars against the French they never showed so much conduct, attention, and perseverence as they do now." If the colonies were to be conquered, it would take time and equal perseverence on the part of England. Strong armies would have to be sent to attack the colonists outside of New England—particularly in New York. Although Gage was soon to leave America, this, in essence, was the strategy the Ministry employed for the remainder of the war.[8]

For the Americans, the lessons learned on Breed's Hill were for a time obscured by the chagrin of defeat. But, eventually, many saw significance in the fact that the defenders had been forced to retreat only when their ammunition ran out. Up to that moment they had held their position against repeated, determined attacks by an enemy superior in numbers, training, and discipline. Unfortunately, some jumped to the conclusion that the raw, undisciplined American soldier was the equal of the British regular. The folly of this notion was amply demonstrated in the costly campaigns of the following year.

The most significant consequence of the battle was not appreciated by either side until long afterward. While suffering a tactical defeat, the

Americans had won a great strategic victory. The heavy losses sustained by the British—particularly in regimental and company officers—crippled the army in Boston. As a result, General Howe, who succeeded to the command in October when Gage was recalled, would not mount another attack against the besieging American army. In fact, the British could not initiate another offensive operation in America for a full year after the battle.

Thus, the defenders on Breed's Hill won for America a year's breathing space: time enough to raise and train a large army; time enough, also, for the "republicans" in Congress to adopt economic and political measures which led inexorably toward independence.

Unaware that the army he now commanded had fought its first battle, George Washington left Philadelphia on June 23, accompanied by Charles Lee and Philip Schuyler. The arrival of this distinguished trio in New York provided an interesting and unexpected demonstration of that city's divided loyalty. Crossing from New Jersey, they were met by a large crowd of dignitaries and inhabitants who conducted them to their lodgings "amidst . . . repeated shouts and huzzas."

That very same evening the royal governor, William Tryon, just returned from England, "came up from Sandy Hook, and landed at the Exchange." He, also, was accorded a warm welcome by the city. To one observer the day's activities were nothing but a hypocritical farce, for "those very people who attended the rebel generals in the morning, and conducted them from place to place with repeated shouts of approbation, . . . one and all joined in the governor's train, and with the loudest acclamations, . . . they shook him by the hand, welcomed him back to the colony."[9]

The commander in chief's party did not tarry long in New York. Leaving Schuyler behind to join his command to the northward, Washington and Lee, hurried by the news of a battle on the 17th, set out for Cambridge. Stopping at Watertown, they were warmly received by the Massachusetts Provincial Congress. That warmth might have been lacking had the battle of Breed's Hill (which has come down in history as The Battle of Bunker Hill) turned out differently. The contemporary historian, William Gordon, believed that "the Massachusetts colony would scarce have been easy under the appointment of General Washington to the chief command, had General Ward been crowned with the laurels of victory." The American defeat, he felt, "will make the appointment go down easily, and prevent objections.[10]

Whether Gordon's speculations are correct or not, the members of the provincial congress greeted Washington with extreme cordiality. They did seem a trifle embarrassed by the outcome of the battle, and attempted to apologize for the performance of the New England troops. "Although naturally brave and of good understanding," they told Washington, "the greatest part of them have not before seen service." They also did their best to prepare him for the squalid conditions in the American camp by observing that "the youth of America are not possessed of the absolute necessity of cleanliness in their dress and lodging, continual exercise and strict temperance to preserve them from diseases frequently prevailing in camps."[11]

This was rather an understatement, as Washington discovered upon his arrival at Cambridge on July 2. The "army" was sprawled around Boston without the least semblance of organization. "Confusion and disorder reigned in every department."[12] Ironically, Washington's first official act only served to increase this confusion and disorder.

Before leaving Philadelphia, he had been entrusted with the Continental commissions of the new general officers at Cambridge. He now discovered for the first time that he had been placed in an embarrassing position by Congress' total disregard for seniority. As might have been expected, the promotion of Putnam over his former superiors (Wooster and Spencer) caused the greatest difficulty. With great displays of indignation, these two officers promptly refused their commissions as brigadiers in the Continental service. Wooster wrote his friend Roger Sherman, enclosing his commission, and requested that he "be good enough to deliver it to Mr. Hancock with my best compliments, and desire him not to return it. I have already a commission from the assembly of Connecticut."[13] The last sentence is significant, for while Wooster eventually consented to accept his commission, he continued to think of himself primarily as a major general in the Connecticut establishment. This was to lead to the first in a long series of command disputes in the Northern department. The taciturn Spencer, without informing Washington of his intentions, simply packed his belongings and returned home.

Washington was enraged and embarrassed by this behavior and many in Congress shared his indignation. Even the Connecticut delegates were incensed, and both Silas Deane and Eliphalet Dyer condemned Wooster's and Spencer's actions in the strongest terms. As Deane remarked, when Wooster was commissioned by Connecticut, he had thought him "totally unequal to the service," and had washed his hands of the consequences. "And if I thought him unfit for a major general of Connecticut forces only," he continued, "could anyone think I would oppose the voice of the Continent and my own sentiments by laboring to prefer him to Putnam . . . ? I wish all such men would leave our army at once."

With regard to Joseph Spencer, Deane admitted that he had held a good opinion of him, "but his leaving the forces in the manner I hear he has, shocks it very greatly, and if true, I wish him to resign at once and let another take his place." When Washington informed Congress that Spencer had indeed left his post without leave, the general opinion was "that he acted a part inconsistent with the character either of a soldier, a patriot, or even of a common gentleman."

However, despite his actions, neither Dyer nor Deane wished to see Spencer lost to the service. He had served in the last two French wars and was considered by most a good soldier. Although 60 years old, he was in good health and could still bear the rigors of active campaigning. In addition, and perhaps most important, he was well liked by his subordinate officers. Forty-nine of these petitioned the Connecticut Assembly to intervene with Congress on his behalf. Dyer, therefore, managed to convince his colleagues to "make some allowance for [Spencer's] first feelings" upon learning he had been superseded by his subordinate. Consequently, the commission was again proffered, and this time accepted. Dyer's efforts on Spencer's behalf were particularly praiseworthy since he coveted the appointment and had reason to believe that he would receive it if Spencer resigned.[14]

The Connecticut generals were not the only ones aggrieved by the Congressional appointments. Some from Massachusetts also felt slighted. As a result, it appeared that the army would lose the highly valued services of John Thomas. Thomas, a doctor in private life, had served with distinction as a lieutenant colonel and surgeon during the French and Indian War. On February 9, 1775, he was one of five generals elected by the Massachusetts Congress, and, on May 19, under a new organization of the province's army, he was commissioned a lieutenant general. As such, he was second only to Artemas Ward in point of rank. In the Continental establishment, however, he was junior to Seth Pomeroy and William Heath, both of whom had been subordinate to him in the Massachusetts line.[15]

The blame for this "unfortunate arrangement . . . which is likely to do so much hurt" was laid by John Adams to the failure of the Massachusetts government to keep the delegates informed of its actions. The delegates knew nothing of the new arrangement of May 19, and, therefore, had used as their guide the list of general officers of February 9. Also, Adams informed James Warren that he and Samuel Adams had attempted to secure his appointment as a general "in room of some others. . . . But, notions, narrow notions, prevented it—not dislike for you," he hastened to add, "but fear of disobliging Pomeroy and his friends."[16]

Determined not to lose Thomas, whom he described as "by far the best officer we [have]," James Warren urged Samuel Adams to "find some way to rectify what really is a mistake."[17] Samuel and John Adams, as soon as they learned of the error, made it their business "to wait upon gentlemen of the Congress at their lodgings and elsewhere to let them into the secret and contrive a way to get out of the difficulty."[18]

Washington also showed deep concern. To prevent a repetition of the resentment aroused by Putnam's appointment, he decided to hold on to the rest of the commissions—including those of Thomas, Pomeroy, and Heath—and await the further directions of Congress. "General Thomas," he informed Congress on July 10, "is much esteemed and most earnestly desired to continue in the service, and as far as my opportunities have enabled me to judge, I must join in the general opinion, that he is an able and good officer and his resignation would be a public loss." Although Thomas had not yet threatened to resign, Washington feared that "postponing him to Pomeroy and Heath, whom he has commanded, would make his continuance very difficult and probably operate on his mind, as the like circumstances did on that of Spencer."

Washington also wrote personally to Thomas on July 23, assuring him of the high opinion he had of his abilities, and promising to do all in his power to make his situation "both easy and honorable." He further advised that the order and rank of the commissions was being reconsidered by Congress, and out of respect for that body, Thomas should not take any action until he heard of its determination.

Charles Lee added his voice to those attempting to dissuade Thomas from resigning. In doing so, Lee revealed the light in which he saw his own subordination to Artemas Ward and George Washington. In view of the rank he had held "in some of the most respectable services in Europe," Lee should have considered his subordination to Washington and Ward "the highest indignity" had he allowed himself to be guided by what he contemptuously referred to as "modern etiquette notions of a soldier's honor and delicacy." However, he had willingly consented to serve in his present position, and he urged Thomas to do the same in order that he might save his country "which a banditti of ministerial assassins are now attempting to utterly destroy with sword, fire and famine."[19]

This eloquent appeal to Thomas' patriotism proved unnecessary, for Seth Pomeroy provided Congress with an easy solution to the problem. Before Washington arrived at Cambridge, that 69-year-old veteran resigned his commission in the Massachusetts army—apparently in protest against the arrangement of May 19. Although he served as a volunteer at the Battle of Bunker Hill, he was determined not to continue in the army. This vacated the first brigadier general's position in the Continental establishment, and, upon a motion by John Adams, Congress elected Thomas to that post. Adams was naturally relieved that the error was corrected, and fervently hoped that this measure would "give all the satisfaction which is now to be given."

In its solution of the problem posed by Thomas' commission, however, Congress created a new predicament. Under ordinary circumstances, the second brigadier, Richard Montgomery, should have been promoted to first brigadier upon Pomeroy's resignation. Instead, Thomas, who under the original arrangement was sixth brigadier, was advanced to that position. Lest Montgomery now feel himself injured and resign, Congress directed James Duane to explain the peculiar circumstances surrounding Thomas' appointment.

When Congress originally appointed the brigadier generals, Duane informed Montgomery, it was decided that the first brigadier should be from Massachusetts. The Massachusetts delegates had then recommended Seth Pomeroy, and he was duly elected. However, before his commission arrived, Pomeroy had resigned. Under these circumstances, Congress thought it proper to adhere to the original agreement by appointing another Massachusetts officer first brigadier general.[20] Fortunately, Montgomery, like Lee, did not hold "to modern etiquette notions of a soldier's honor and delicacy," and he made no complaint against Thomas' appointment.

While the disputes over commissions were being settled, the commander in chief attempted to bring some order out of the chaos he found at Cambridge. The men were for the most part inadequately clothed, housed, and armed. There was little or no discipline and provincial jealousies which, he glumly wrote Schuyler, "in a little time must have ended either in a separation of the army, or fatal contests with one another."[21]

The command structure—or lack of one—was partially responsible. Steps were immediately taken to rectify it, and, on July 22, Washington announced a new arrangement. He divided the army into three divisions: the first commanded by Major General Ward, with Brigadiers Thomas and Spencer under him; the second, commanded by Major General Lee, and consisting largely of New Hampshire and Rhode Island men under the immediate command of Brigadiers Sullivan and Greene; and the third division which he entrusted to Major General Putnam.

On paper, at least, the American army now looked truly formidable. And in point of numbers it was. Congress originally voted to maintain an army of 15,000 men in Massachusetts. By July, however, it numbered some 17,000 rank and file and was still growing! Moreover, if every regiment was brought up to full strength, Washington estimated that he would have about 24,500 men. While it was unlikely that the regiments could be recruited to full strength, he felt that the army should be increased to at least 22,000.[22]

Washington justified this increase by referring to his instructions which authorized him to recruit the army to a sufficient strength, as long as it did not exceed twice the strength of the enemy. And Washington reported that the British had 11,500 men in Boston. This was a gross exaggeration. Even with the reinforcements that arrived in late June and early July, General Gage had barely 6,000 effectives under his command.[23]

As the army increased in size, the problems attending its régulation grew apace. The efficient purchase and distribution of essential supplies and provisions was absolutely necessary to the maintenance of the army. However, the staff officers whose job it was to attend to these administrative matters had not been appointed by Congress when it elected the general officers. Since such officers would be entrusted with large sums of money, it was natural that Congress should take some care in their selection. Also, there was a good deal of provincial rivalry for these important posts. As a result, it was the middle of July before Congress took formal action.

George Washington, on July 10, impatient to have the staff positions filled, wrote Congress that it "was indispensibly necessary for the good government of the army" that there should be appointed immediately "a quartermaster general, a commissary general, a commissary of musters, and a commissary of artillery." In addition, the inefficiency of the present system of supplying provisions (each provincial contingent having its own commissary) made the appointment of a commissary general of particular importance. To fill this post, he recommended Colonel Joseph Trumbull, and commented upon his excellent record as commissary for the Connecticut forces.

When Congress received this letter, the delegates responded with alacrity in unanimously electing Joseph Trumbull commissary general. They also managed to agree upon James Warren for paymaster general and Jonathan Trumbull, Jr., to be his deputy with the army in New York. This seemingly exhausted their talent for cooperation, for they could not agree on proper persons to fill the remaining posts. Instead, they instructed Washington to make the appointments himself.[24]

This action enraged John Adams. He had worked behind the scenes to get "proper persons" recommended for quartermaster general, commissary of artillery, and commissary of musters—"but in vain." Leaving these appointments to Washington, he believed, was "against every proper rule and principle, as these officers are checks upon his." As such, "they ought not to be under any dependence upon him or so great obligations of gratitude as those of a creature of the creator."

Quite aside from the question of principle, however, John Adams was concerned lest Massachusetts men be passed over in the appointments. Apparently he already suspected that Washington did not have a high opinion of New Englanders in general, and Massachusetts men in particular. Powerless now to directly influence "the appointment of these important and lucrative officers," he urged James Warren and his friends to recommend "proper persons" to the General. In this way, he hoped, "a great misfortune to our colony" could still be averted.[25]

Adams's fears on this point proved well founded. Washington, armed with congressional authorization, promptly appointed two Philadelphians, Thomas Mifflin and Stephen Moylan, quartermaster and mustermaster general, respectively. Mifflin had been Washington's aide-de-camp since June 23, and had accompanied him to Cambridge from Philadelphia. Thus, he was in an excellent position to obtain the highest staff appointment in the army.

Moylan, on the other hand, came to his appointment by a more indirect route. Originally, Charles Lee had intended to make him one of his aides-de-camp. However, Moylan, according to Lee, "dangled his time after some intrigue (for he calls every woman who has a body to her shift an intrigue) until my two aide-de-campships were filled up." Therefore, Lee, on July 27, requested that Robert Morris "would recommend him to the members of the Continental Congress . . . for some provision." At the same time, Lee promised to "write to every one with whom I have an interest on the same subject." Thus Moylan's dalliance unexpectedly made possible his appointment as mustermaster general.

By the end of August, the major staff positions were filled—mostly with appointees of the commander in chief. Although Congress relinquished its appointive power in this instance, the consequences were by no means as dire as John Adams had thought they would be. At the same time, however, Congress tacitly surrendered its power to appoint field-grade officers, and this proved far more serious.

Until the formation of the Continental army, field-grade officers (colonels, lieutenant colonels, and majors) were appointed by the assemblies or conventions of their own colonies—as were the general officers. The difficulties encountered in the selection of a handful of Continental generals probably induced Congress to refrain from exercising the same power over the commissioning of hundreds of field-grade officers. As early as June 20, Caesar Rodney reported that Congress had decided merely to confirm the field-grade officers in their rank "according to their appointments by the colonies where the troops they commanded were raised."[26]

Consequently, Washington, when he arrived at Cambridge, had with him a packet of commissions to be made out in the names of the field-grade officers already with the army. Similarly, the New York Provincial Congress was requested to recommend suitable field-grade officers to the general commanding in that department. The general would then fill out the commissions accordingly. So, while field-grade officers were commissioned by the Continental Congress, in practice their actual appointment was retained by the individual colonies.[27]

Not everyone was pleased with this arrangement—least of all George Washington. In effect, such a policy gave the New England colonies a virtual monopoly in the appointment of all officers below the rank of general, and he viewed this prospect with misgivings. On August 29 he confided to his fellow Virginian, Richard Henry Lee, that one of the reasons he appointed Mifflin quartermaster general was that "he stands unconnected with either of these governments, or with this, that, or the other man; for between you and me, there is more in this than you can easily imagine." Considering Lee's close connection with the Adamses, this confession was indiscreet to say the least.

Washington went on to question whether, "now the army is become Continental," it was proper to leave the "ultimate apointment of all officers below the rank of generals to the governments where the regiment originated." To Washington it seemed improper for two reasons. First, it gave "that power and weight to an individual colony, which ought of right to belong only to the whole; and, next, it dampens the spirit and ardor of volunteers from all but the four New England governments, as none but their people have the least chance of getting into office." The only solution, he informed Lee, was to have all commissions which the commander in chief was authorized to give, "approved or disapproved by the Continental Congress, or a committee of their body." Only then would "every gentleman . . . stand an equal chance of being promoted according to his merit."

Washington's vehemence on this point was largely attributable to his disgust with the New England officers and men—particularly those from Massachusetts—which he made little effort to conceal. He had informed his brother, Lund Washington, on August 20 that they "by no means deserved" the reputation they had acquired. The officers were "the most indifferent kind of people" he had ever seen. Soon after his arrival he had had to break one colonel and five captains for cowardice and fraud, and there were two more colonels under arrest for the same offences. "In short they are by no means such troops, in any respect, as you are led to believe of them from the accounts which are published, but I need not make myself enemies among them, by this declaration, although it is consistent with truth." The men, he concluded, might be made into acceptable soldiers if they had different officers, but "they are an exceeding dirty and nasty people."

In the same vein, Washington complained to Richard Henry Lee in his letter of August 29 that there was "an unaccountable kind of stupidity in the lower class of these people which, believe me, prevails but too generally among the officers of the Massachusetts *part* of the army who are *nearly* of the same kidney with the privates!" Washington kept up a steady stream of indiscreet remarks concerning the New England officers and men for some months, although he "studiously avoided in all letters intended for the public eye, I mean for that of Congress, every expression that could give pain or uneasiness." Joseph Reed finally warned him that the contents of his private letters were known to the New England delegates, and he had made enemies by his unguarded remarks. Too late, Washington decided to "observe the same rule with respect to private letters" that he had followed in public ones.[28]

Perhaps the most important political enemy he made was ironically the man who had worked hardest for his appointment as commander in chief—John Adams. Deeply resenting Washington's aspersions, Adams asked Colonel Henry Knox to tell him if "every man to the southward of Hudson's River behave like a hero, and every man to the northward of it like a poltroon, or not?" Certainly Washington's letters gave that impression, and it bothered Adams that "he often mentions things to the disadvantage of some part of New England, but seldom anything of the kind about any other part of the Continent."[29] Much of the subsequent hostility shown by New Englanders toward the commander in chief can be traced to the impolitic remarks he made during the first year of the war.

Another high-ranking officer who antagonized John Adams was Major General Charles Lee, who also owed his commission in large part to Adams' efforts in his behalf. On July 4, shortly after his arrival at Cambridge, Lee informed Robert Morris that he had "found everything the reverse of what had been represented." The perpetrators of this misrepresentation, he clearly implied, were the Massachusetts delegates.

When Adams learned of this accusation, he was highly incensed. "What General Lee could mean by this," he declared, "I know not." But, "I think he should have been particular, that he might not have run the risk of doing an injury. If General Lee should do injustice to two of the Massachusetts delegates [John and Samuel Adams], he would commit ingratitude at the same time;" for to those two "he certainly owes his promotion in the American army, how great a hazard so ever they ran in agreeing to it." Adams still believed that Lee could "do great service in our army at the beginning of things, by forming it to order, skill, and discipline." But, in his anger, Adams now hinted that Lee's services could before long be dispensed with, for "we shall soon have officers enough."[30]

It was now time for John Adams to be indiscreet. In a letter to his close friend James Warren, he observed that Lee "is a queer creature; but you must love his dogs if you love him, and forgive a thousand whims, for the sake of the soldier and the scholar.[31] The British intercepted this letter and, to Adams' mortification, published it in the *Massachusetts Gazette.*

Charles Lee, ever the diplomat, assured Adams that he was not offended by anything contained in the intercepted letter. On the contrary, that Adams considered him whimsical and eccentric he took "rather as a panegyric than sarcasm." He also hastened to inform Adams that his love for dogs did not make him a misanthrope. For, he proclaimed, "when I meet with a biped endowed with generosity, valor, good sense, patriotism, and zeal for the rights of humanity I contract a friendship and passion for him amounting to bigotry or dotage; and let me assure you without compliments that you yourself appear to be possessed of these qualities." In closing, Lee indulged himself in a bit of that whimsy for which he was famous. "Spada [his favorite dog] sends his love to you," he informed Adams, "and declares, in very intelligible language, that he has fared much better since your allusion to him, for he is caressed now by all ranks, sexes, and ages."[32]

This letter had its desired effect. The moment he received it, John Adams wrote Lee that "no letter I ever received gave me greater pleasure." He confessed that he had been "under some apprehensions, that a certain passage, in a very unfortunate as well as inconsiderate letter, might have made some disagreeable impressions on your mind." Adams also found Lee's opinion of his qualities highly flattering, and he returned the favor by observing that his oft expressed opinion of Lee's "attainments as a scholar and soldier" might easly have been expressed in even stronger terms "with the same sincerity."[33] Paradoxically, then, the intercepted letter served to forge a bond of friendship between Lee and Adams. For Lee this was indeed fortunate, because in a few months he would need powerful friends in Congress in order to retain his commission in the Continental army.

Perhaps "the wanton expressions" in Adams' intercepted letter were symptomatic of the mental duress engendered by overwork and Philadelphia's oppressive heat. Certainly, many of the delegates were feeling the strain of both by late July. Much had been accomplished since they convened on May 10—but much remained undone. In particular, many of the organizational problems necessary to support the army through the fall and winter had yet to be solved. Consequently, Washington requested, through his friend Benjamin Harrison, that Congress either move closer to Boston or send a committee to camp so that he might confer with them.

Congress, however, did not look with favor on either of these steps. The delegates were anxious to return home, and would not consider postponing their adjournment. But Congress balked at appointing a committee to confer with Washington because it "could not think of parting with the least particle of power."[34] Consequently, fatigued by their labors—but jealous of their authority—the delegates on August 2 adjourned to the 5th of September, and the many pressing problems facing the army in Massachusetts and New York would have to be resolved by Washington and Schuyler or held in abeyance until Congress reconvened.

The Creation of a Northern Army

WHILE the organization of the army gathered before Boston was uppermost in the minds of most members of the Continental Congress during the summer of 1775, affairs to the northward daily assumed a more ominous complexion. By the end of May, the American forces in that quarter held Ticonderoga and Crown Point, and controlled the waters of Lake Champlain. These posts while strategically located, were little more than ruins, and extensive repairs were required to put them in a state of defense. American control of the lake was also tenuous. Reports emanating from St. Johns, at the foot of the lake, indicated that the British were constructing two large vessels to replace the sloop captured by Arnold in May. If these were completed, nothing could prevent the British from regaining control of the lake and launching a counterattack against the small American garrisons at Ticonderoga and Crown Point.

When Congress rescinded its order to abandon the Champlain posts, it was forced to adopt new measures which led toward a deeper involvement in that quarter. The handful of New Hampshire and Massachusetts men under the joint command of Colonels Arnold and Allen had to be reinforced. Since each of the New England colonies had sent large contingents to the army besieging Boston, and the posts on the lake were located in New York, it seemed reasonable to expect that province to supply the additional troops. However, New York, unlike New England, had made few preparations for war. Indeed, by late June, New York had yet to raise a single regiment, despite the warning of her delegates in Congress that the "honor as well as the interest of the province" required the raising of troops with "alacrity and dispatch." Consequently, even before Congress suggested it, the New York Congress was forced to ask Governor Trumbull to send Connecticut troops to secure the northern posts.[1]

Trumbull responded promptly, ordering Colonel Benjamin Hinman to proceed at once to Ticonderoga with 1,000 men.[2] The alacrity of Connecticut's response was due to an appreciation of the strategic importance of the northern posts, and to a deep-seated suspicion concerning New York's reliability. Many New Englanders thought New York's failure to provide for her own defense was symptomatic of a lukewarm enthusiasm for the American cause.[3] Moreover, the longer she procrastinated, the greater the danger that the British would seize control of the northern lakes and the Hudson River and isolate New England from the rest of the colonies. Such fears were not without foundation. General Gage suggested such a plan to Lord Dartmouth in June, and for the next two years it dominated British strategy for the subjugation of the colonies.[4]

It is not surprising, then, that many of the colonial leaders were dissatisfied with a mere reinforcement of the garrisons at Ticonderoga and Crown Point. The fortifications were in a ruined condition, and, even if they were repaired and the garrisons strengthened, they would be unable to stop a British invasion in force from Canada. The only way that that could be prevented was to wrest Canada from the British.

Such a step would not only forestall any British invasion, it would also prevent a repetition of the Indian raids experienced by the colonists during the French wars. While some found it hard to believe that Englishmen could be guilty of such barbarism, John Adams warned that while it would be horrible "to let loose these blood hounds to scalp men and to butcher women and children . . . still it [is] such kind of humanity and policy as we have experienced from the ministry."[5] Indeed, only a few days after Adams penned this warning, General Gage advised the Secretary of War, Lord Barrington, that he should not "be tender on using the Indians," and offered his opinion that the governor of Quebec, General Sir Guy Carleton, would be justified in raising as many Canadians and Indians as he could to attack the frontiers of New York and New England.[6]

As if to confirm the colonists' worst fears, reports reaching Congress in June indicated that Louis St. Luc de la Corne was urging the Indians to take up the war hatchet against the Americans. La Corne earned the fear and hatred of the colonists when, as Indian Superintendent under the French regime, he was instrumental in directing the devastating Indian raids on the frontier. His son-in-law, Major Campbell, now held a similar position in British Canada, and together they urged their savage allies to paint for war.[7]

Colonels Ethan Allen and James Easton added their voices to those urging Congress to invade Canada. They also wrote the provincial congresses of New York and Massachusetts and assured them that two or three thousand men could secure Canada if they acted promptly. But all to no avail.[8]

The members of Congress were impressed by the danger posed by British Canada, but not sufficiently so in June to authorize the invasion of that province. After all, they had not yet agreed to adopt the army besieging Boston. When that was done, perhaps a second army could be raised to invade Canada—but not before. Also, an invasion of Canada would certainly shatter the image many of them cherished of American colonists fighting only in defense of hearth and home. Congress therefore decided that if an American army were eventually sent to Canada, it would be done only after the Canadians indicated they would welcome such a move and join wholeheartedly in the cause of America.[9] Under these conditions, it would not be an invasion. Rather, Congress would be merely extending aid to another American colony acting in defense of its rights and liberties.

While Congress debated its policy toward Canada, the first in a long series of command disputes took place in the embryonic Northern army. On May 3 the Massachusetts Committee of Safety had given Benedict Arnold a colonel's commission and authorized him to raise a force of 400 men to capture Ticonderoga and Crown Point. Before he could recruit his men, however, he learned that an expedition of Green Mountain Boys under Colonel Ethan Allen was being assembled for the same purpose. Hurrying to Castleton, where Allen was gathering his men, Arnold claimed the right of command in consequence of his Massachusetts commission. Since Allen had some 200 men and Arnold had none, his demand was rejected, and he was permitted merely to accompany the expedition as a volunteer.

By June the roles of the two "commanders" were reversed. Most of Allen's men drifted away to their homes, while Arnold's command grew to about 150 men as recruits were forwarded from Massachusetts. Then Arnold's command was contested from another quarter. Colonel James Easton, a Massachusetts officer, had raised about 50 men in the vicinity of Pittsfield in late April and joined the Allen expedition. At the council of war held before the attack on Ticonderoga, Easton had been named second in command. Thus, with Allen removed from contention, Easton felt the command should devolve upon him.[10]

To bolster his pretensions, Easton made a report to the Massachusetts Congress in which he portrayed himself as the hero of Ticonderoga. He claimed he was not only the joint leader of the expedition, but, also, that it was he who had first entered the fort and called upon its commander, Captain William Delaplace, to surrender. Colonel Arnold was not even mentioned in this report.

More than a month elapsed before an anonymous eye-witness to the capture of Ticonderoga contradicted Easton's report in a letter to the press. Styling himself "Veritas," he labeled Easton a liar and a coward. It was Allen and Arnold who entered the fort and received its surrender. Easton, far from being the first, was the last man to enter the fort, "and that not till the soldiers and their arms were secured, he having concealed himself in an old barrack near the redoubt, under the pretense of wiping dry his gun, which he said had got wet in crossing the lake." Furthermore, since the capture of the post, "Veritas" had "often heard Colonel Easton, in a base and cowardly manner, abuse Colonel Arnold behind his back, though always very complaisant before his face." When Arnold learned of Easton's duplicity, he demanded satisfaction, but Easton refused. Whereupon, "Veritas" "had the pleasure of seeing him heartily kicked by Colonel Arnold, to the great satisfaction of a number of gentlemen present."

Another who bridled at Easton's account was Captain Delaplace. A prisoner in Hartford, he chanced to see Easton's report published in the paper, *American Oracle*. "In justice to myself," he declared, I cannot "do less than contradict the many particulars therein contained, knowing them to be totally void of truth." He had neither seen nor conversed with Easton on the day of the surrender, he asserted, and was "quite at a loss to conjecture what could incline . . . Colonel Easton to publish a conversation said to be had with me, except he, knowing that I was a prisoner, and restricted from giving any account at all of this affair, took the advantage of my situation, in order to answer his own purposes, at the total expense of his veracity." Nevertheless, long before either of these refutations could be made, Easton's tale had its desired effect.

Arnold, tired of the endless bickering over command, and wishing to clarify his own position, asked the Massachusetts Congress for permission to resign. That body responded on June 1, and assured him that they placed the greatest confidence in his "fidelity, knowledge, courage, and good conduct," and they asked him to "dismiss all thoughts of quitting [his] important command at Ticonderoga, Crown Point, [and] Lake Champlain." Almost as an afterthought it added that he was to retain this command only "until the colony of New York or Connecticut shall take on them the maintaining and commanding the same agree-

able to an order of the Continental Congress." Thus, while he was confirmed in his command of the Massachusetts troops, Arnold's command
of Ticonderoga and Crown Point was temporary—contingent upon the
arrival of Connecticut or New York troops.

Despite such assurances of their confidence in him, the members of
the provincial congress thought it prudent to send a committee to Ticonderoga to investigate rumors of Arnold's misconduct. This committee,
consisting of Walter Spooner, Jedediah Foster, and James Sullivan, was
instructed to make itself fully acquainted with Arnold's "spirit, capacity,
and conduct," and decide on the spot whether he was fit to continue in
the commission and pay of Massachusetts.[11]

When the committee arrived at Ticonderoga, it found a chaotic
situation. Colonel Hinman, in compliance with orders from Governor
Trumbull, had arrived at the post with a portion of his Connecticut
regiment. By the authority of the resolves of the Continental Congress,
and the mutual agreement of New York, Connecticut, and Massachusetts, he claimed the command of the northern posts. Arnold's force,
however, outnumbered that of Hinman, and he refused to relinquish his
position. Establishing his headquarters at Crown Point, Arnold placed
a subordinate, Captain Herrick, in charge of Ticonderoga, and Hinman
and his men were forced to take orders from this officer. If they refused, they were threatened with restriction to the post.

The committee therefore made the short trip to Crown Point, presented its instructions to Arnold, and informed him that the Massachusetts Congress recognized Colonel Hinman (the ranking officer of the
Connecticut troops) as the commander of the posts on Lake Champlain.
Arnold was to consider himself as second in command and place himself
under Hinman's orders. In a towering rage, Arnold damned the provincial congress which could "first appoint an officer, and afterwards,
when he had executed his commission, . . . appoint a committee to see
if he was fit for his post." In righteous indignation he informed the committee that he could not surrender the fortresses and vessels he had captured to a younger officer of the same rank without bringing disgrace
upon himself and the troops he commanded. Determined not to serve
under Hinman, Arnold resigned.

There are two accounts of the events which then transpired. The
committee reported to the provincial congress that, upon his resignation,
Arnold ordered his men to disband. Since many of the troops had not
been raised by Arnold, the committee took it upon itself to reform them
into a new regiment under Arnold's rival, Easton. At the same time, the
committee designated Easton as Hinman's second in command. However, some of the men showed "a mutinous spirit" because they appre-

hended that they were not going to be paid for their past services. The committee quieted these fears, assured the men they would be paid, and, in addition, promised them the bounty given by Massachusetts to new recruits. This ended the "mutiny" and the committee returned home.

A more colorful account of these events was given to Governor Trumbull by Captain Edward Mott, one of Hinman's subordinates. According to Mott, Arnold and some of his men went on board the vessels anchored off Crown Point, and "threatened to go to St. Johns and deliver the vessels to the [British] regulars." The Massachusetts committee attempted to reason with him, but "they were treated very ill and threatened, and after they came away in a bateau, they were fired upon with the swivel-guns and small arms by Arnold's people." Whereupon, Mott, in company with a Lieutenant Halsey, Mr. William Duer of New York, and James Sullivan, proceeded to board the vessels to reason with the mutineers. (William Duer was a judge in Charlotte County, New York, and had availed himself of Captain Mott's services before. Early in June, when a mob attempted to force him to close his court at Fort Miller, Duer refused to do so and called upon Captain Mott to disperse the agitators. Thus, Duer came to be viewed by the inhabitants of the area as an enemy to "the rights and liberties of America." His inclusion in the group bargaining with the mutineers was less than wise.) Mott's party was promptly made prisoner, and men set over them with fixed bayonets. Nonetheless, they managed to convince their captors of the error of their ways, and the next day the vessels were brought back to Ticonderoga.

Captain Mott's account of the affair would appear somewhat exaggerated. If it were true that Arnold threatened to return the vessels to the British, or that his men fired upon the committeemen, the committee certainly would have made some mention of it in its report. It is also significant that Walter Spooner, the chairman of the committee, made no mention of such incidents in his letter to Governor Trumbull of July 3. He merely observed that some of Arnold's men refused to reenlist in the new regiment formed under Easton. He did acknowledge the valuable assistance rendered by the Connecticut officers and Judge William Duer in making these recalcitrants change their minds. So there might be some truth in Mott's account of being detained aboard the vessels and finally persuading Arnold's men to accede to the committee's wishes.[12]

While these events were transpiring on Lake Champlain, the issue of command was resolved by the Continental Congress. On June 27 that body directed Major General Philip Schuyler to take command of the Continental forces on or about Lakes George and Champlain. In addition, he was instructed to take steps to assure American command of the lakes, foil the threatened invasion by Governor Carleton, and take possession of St. Johns, Montreal, and any other post in Canada necessary to guarantee the security of the United Colonies. But the occupation of any part of Canada was made contingent upon its not being disagreeable to the Canadians.[13]

These instructions represented a marked change in Congress' policy toward Canada. Previously, Congress had stipulated that no American troops were to enter that province unless they were assured of the active support of the Canadians. Now the only condition required for such a move was that the Canadians should not actively oppose it. This alteration of policy, Hancock informed George Washington and Schuyler, was prompted by a warning received from the Albany Committee that Governor Carleton was preparing to invade northern New York. Richard Henry Lee also informed Washington that Congress had "again taken up the business of entering Canada, and have left the propriety of it to General Schuyler."

The manner in which Schuyler received these instructions is of some significance. Since Washington was the commander in chief, the instructions should have been sent to him. He would then have transmitted them to Schuyler, his subordinate. Instead, Congress issued its orders directly to Schuyler. To have done otherwise, Washington was informed, would have occasioned a delay that "might prove detrimental to the service."[14] Indeed, it took several days for express riders to reach Albany from Philadelphia, and the communication problem would worsen as the army moved closer to Canada. Consequently, while the officer commanding the Northern department remained theoretically responsible to the commander in chief, in practice he henceforth received his orders directly from the Continental Congress.

Apparently neither Washington nor Schuyler was overly concerned about this breach of the chain of command. They were too preoccupied with the organization and disciplining of the armies entrusted to their care. Schuyler's first intimation of the chaotic state of his army came when he met Benedict Arnold at Albany. He was informed that the army consisted of about 1,200 men, but had thus far made no move to harass the enemy or repair the fortifications at Ticonderoga and Crown Point. On the other hand, the British were very busy building vessels at St. Johns and making preparations to recapture those posts. Schuyler was impressed with Arnold's knowledge and directed him to transmit this information to the president of Congress.[15]

Schuyler believed that the first order of business should be to inculcate a sense of discipline in the soldiers. Once he had actually seen some of them, however, he was far from confident. While he assured

Washington that he would do his best to bring order and a sense of discipline to the troops he commanded, he was anything but optimistic. It would be extremely difficult, he gloomily predicted, "to introduce a proper subordination amongst a people where so little distinction is kept up."[16] It was evident from the beginning that the aristocratic Schuyler was not going to get on well with the democratic New Englanders. And since the Northern army was composed largely of officers and men from that section, this boded ill for his success as their commanding general.

Although provincialism was a factor in the rift which developed between Schuyler and the New Englanders, it is well to remember that Brigadier General Richard Montgomery, Schuyler's second in command, had a close relationship with the officers and men of the Northern army. This was despite the fact that Montgomery was a half-pay British officer as well as a New Yorker by adoption, having married into the powerful Livingston family. Nevertheless, Montgomery's aggressiveness and courage weighed more heavily with the New Englanders than his background, and so they accorded him the respect which they withheld from Schuyler.

It was immediately apparent to Schuyler that much of the disorder in the Northern army was due to the lack of a staff organization. To remedy this, Congress, on July 17, appointed Walter Livingston commissary of stores and provisions for the duration of the campaign. Donald Campbell was elected deputy quartermaster general and Gunning Bedford deputy mustermaster general in the same department. A few days later, Jonathan Trumbull, Jr., the son of Governor Trumbull of Connecticut, was named deputy paymaster general. Congress could not agree, however, on a proper person to be Schuyler's adjutant general. Instead, it resolved that the convention of New York should recommend someone for that post to General Schuyler. At the same time, the delegates from New York wrote the New York Congress that Morgan Lewis would make a good adjutant general.[17]

The appointment of an adjutant general should have been a relatively simple matter. A peculiar set of circumstances dictated otherwise. Ordinarily, the choice of the delegates, Morgan Lewis, would have been quite acceptable to the provincial congress. But before their recommendation was known, that body had decided that William Duer should have the appointment. Finally, unknown at first to either group, Schuyler had decided that Benedict Arnold would make the best adjutant general.

His first encounter with Arnold had impressed Schuyler with that officer's outstanding ability. His knowledge of the Northern department and his present unemployment made him a natural choice for the staff appointment. Consequently, Schuyler wrote Silas Deane and asked him to get Arnold appointed adjutant general. Fully aware that Arnold's recent run-in with the officers now commanding the troops at Ticonderoga made his choice somewhat impolitic, Schuyler admonished Deane to keep secret the source of the recommendation.[18]

Deane, though unsuccessful in obtaining the appointment, apparently did remain silent about Schuyler's involvement. Not so Arnold. He showed no restraint in telling his friends that Schuyler had offered him the staff position, and eventually this information reached William Duer. Duer, of course, had been an active participant in the command embranglement which led to Arnold's resignation. While he could not believe that Schuyler would show such a "mark of favor to anyone, whose unaccountable pride" had led "him to sacrifice the true interests of the country," Duer nevertheless urged that if Schuyler did entertain any such action, he first investigate Arnold's conduct at Ticonderoga. Then, should Schuyler still persist in favor of Arnold, Duer would view it as "a tacit reproach of [his] conduct."[19]

Judge Duer was a merchant and politician of some note and was soon to represent New York in the Continental Congress. Furthermore, he was a conservative Whig and associated with the Livingston faction of which Schuyler himself was a leader. Thus, with the cat out of the bag, Schuyler quickly lost interest in Arnold's appointment.

As far as Arnold was concerned, it is unlikely he ever seriously considered accepting the position. By doing so, he would have taken himself out of the list of line officers and forfeited his jealously prized seniority. This would hardly have been characteristic. It is also a little difficult to imagine that fiery individual trading his sword for a pen! It is more likely that his indiscreet talk about Schuyler's intentions was calculated to anger his enemies—particularly Duer. This accomplished, he left for Massachusetts to settle his accounts with the provincial congress.

It may or may not be a coincidence, but, on July 20, the day after Duer wrote Schuyler, the New York Provincial Congress unanimously elected him adjutant general with the rank of colonel. The letter informing him of his appointment miscarried however, and it was nearly a month before he learned of it. He received the news with mixed emotions, and eventually declined the position. His reason for doing so, he explained, was a concern for his brothers' mercantile interests in the island of Dominica. Accepting the appointment, he informed the congress on August 15, would be to "risk . . . their fortune by my political conduct." The committee appointed by the congress to confer with Duer on this point agreed. Consequently, a few days later, Edward Flemming was nominated for the post and accepted.

While politicians squabbled over staff appointments, and Schuyler struggled with problems of discipline and supply, the army did little but consume rations. The sense of urgency and impatience to push on to Canada which gripped the army during May and June seemed to dissipate under the hot July sun. Chafed by the weeks of inactivity, some of the officers, General Montgomery among them, urged Schuyler to move on St. Johns. Governor Trumbull, who had strained the resources of Connecticut to provide men and supplies for the Northern army, was also vexed. Losing patience, he directed Connecticut's delegates to Congress to raise the question: "Is it not high time to proceed into, and even to hasten forward to secure the government of Quebec?" and informed Schuyler of his action. If more troops were needed, he offered to send Colonel Waterbury's regiment to the northward with all dispatch.

In responding to this criticism of his inactivity, Schuyler complained that while hitherto every prospect seemed favorable for a move into Canada, he now found such an enterprise impossible for want of transportation and sufficient provisions. All supplies were hauled from Albany to either Fort George or Skenesboro, and thence carried by bateau to Ticonderoga. The shortage of wagons and bateaux made these operations extremely slow. As a result, by the end of July, there were only 10 days rations at Ticonderoga, and Schuyler was forced to hold troops at Albany to keep them from starving at the northern posts.[20]

To further complicate matters, Congress continued to insist that the good will of the Canadians was a necessary condition for any venture into that province. "You will please particularly to notice," President Hancock cautioned Schuyler, "that although the Congress have given you peremptory instructions to take or destroy all vessels, boats, etc. preparing by Gov. Carleton on or near the lake, yet with respect to your proceeding to Montreal and Quebec such circumstances are pointed out by their resolutions which they expect you be fully possessed of previous to your undertaking the prosecution of that expedition."

Congress' admonitions concerning the invasion of Canada seemed contradictory to Schuyler. The resolution of June 27 had placed only a negative condition on an expedition into Canada. Only if the Canadians should appear displeased by the prospect of such a move, the resolution stated, should Schuyler hesitate to advance into that province. The latest letter from the president, however, lent a positive quality to that qualification by the emphasis placed upon it. Unsure of the intent of Congress, Schuyler asked Samuel Chase, a delegate from Maryland, with whom he had become acquainted in Philadelphia, for his opinion on this point. Chase promptly replied that "a previous condition, a *sine quâ non,* of marching into Quebec, is the friendship of the Canadians.

Without their consent and approbation," he warned Schuyler, "it is not [to] be undertaken."[21]

While such a condition may have seemed reasonable in theory, it quickly proved the opposite in practice. Reliable reports concerning Canadian public opinion were hard to come by. Soon after his arrival at Ticonderoga, Schuyler informed Congress that he could not "find that any intelligence has been received from Canada, on which any great dependence can be made." On the other hand, "accounts from all quarters agree that the Canadians are friendly to us."[22] Until these "accounts" were verified, Schuyler felt he should not move.

To obtain this information, Schuyler sent Major John Brown into Canada on July 24. Three weeks later, after several hairbreadth escapes, that officer returned with a report which should have removed all doubts from his superior's mind. While in that province, he reported, I was "protected by the Canadians, who I can assure you, are our friends. . . . Though they refuse to take up arms against the colonies," he asserted, "they wish and long for nothing more than to see us, with an army, penetrate their country."

Brown also reported that there were only about 700 of the King's troops in Canada; 300 at St. Johns and the remainder scattered among posts at Quebec, Montreal, and Chambly. "Now," he urged, "it is time to carry Canada. It may be done with great ease and little cost, and I have no doubt but the Canadians would join us." But there was great danger in further delay. "Should a large reinforcement arrive in Canada," he warned, "it will turn the scale immediately. The Canadians must then take up arms, [i.e., against the Americans] or be ruined."[23]

With his mind temporarily at ease concerning the disposition of the Canadians, Schuyler still refused to advance because of the deficiency in men, supplies, and transportation. These shortages were blamed by Major Brown on New York. "It seems that some evil planet has reigned in this quarter this year," he informed Governor Trumbull, "for notwithstanding the season far advanced, and a fine opportunity presents of making ourselves master of a country, . . . New York have acted a droll part, and are determined to defeat us, if in their power; they have failed in men and supplies." Colonel Hinman also sarcastically observed that while "the province of New York abounds with officers, . . . I have not had my curiosity gratified by the sight of one private." The New York Congress had authorized the raising of four battalions of 750 men each in late June, but the first of these troops did not join the Northern army until August.[24]

Dominated by the conservative Livingston faction, the extralegal government of New York moved with some reluctance to support the

incipient rebellion. In the Continental Congress, the New York delegates provided the leadership for those who sought reconciliation with
England and a limitation of the war to Massachusetts. Within their own
province, the New York leaders attempted to follow a cautious policy
which embraced allowing the royal governor, William Tryon, to remain
in New York City and supplying British men-of-war in the harbor, while
at the same time agreeing to raise several battalions for the Continental
service. Little wonder that Connecticut viewed New York's attachment
to the American cause with some suspicion. Nor is it surprising that
Philip Schuyler, one of the leaders of the Livingston faction, showed
considerable reluctance to initiate the invasion of Canada and the con-
sequent expansion of the war.

Philip Schuyler's continued procrastination eventually proved fatal
to American ambitions in Canada. The deficiencies he complained of
were real enough, but they were not sufficient justification for his inactivity. By the middle of August he had at least 1,500 men with which
he could attack St. Johns and its 300 British defenders. In addition, he
had complete command of the lake. But time was running out. If the
British were allowed to finish the vessels they were building at St. Johns,
this advantage would be lost. Schuyler was faced with a critical command decision. He must either go forward with the forces he had and
attempt to destroy those vessels and capture St. Johns, or allow the
British to regain control of the lake and prepare to meet the invasion
which would inevitably follow. At this critical moment, Schuyler had
to leave for Albany to attend an Indian conference.

Schuyler's departure on August 17 left Brigadier General Richard
Montgomery in command at Ticonderoga. Montgomery, unlike his
superior, could act decisively and vigorously when the occasion demanded. On August 23, 1775, Major Brown, stationed at the foot of
the lake to keep an eye on British preparations, reported that the two
vessels were nearly complete and Montgomery must act immediately to
prevent their entering the lake. Since St. Johns is located several miles
down the Richelieu River, which connects Lake Champlain with the St.
Lawrence, Brown suggested that should the army be unable to move, a
strong detachment should be sent at once to occupy either Rouse's
Point or the Ile aux Noix—a small island in the river above St. Johns.
With a few cannon, such a detachment might prevent the vessels from
getting out into the lake.

Montgomery immediately informed Schuyler that in his opinion it
was "absolutely necessary to move down the lake with the utmost dispatch." Without waiting for a reply, he embarked on the 28th for the
Ile aux Noix with two cannon and about 1,200 men.[25]

Montgomery did not hesitate a moment in taking the step where his superior had balked. In doing so, he was guilty of insubordination—and he knew it. "The moving without your orders," he informed Schuyler, "I don't like; but, on the other hand, the prevention of the enemy is of the utmost consequence. If I must err I wish to be on the right side." Knowing the circumstances, he hoped Schuyler would approve his actions. At the same time Montgomery was aware of the diminishing respect the men had for Schuyler, and he urged his chief to rejoin the army as soon as possible. "It will give the men great confidence in your spirit and activity," he advised, and "how necessary this confidence is to a general, I need not tell you."[26]

Although usually sensitive to any challenge, real or imagined, to his position as commander, Schuyler received the news of his subordinate's independent action "with pleasure." He had no doubts concerning the propriety of entering Canada, he declared; "to do it has been my determination, unless prevented by my superiors, for some time." Perhaps he had so determined, but he was quite obviously relieved that Montgomery had assumed the responsibility, "weak and ill-appointed as we are," for launching the invasion.[27]

Montgomery had secured Ile la Motte by the time Schuyler joined him on September 4. Resuming the command, Schuyler proceeded to St. Johns on the 5th, and disembarked 1,000 men within one and a half miles of the fort. Since the Americans outnumbered the defenders by at least three to one, they should have encountered little difficulty investing the fortress. However, Schuyler had disembarked them in a swamp, and most of the first day was required to reach the enemy's advanced lines. This accomplished, the troops entrenched for the night.

That night Schuyler received a visitor—a man whose name he revealed only to Washington—who provided the latest intelligence from Canada. With the exception of 50 men at Montreal, all of the British regulars were apparently at either St. Johns or Chambly. In addition, he reported that the fortifications at St. Johns were complete and well furnished with cannon. As to the disposition of the Canadians, he asserted that while they would welcome an American invasion they would do nothing actively to support it.[28]

The most remarkable thing about this information was that none of it was new. It merely confirmed what Schuyler had been told by Major Brown and others for the past month. Although his informant had told him that the presence of an American army would not be displeasing to the Canadians, Schuyler unaccountably decided that more information was necessary concerning the disposition of the Canadians before he proceeded! Consequently, on the following morning he retreated with his army to the Ile aux Noix, where he was joined by 700 additional New York and Connecticut troops.

The American army now outnumbered the defenders in St. Johns by five to one. In addition, Schuyler had five cannon and two mortars. The only thing he lacked was resolution. The little he had mustered to join Montgomery ebbed away as he suffered one of his recurrent fits of illness. So, two days after his withdrawal from St. Johns, he informed Congress that he planned to return up the lake to recover his health unless they ordered him to remain with the army. Without waiting for a reply, he entrusted the direction of the army to Montgomery, and, on the 16th, departed for Ticonderoga.[29] Almost two years were to elapse before Philip Schuyler again ventured to assume the direct command of the Northern army, and in the interim the men's confidence in his "spirit and activity" was not enhanced.

With Montgomery once again in command, the siege of St. Johns began in earnest. However, the delay occasioned by Schuyler's indecision allowed the British—between the abortive attempt of the 5th and the commencement of the siege on the 18th—to increase the garrison from a little over 300 men to about 725. As a result, the fort was able to withstand the American siege for 55 days. This proved an important strategic victory for the British. For while Montgomery was able to take Montreal on November 13, two weeks after the fall of St. Johns, the onset of winter and the expiration of enlistments dashed American hope of a decisive victory and afforded the British an opportunity to reinforce their beleaguered forces in Quebec.[30]

Discord and Disaster in the North

The American Failure in Canada

CONGRESS was not pleased with the performance of its Northern army, nor with the officer who commanded it. News of Montgomery's embarkation temporarily dispelled the impatience occasioned by Schuyler's procrastination, but this proved short-lived. When Schuyler's letter of September 8 reached Philadelphia, describing his abortive attempt on St. Johns, the delegates were once more filled with misgivings. Congress debated the wisdom of Schuyler's action, and finally appointed a committee of four to draft a letter advising him of Congress's verdict on his past decisions and the future course it wished him to pursue.

The four men chosen for the committee—Silas Deane, Samuel Chase, John Rutledge, and John Jay—were all friends and political supporters of General Schuyler and in the letter they submitted the next day, September 20, they warmly praised him for the action he had taken at St. Johns. This touched off a "large controversy," for many of the delegates objected to giving their "approbation of his late proceedings in retreating to Nut Island [Ile aux Noix]." After a lengthy debate, a letter was finally accepted which commended Schuyler for *taking possession* of Ile aux Noix! The unsuccessful attack on St. Johns and the subsequent retreat were not even mentioned, but he was admonished not to abandon the island "without the most mature consideration or the most pressing necessity." The rebuff at St. Johns, seemed to instill Congress with a determination to conquer Canada that had been lacking before. Even if the Canadians remained neutral, Schuyler was informed, Congress expected his "enterprize will be crowned with success . . ." and that neither men nor money would be spared.[1]

To fulfill this pledge, Congress directed immediate reinforcements to the Northern army. The New York Provincial Congress was asked to send forward all of the troops it had raised, and General Wooster was ordered to march at once with his Connecticut troops for Albany. That some of the delegates anticipated trouble between Wooster and Schuyler is evident from an entry that was deleted from the Journals. This directed the president to write Governor Trumbull "to request [him] to issue such orders and give such directions . . . as may effectually prevent all disputes in point of rank or command."[2]

It will be remembered that David Wooster was more than a little miffed at his demotion from major general in the Connecticut establishment to brigadier in the Continental army. After first refusing his commission, he was eventually prevailed upon to accept it—but he did so with reluctance and important mental reservations. Several incidents during the summer of 1775 illuminated these reservations, and should have warned Congress of the dangerous consequences of sending Wooster to serve under Schuyler.

The first of these incidents occurred during June. On the 15th, the New York Congress requested Wooster to march the troops under his command to New York. If necessary, the congress informed him, he should consult with Governor Trumbull before complying with the request. This he did promptly, and urged the governor to approve the application made by the New York Congress.

The circumstances which prompted the members of the provincial congress to ask for the Connecticut troops—and which convinced Wooster of the expediency of acceding to their request—were not spelled out in their letter. However, on the same day, Wooster was informed by Isaac Sears that the reason was the anticipated arrival of a large contingent of British regulars from Cork, Ireland. Sears, a leader of the New York Sons of Liberty, also informed Wooster of an interesting fact that the New York Congress had failed to mention. While Wooster was to march into the province, he was not to occupy the city of New York. Instead, he was to camp some five miles distant. In keeping with the strictly defensive policy outlined by James Duane in May, it appeared that while the penetration of the province would be opposed, the landing of British troops in the city would not.[3]

Substantiation of this soon came to hand. Just before midnight on June 15, Isaac Sears arrived at Wooster's Greenwich headquarters and roused the general from his bed. Not only was the landing of British troops to be unopposed, Wooster learned, but "the people of New York intend[ed] to quarter the troops in the city!" This ambivalence disturbed Wooster, and he was reluctant to place himself under a body of men who could formulate such a policy. "I should be glad to be informed," he wrote Trumbull, "how far I shall subject myself and the troops under my command to the direction of the Continent or provincial congress;

whether, (if I proceed to New York), when the Irish troops arrive, I shall wait for directions from the Continental Congress whether to oppose them or not." In addition, he made it clear to the governor that it was his opinion "that they ought not to be suffered to land."

Governor Trumbull therefore ordered Wooster to proceed to within five miles of the city of New York with 1,700 Connecticut troops. At the same time, he informed the New York Congress that this force would be subject to the orders of the Continental Congress as well as those of the provincial congress. Two days before this decision was reached, however, the New York Congress complicated matters by changing its mind. Learning that the transports destined for New York were going instead to Boston, it informed General Wooster that his services were no longer required.[4] But the matter did not end here.

Completely unaware of all this, the Continental Congress passed a resolution on June 16, 1775, which asked the New York Congress to request troops from Governor Trumbull to garrison certain important posts in their province. According to Eliphalet Dyer, this resolve was prompted by an apprehension that "cautious men" in New York were intent upon "saving for themselves and their province a safe retreat if possible. We readily see that they most carefully avoid taking any hand in these matters [i.e., opposition to the British]," he told Governor Trumbull, "therefore the more they are brought to move and apply the more they will involve themselves in the same predicament with the other colonies, which will give us a stronger security for their future firmness in the general cause."

The delegates in Congress were therefore pleasantly surprised when they learned that the New York Congress had anticipated their resolution. But their pleasure again gave way to apprehension when they learned that the provincial congress had cancelled its request for Connecticut troops. "This Congress notwithstanding," Dyer reported on June 20, "persist in their resolutions, that General Wooster without western forces go forward to New York as soon as possible." In part, this decision was based upon the fear that the reported rerouting of the Cork transports was a trick, and that when the British found New York unprotected, they would "return of a sudden and get a footing there." "But that is not the only reason," Dyer wryly commented to Trumbull, "your imagination I dare say will suggest others." Thus prodded by Congress, New York again requested Connecticut troops, and by the first week in July, Wooster was camped within a mile and a half of New York City.[5]

As it turned out, the Connecticut troops were not needed after all. A packet boat sent by General Gage intercepted the transports off Sandy Hook and the four regiments aboard were redirected to their original destination—Boston. Although aware of this by July 6, the Connecticut troops, lacking orders to the contrary, remained in New York. At first, relations between Wooster and his men and their New York hosts were cordial enough. A banquet held in their honor by the New York Military Club provided Wooster and his officers a day of good food, drink, and entertainment and concluded with the drinking of 18 toasts, including one to "the daughters of America in the arms of their brave defenders only!"[6]

However, relations did not remain cordial. Indentured servants in large numbers ran away from their masters in the city and joined the Connecticut troops, and the provincial congress had to order Wooster to return them to their owners. More serious were the confiscation of King's stores and the destruction of a boat belonging to the British man-of-war *Asia*. Despite the censure of her neighbors, New York still supplied His Majesty's war ships in the harbor and the congress did all in its power to prevent any incident which might invite British retaliation against the city. The Connecticut troops demonstrated that they had no such inhibitions and, while the King's stores were recovered and eventually returned, the *Asia*'s boat was burned.

The city magistrates found they could do little to control the New England troops, and General Wooster himself finally concluded that the only solution lay in moving the camp further from town. The provincial congress heartily agreed, and named a special committee to expedite the move. Then, to placate the Captain of the *Asia,* the congress ordered the construction, at their expense, of a replacement for the boat which had been burned. (This boat too was destroyed "by some disorderly persons" when nearly completed and another was constructed under a special guard of the city militia.)[7]

As the immediate threat to New York dissipated, Wooster and his men were withdrawn to defend Connecticut's coastline from depredatory British foraging parties. The dust of their departure had hardly settled when the New York Congress, to its chagrin, found it lacked the necessary manpower to construct and guard the fortifications in the Hudson Highlands recommended by the Continental Congress.

Thus, in August, New York again requested Connecticut troops, and Governor Trumbull once again ordered Wooster to proceed there and place himself under the direction of the provincial congress. This time Wooster objected vehemently. "Your honor knows the suspicious light in which the New York Congress are viewed by the rest of the Continent," he complained to Trumbull on August 24. "I must therefore beg of your honor to alter that part of your orders to me, in which you subject me to the direction of that body of men." Furthermore, he personally had no faith in their loyalty to the cause, and thought "it not only a disgrace to me, but a dishonor to my employers, that I am subjected to them. You know not, sir, half their tricks." Knowing Wooster's opinion of the New York Congress, Trumbull should never have sent him to that province—but he did. Moreover, he left unresolved the question of whose orders Wooster was to obey.

The issue of subordination was squarely joined on September 13, when the New York Committee of Safety ordered Wooster to detach a company for the erection and guarding of the Highland fortifications. This order, the committee claimed, was in response to a directive received from the Continental Congress. Wooster, from his camp at Harlem, replied that he neither could nor would detach any troops without a specific order from either General Washington or the Continental Congress. If the committee had such an order from the Continental Congress, he wished to see it.

John Haring, the chairman of the committee promptly informed Wooster that the congressional resolve referred to was that of June 16, by which the Connecticut troops sent to New York to secure certain posts and aid in the erection of fortifications were to be under the direction of the New York Congress. The resolve of June 16 was quite clear on this point. However, there were certain circumstances, as Wooster carefully pointed out, which cast doubt upon the relevancy of that resolve in the present instance.

In the first place, the resolution had been passed "before the Continental forces were properly organized." It therefore pertained to Connecticut, rather than Continental troops. And, second, he and his troops had received their orders—by way of Governor Trumbull—from the commander in chief, and were therefore acting in a Continental capacity. "No provincial congress can," he informed the committee on September 17, "with any propriety, interfere in the disposition of Continental troops, much less *control* the orders of any general officer. If the Continental Congress or the commander-in-chief, think proper to employ the whole or a part of the troops under my command, in erecting and defending batteries, at the Highlands or elsewhere," he assured the committee, "I shall expect *their orders* direct, and no man will with greater alacrity obey their *lawful summons.*"

Clearly, the central issue in this controversy was whether General Wooster's command consisted of Connecticut or Continental troops. If the former, the resolution of June 16 applied, and the orders of the provincial congress were valid. If the latter, the resolve was irrelevant, and the orders based upon it invalid. Similarly, it was of importance whether Wooster was acting in the capacity of a Continental brigadier or a Connecticut major general.

To the extent that these troops were acting under orders from the commander in chief, outside of Connecticut, they had to be considered Continental soldiers. The fact that a sizable portion of this regiment had previously been detached and sent to join the Northern army by order of Congress tended to reinforce this contention. Thus, General Wooster was probably correct in questioning the authority of the New York Congress.

Strangely enough, the one man who did not find this line of reasoning conclusive was General Wooster. A few weeks before his dispute with the New York Committee of Safety, Wooster had refused to allow Gunning Bedford, deputy mustermaster general, to muster the troops under his command. His reason: he did not consider himself a Continental officer! Thus Wooster had two hats—one a Continental brigadier's, the other, a Connecticut major general's—and he could with dexterity put on one or the other as the occasion demanded.

Congress was aware of this ambivalence when it ordered Wooster to Albany to join the Northern army. However, the delegates themselves were apparently unsure of Wooster's status. At the same time that they issued the order sending him north—which clearly indicated he was a Continental officer—they requested Governor Trumbull to "issue such orders and give such directions" to Wooster "as may effectually prevent all disputes in point of rank or command." This latter resolve tacitly acknowledged that he was a Connecticut officer. The realization of this inconsistency is probably what prompted Congress to expunge the resolve from the record and to refrain from making the request of Trumbull. Consequently, Wooster's status remained unclarified, and his arrival in the Northern department precipitated a command crisis at a most inopportune moment.

General Schuyler's first intimation of his impending difficulties with the Connecticut troops came in August with the arrival of Gunning Bedford at Ticonderoga. Bedford informed Schuyler of Wooster's refusal to muster his men and his reason. To his distress, Schuyler soon discovered that a similar attitude prevailed among the Connecticut troops already under his command.

As soon as Bedford arrived, Schuyler issued a general order directing the company captains to prepare muster rolls in conformance with forms to be distributed by the deputy mustermaster. Acting in conformance with this order, Bedford soon discovered that the Connecticut troops were different from the rest of the army in one important respect. "When I gave them the forms," he reported, "I showed them the articles (in the general body of rules for the regulation of the army) which respect my particular department. I found the Connecticut troops had none of them signed them [the Articles of War]." Since Schuyler had issued specific orders that everyone should sign the Continental

Articles, he immediately summoned the officers and demanded an explanation.

The Connecticut officers admitted that they had disobeyed orders in not urging their men to sign the Articles. However, to do so, they warned Schuyler, "would raise a defection . . . which would injure the cause, as the soldiers thought their signing the articles would dissolve their present obligations, for a limited time, to their own colony, . . . and involve them in a service, the end of which was uncertain, and would leave them, perhaps, on no better footing than that of regulars."

This was an extremely serious matter. Soldiers who had not signed the Articles of War were not liable to discipline by Continental officers. Of course the men could be court-martialed and punished under the Connecticut articles of war, but such courts could consist only of Connecticut officers. Thus, Continental officers, as such, had no disciplinary authority over their subordinates. One can imagine Schuyler's reaction when he learned that he had no authority over the internal regulation of more than half his army. However, if he insisted upon their signing the Articles, the Connecticut regiments might pack up and go home. Wasn't it better to have an undisciplined army than no army at all? Schuyler decided it was, and "thought prudent to drop the matter for the present."[8]

The matter did not stay dropped for long. During the second week of October General Wooster arrived at Fort George. "And now, my good sir," wrote Bedford to Schuyler, "suffer me to condole with you at the approach of troubles, I see ready to be heaped upon you. General Wooster and his regiment, in a few days will be with you." Indeed, Wooster was already guilty of insubordination on two counts. On the march from Albany to the post at the southern end of Lake George, he had discharged some of the troops under his command.[9] And, soon after his arrival, he convened a general court-martial, despite the regulation that only the commanding officer of a department—in this case, Schuyler—could discharge the men serving under him or order a general court-martial.

Wooster justified his dismissal of the troops by declaring that "he was major general of the Connecticut forces, and that no man on this side of Connecticut had a right to discharge one of his soldiers but himself."

In the case of the court-martial, however, Wooster ran into a bit of trouble. Mr. Cobb, the commissary at Fort George, "as he was a Connecticut man, (but who despises them thoroughly in his heart) was let into their counsels," and he was present when Wooster determined to call the court-martial. Acting as major general of the Connecticut forces, Wooster had no qualms in ordering the court, but the matter was complicated by a shortage of qualified Connecticut officers to sit on it. The only way he could get additional officers was to sign the order as a brigadier in the Continental service. But even he balked at so gross an act of insubordination. "He mentioned the difficulty to his officers—'Why, one of them replies, you have two strings to your bow'—another, 'Take care you don't pull the weakest' and a third, 'You may pull on both on occasion.' " Cobb believed that he finally signed the order as a brigadier general.[10]

Schuyler seethed with indignation when news of Wooster's "extraordinary conduct" reached him at Ticonderoga. Characteristically, he viewed Wooster's insubordination as a personal insult, rather than as the serious breach of military discipline it was. "I assure you," he informed the president of Congress on October 14, "that I feel these insults from a general officer with all that keen sensibility that a man of honor ought, and I should be ashamed to mention them to Congress, but that the critical situation of our public affairs at this period require that I should sacrifice a just resentment of them—and I would wish to have it remembered that to that cause only must be imputed that I have suffered a personal indignity to go unpunished."[11]

Schuyler, for all his fury, was impotent. General Montgomery was urgently requesting reinforcements for the siege of St. Johns. Many of Schuyler's men were not fit for duty because of sickness—real or feigned—and others, officers and men alike, either malingered or deserted. Consequently, Wooster's regiment was desperately needed, and it soon became painfully evident that the regiment would not go forward if Schuyler chose to punish its general's insubordination by either removing him from command or holding him at Ticonderoga for a court-martial.

When 353 of Wooster's men arrived at Ticonderoga, Schuyler ordered them to proceed to St. Johns. General Wooster, however, had not yet arrived, and the men informd Schuyler that they did not "choose to move until he does." "Do not choose to move! Strange language in an army; but," complained Schuyler, "the irresistible force of necessity obliges me to put up with it." Another incident demonstrating how much his authority had been curtailed, occurred on October 18. "This morning," he informed President Hancock, "I gave an order to Lieutenant Colonel Ward to send a subaltern, a sergeant, corporal, and twenty privates, in two bateaux, to carry powder, artillery stores, and rum [to St. Johns]. The colonel (who is a good man) called on me to know if he would not be blamed by General Wooster for obeying my orders. I begged him to send the men, and urged the necessity. The men," he sarcastically concluded, "I believe, will condescend to go."

General Wooster arrived at Ticonderoga during the afternoon of October 18 and was met by Schuyler who informed him that he was to remain at that post until he acknowledged his subordination to his immediate superior—General Montgomery. Wooster bluntly replied that if he remained at Ticonderoga, so too did his regiment. However, he assured Schuyler that "he would most readily put himself under the command of General Montgomery; that his only views were the public service." Having heard this "spirited and sensible declaration" with "inexpressible satisfaction," Schuyler decided to allow him to proceed on the morrow to St. Johns.[12]

The matter might have ended here, but that night Schuyler received Bedford's letter of the 15th which contained the detailed account of the court-martial called by Wooster. Apparently this was the first that Schuyler had heard of that incident (his previous doubts concerning Wooster's subordination having been aroused by that officer's controversy with the New York Committee of Safety and his dismissal of troops on the way to Fort George). Therefore Wooster's "spirited and sensible declaration" of that afternoon no longer filled Schuyler with "inexpressible satisfaction."

Early the next morning, October 19, Schuyler informed the Connecticut general that he could not permit him to proceed to St. Johns. Everything, Wooster was told, seemed to indicate that he was a brigadier general in the Continental army. That rank had been conferred upon him by the Continental Congress, the regiment he commanded had been taken into the pay and service of the Associated Colonies, and he had "in a variety of instances obeyed the orders of Congress. . . . But," Schuyler added, "I am just now informed that you have called a general court-martial at Fort George on your way up here, a conduct which I cannot account for, unless you consider yourself as my superior. . . . You are a younger brigadier general than Mr. Montgomery, and unless you consider yourself as such, I cannot consistent with the duty I owe the public, permit you to join that part of the army now under Brigadier General Montgomery's command." Wooster was asked to give an immediate and explicit answer to the question: "Whether you consider yourself and your regiment in the service of the Associated Colonies, and yourself a younger brigadier general in that service than Mr. Montgomery or not?"

Wooster's reply was prompt and explicit as far as it dealt with his rank in the Continental army. "You are sensible," he informed Schuyler, "that my rank could not be very agreeable to me." Nonetheless, "I have the cause of my country too much at heart to make any difficulties or uneasiness in the army." Consequently, he assured his superior, "I shall consider my rank in the army what my commission from the Continental Congress makes it, and shall not attempt to dispute the command with General Montgomery at St. Johns."

The status of his regiment, however, was another matter. "As to my regiment," he declared, "I consider them as what they really are, according to the tenor of their enlistments and compact with the Colony of Connecticut, by whom they were raised." They were Connecticut troops "acting in conjunction with the troops of the other colonies in the service and for the defense of the Associated Colonies in general." In addition, having unanimously refused to sign the Continental Articles of War, his men were subject only to the "Law Martial of Connecticut under which they were raised." This made Wooster, by virtue of his commission from that colony, and not Schuyler, the supreme disciplinary authority of the Connecticut troops. "Upon the same principle," he asserted, "I ordered a general court-martial at Fort George."[13]

One can only imagine Schuyler's consternation following this exchange. Forcing Wooster to recognize his subordination to Montgomery in the Continental line, would not assure harmony in the Northern army. As long as the status of the Connecticut troops remained equivocal and they acted with, but not as a part of, the Continental army, then the entire command structure was jeopardized. For all intents and purposes, whenever he chose to act in his capacity as a Connecticut major general, David Wooster would enjoy all of the prerogatives of an independent command. And it was clear to Schuyler that Wooster both realized and planned to take advantage of the dichotomous role in which he had been cast.

An immediate danger posed by such an arrangement involved the question of provisions. One of the gravest problems in the Northern department was the lack of sufficient supplies. By dint of strenuous efforts, Schuyler and the department's commissary, Walter Livingston, had managed by the fall of 1775 to create a barely adequate system which funneled supplies from central New York to the army before St. Johns. In conformance with their unique status, the Connecticut regiment decided it would not draw supplies from the department's commissary. Instead it set about provisioning itself.

The always informative Gunning Bedford reported to Schuyler on October 15 that Wooster had contracted with the mercantile firm of Lockwood and Colt to supply the needs of his regiment. To assure the faithful and interested services of the merchants, Wooster made Lockwood his personal secretary and Colt the regimental commissary. As a result the regimental stores included large quantities of molasses, sugar, peas, rice, chocolate, and soap—all of which were either in short supply or entirely lacking in the Northern army. This not only assured that they would not be dependent upon the Continental Congress in any way ("they will not touch Continental stores, nor eat Continental provisions: they boast [of] having nothing to do with the Continent") but it was darkly hinted that they had more stores than they could consume, and intended to sell the surplus to their less fortunate comrades in arms. Consequently, the entire army might be disrupted "by the jealousies Wooster's regiment must create among the other troops, when they see them so much better provided with everything than they are, or can be."

As in the case of their refusal to sign the Articles of War, Schuyler felt it imprudent to attempt to force the Connecticut troops to conform to the regulations governing the rest of the army. Nor could he effectively discipline General Wooster. In either case, had he tried, Wooster's regiment probably would have refused to reinforce General Montgomery. As it was, on October 21, some of the officers and most of the men declared that they thought it imprudent to proceed to St. Johns at that late season. The army, they reasoned, would be inevitably overtaken by winter in Canada, and the men would either perish from the cold or be forced to make a hurried retreat. In the latter case, a deficiency of boats would force the sacrifice of many of them to the enemy.[14]

With the aid of Wooster, Lockwood, and the regimental chaplain, Schuyler finally induced the men to proceed at least as far as St. Johns. At one o'clock in the afternoon of the 22nd, the regiment embarked for the foot of the lake. As they were leaving, however, Schuyler could not resist a parting shot at Wooster. "Being well informed," he dryly remarked, "that you have declared on your way to this place that if you were at St. Johns, you would march into the fort, at the head of your regiment, and as it is just, that you should have an opportunity of showing your prowess and that of your regiment, I have desired General Montgomery to give you leave to make the attempt, if you choose."

While provocation was certainly not lacking, Schuyler should never have indulged himself in this witticism. It was peevish, petty, and ill suited to a commanding officer. Such behavior would diminish the respect a subordinate should hold either for him or for the orders he issued, and General Wooster had very little of either to begin with. Perhaps Schuyler felt he could indulge himself since he could rely upon Montgomery to keep Wooster in line. However, in the event that something happened to Montgomery, Wooster would then succeed to the actual command of the army in Canada, and then Schuyler might have occasion to regret such a display of petulance.

Any fears that Wooster might contest Montgomery's superiority were soon allayed. "Mr. Wooster," Montgomery wrote on October 31, "has . . . behaved much to my satisfaction at least as far as has come to my knowledge." In addition, he informed Schuyler that he had shown the old general every courtesy and even invited him to live with him. Montgomery seems to have realized, as Schuyler did not, that Wooster's advanced years as well as his dissatisfaction with his rank demanded tactful handling by his superiors. Wooster, after all, was 64 years old, while Montgomery, his immediate superior, was only 37! Even General Schuyler was only 42 years of age—a young upstart compared to the old Yankee general. It would be strange indeed if Wooster did not feel the incongruity of his subordination to men so much his junior in years. Consequently, Montgomery's tact and courtesy succeeded in winning Wooster's loyal cooperation where Schuyler's threats and sarcasms failed.

Reinforced by Wooster's regiment, Montgomery was able to press his siege to a successful conclusion. With the capitulation of St. Johns on November 2, the road to Montreal was open. This bright prospect was dimmed, however, by the fact that a majority of the troops refused to leave St. Johns.

Led by Wooster's regiment, the men rebelled at proceeding further into Canada at such a late season. They were poorly clad and already felt the effects of the November wind and rain. What would become of them, they asked, when the harsh Canadian winter began in earnest? Also, and perhaps most important, the Connecticut enlistments expired at the end of December, and many felt that the snow and ice would prevent them from returning home before the spring thaw.

Such obstructionism angered and dismayed even members of the Connecticut delegation in Congress. "The behavior of our soldiers had made me sick," Silas Deane bitterly commented, "but little better could be expected from men trained up with notions of their right of saying how, and when, and under whom, they will serve; and who have, for certain dirty, political purposes, been tampered with by their officers, among whom no less than a *General* has been busy." The "General" referred to was obviously Wooster.

In the end, General Montgomery was forced to promise the men new winter clothing if they would proceed to Montreal. In addition, he promised that once the city fell, all those who wished it would be promptly dismissed.[15]

Without a shot being fired in its defense, the civil authorities of Montreal surrendered the city to Montgomery on November 13. What remained of the British army in Canada was now concentrated at

Quebec. If that citadel could be reduced, the conquest of Canada would be complete.

Sir Guy Carleton, Governor of Canada and commander of British forces in that province, had started the campaign with only two regiments of British regulars—the 7th and the 26th. After the fall of St. Johns, only 70 men of the 7th Regiment remained. These, combined with some 200 British and 300 French militia, had the task of defending Quebec. In addition, the Royal Navy contributed 37 marines and 345 sailors. In all, Carleton had no more than 1,200 men to hold the extensive lines guarding the city. Nearly half of this force—the militia—was completely unreliable and might well throw down their arms at the appearance of the American army. Thus, the city's governor, Hector Cremahé, pessimistically informed General Howe that "there is too much reason to apprehend the affair will be soon over."[16]

On the 9th of November, while Montgomery closed in on the doomed city of Montreal, a starved and ragged band of Americans emerged from the wilderness on the southern bank of the St. Lawrence opposite Quebec. This was the remnant of Colonel Benedict Arnold's command which, 1,100 strong, had set out from Cambridge on September 6. Now, 64 days later, their numbers reduced by half, they gazed upon the mighty fortress they had come to conquer—Quebec.

The feasibility of such an expedition had first attracted Washington's attention in early August. The plan, as he explained it to Schuyler, was to push an army of between 1,000 and 1,200 men up the Kennebec River, directly to Quebec. This would force General Carleton to split the force he had gathered to oppose Montgomery. "He [Carleton] must either break up and follow this party to Quebec," he informed the Northern commander, "by which he will leave you free passage, or he must suffer that important place to fall into our hands."[17]

Theoretically, this was sound strategy. However, both Washington and Arnold grossly underestimated the physical obstacles that would have to be surmounted. Consequently, instead of arriving at his objective about the first of October as originally planned, Arnold was not in position to cooperate with Montgomery until the second week of November.[18]

Arnold's late arrival set back the timetable for the conquest of Canada by a full month. This proved fatal. Had he arrived in early October, Carleton would have been forced to divide his small force and St. Johns would have fallen quickly. Montgomery could then have taken Montreal and marched with his army to join Arnold for an assault upon Quebec. This could all have been accomplished before Montgomery's men became restive at the lateness of the season. As it was, with the surrender of Montreal, many of the troops demanded that Montgomery make good the promise of dismissal he had been forced to give at St. Johns. Of the several hundred New England troops in his army, fewer than 200 reenlisted. The rest, even before their enlistments had expired, promptly left the army for their homes—hastened on "by their fear of being detained in Canada, by the severity of the weather." Montgomery was left with about 1,000 men, which, he warned Schuyler, while sufficient to "hold the ground already gotten," could not hope to conclude the conquest of Canada. He therefore desperately pleaded that he be reinforced with "a large body of troops . . . in order to make a vigorous attack on Quebec, before the arrival of succors in the spring."[19]

Reinforcements—large or small—were not forthcoming. When Montgomery joined Arnold before Quebec on December 2, he brought with him only 300 men. He had left about 500 men at Montreal under the command of General Wooster. With Arnold's tatterdemalion force, the besiegers could muster barely 800 men. The besieged, on the other hand, numbered about 1,200 fighting men and were ensconced behind the strongest fortifications in North America. Nonetheless, Montgomery and Arnold decided to attack on the first dark and stormy night.[20]

Such a night was New Year's Eve. Shortly after midnight, in a howling blizzard, the Americans launched a two-pronged attack against the lower town and the bastion on Cape Diamond. Within minutes Montgomery, leading the attack on Cape Diamond, was shot dead, and Arnold, directing the attack in the lower town, was severely wounded and carried back to the hospital.

The night then became a horror for the Americans remaining in the lower town. Groping up pitch-black, snow-filled streets, they ran into barricades defended by cannon as well as muskets. Terrible carnage was wrought by the cannon in the narrow streets. Many of the wounded fell in the deep snow and soon perished. Others, more fortunate, were captured. Of the 800 men who made the attack, 48 were killed, 34 wounded, and a staggering 372 captured. Most of these casualties were suffered by Arnold's column. The New Yorkers, who had turned back after the death of Montgomery, suffered only 14 casualties. The British lost only 18 men—5 killed and 13 wounded. The handful of Americans that survived that New Year's massacre could not hope to renew the attack. Indeed, they would be very fortunate if Carleton did not sally forth and complete their destruction.[21]

The midnight attack on Quebec marked the last desperate effort of American arms in Canada. With its failure, the hope that Canada might become the fourteenth member of the United Colonies went aglimmering. The causes of this final defeat were legion. If Congress had been more generous in supplying the Northern army with men and supplies, if Arnold had arrived at Quebec earlier, and if Montgomery and Arnold had not been shot down, the outcome of the assault might have been different. Nevertheless, as entertaining as the "ifs" of history may be to armchair strategists, they throw little light on why events occurred as they did. In this case, it is clear that a contributory cause of the American failure in Canada was Philip Schuyler's lack of initiative as commander of the Northern department.

It is true that Congress's attitude toward the invasion of Canada was somewhat equivocal during the summer of 1775. It must therefore assume partial responsibility for the fatal delay in launching the invasion. However, it is clear from the correspondence between Congress and General Schuyler that the ultimate decision to proceed into Canada had to be made by the latter. Throughout July and August he found numerous reasons to put off making such a decision. It was finally up to General Montgomery to initiate the move into Canada during his superior's absence. The delay caused by Schuyler's indecision gave Governor Carleton valuable time in which to strengthen the critical post at St. Johns.

Even so, the invasion might have been successful if Schuyler had then acted with firmness and resolution. Instead, he ordered a retreat to the Ile aux Noix after a minor skirmish with the enemy. This gave Carleton even more time in which to strengthen and reinforce St. Johns. Having accomplished nothing, Schuyler retired to Ticonderoga, leaving the more energetic Montgomery in command of the army. But it was then too late. The months of procrastination made a long siege of St. Johns inevitable, and by the time that post surrendered, the approach of winter and the expiration of enlistments combined to thwart an American conquest of Canada.

Besides his indecisiveness, Schuyler had a flaw in his personality which had serious consequences. As a self-conscious aristocrat, he had from the first been annoyed by the independent and democratic spirit of the New England troops which defied his attempts to instill a "proper subordination" in the army. The New Englanders, officers and men, were aware of his dislike for them and returned it with interest.

By itself, this situation was neither unique nor particularly serious. Many high-ranking officers in the Continental army, including Washington, viewed Yankee independence in the army with distaste. Whatever their views concerning democracy in the political realm, they all agreed that it had no place in the army. As General Montgomery commented, "troops who carry the spirit of freedom into the field, and think for themselves," will not bear either subordination or discipline.[22] However, he, with Generals Washington, Lee, and Gates, knew the art of compromise and the necessity of using it judiciously to get the most out of the men under his command.

Schuyler either could not or would not compromise, and, as a result, the New England troops, and even many of those from New York, came to regard him as a narrow-minded, aristocratic tyrant. To one observer this clearly indicated the need for a general officer to be "well acquainted with the genius, temper & disposition of the people who compose his army." And while this officer asserted that he did not "believe one fiftieth part of the complaints against General Schuyler," he was convinced "that the greater part of the uneasiness" in the Northern army was due to Schuyler's attempt to impose upon the troops "usages frequently practiced among regular troops." Consequently, the New Englanders were "universally disaffected with General Schuyler."[23]

Although personal popularity was important for a general who had to lead men imbued with "the spirit of freedom," it was not absolutely essential. Schuyler might still have been a good general if he had gained the respect and confidence of the men by displaying personal courage and enterprise. This he certainly did not do. Despite Montgomery's warning that his presence with the army, and a show of "spirit and activity" would be necessary to win the confidence of the men,[24] Schuyler spent only two weeks with the army in September. Thereafter, he spent his time either at Ticonderoga, Albany, or at his Saratoga home, while his army perished in Canada.

To be fair, it should be noted that one of the reasons for Schuyler's absence from the army was the poor state of his health. He seemed particularly susceptible to indispositions when faced with the need to make important decisions or when a battle was in the offing. This does not necessarily mean that he was a coward—although some of his enemies hinted that this was the case. Certainly it appeared to indicate a lack of "strong nerves" which Montgomery, as early as June, feared would be a handicap should Schuyler be given a military command.

Schuyler's absence from the army he commanded, whatever the reasons for it, had an incalculable effect upon the morale of the officers and men. An energetic and courageous commander can often set a personal example which at a critical moment can turn defeat into victory. The Northern army lacked such a commander. Thus, Philip Schuyler's inadequacies as a commander contributed significantly to the low morale, lack of discipline, and poor performance in battle of the Northern army and the resultant failure of the Canadian campaign.

The American Army Becomes Truly Continental

$\mathbf{M}$ANY of the difficulties experienced by both the Northern army and the army besieging Boston during the fall and winter of 1775 were the result of poor organization. The basic problem was simply that Congress lacked effective control over these armies. The general officers were appointed by and responsible to Congress, as were the major administrative officers. However, the individual colonies still had the appointment of all officers below the rank of general and the sole responsibility for maintaining their regiments at full strength. Both Washington and Schuyler were hindered by a lack of men and supplies, and too often found themselves at cross purposes with subordinates over whom they had little control. Thus, by and large, the American army was "Continental" in name only.

Eventually, the question of whether Congress or the individual colonies would have the appointment of field-grade officers came to have political overtones. Those who favored a strong central government naturally wished to increase the dependence of the army on Congress, while those who wished to preserve the autonomy of the colonies resisted any such development. Initially, however, George Washington's objections to the appointment of such officers by the individual colonies had nothing to do with political theory.

Since the army besieging Boston was composed of New England regiments, the field officers were also New Englanders, and, much to Washington's despair, this arrangement was likely to be perpetuated indefinitely. As noted before, the commander in chief had taken an immediate dislike to the New England soldiers whom he described as "an exceeding dirty and nasty people," and he felt that the officers were of the "same kidney with the privates." But with the disposition of all

61

commissions below that of general in the hands of the individual colonies, Washington was forced to conclude that "volunteers from any other colonies, however deserving they may be of notice . . . will stand little chance whilst there is an application from any person of the government from whence the regiment came." Such being the case, he observed to Lewis Morris on August 4, the only remedy was for Congress to grant all field-grade commissions and, using merit as the sole criterion, impartially consider applicants from all of the colonies.

To make matters worse, Washington was convinced that a variety of low politics was involved in the selection of many of his junior officers. When giving his reasons for appointing Thomas Mifflin quartermaster general, Washington hinted at this when he observed that "he stands unconnected with either of these governments, or with this, that, or the other man; for, between you and me, there is more in this than you can easily imagine." Also, by the end of August, he was showing an awareness of the political implications of the policy being pursued. He confided to Richard Henry Lee that in his opinion "it is giving that power and weight to an individual colony, which ought of right to belong only to the whole."[1]

Washington's objections to the system of appointing officers were made too late for Congress to act upon, that body having adjourned on August 2. However, had Congress been in session, it is extremely doubtful whether it would have taken any action. Confidence in the newly adopted army was high during the summer of 1775, and few were yet prepared to look at it critically. James Warren, understandably proud of his fellow Yankees, confidently declared to Sam Adams on August 2 that "the army of the united colonies are already superior in valour, and from the most amazingly rapid progress in discipline, we may justly conclude will shortly become the most formidable troops in the world." Some, including Washington, may have been less optimistic, but with General Gage and the British army penned up in Boston, many began to believe that the colonies had little to fear from the British military.

There was another reason why many in Congress were reluctant to accede to Washington's suggestions concerning the appointment of officers. To do so would strengthen congressional control of the army and hasten the transformation of the individual provincial militias into a regular, standing army under the sole direction of the central government. Both of the major congressional factions opposed such a development during the summer of 1775. Those favoring reconciliation viewed it as a step away from their goal, while those secretly in favor of independence viewed with misgivings any proposal that would strengthen the central government at the expense of the individual colonies. Furthermore, many members of Congress sincerely believed that the creation of a standing army would subvert and ultimately destroy the very liberties it was meant to protect.

The most fervent attack on standing armies appeared in a Philadelphia newspaper in late August of 1775. The author, who chose to use the sobriquet "Caractacus" [the first Briton who led resistance to the Roman invasion], not only condemned regular armies but also a paid militia—by accepting pay, a militiaman was transformed into a mercenary. The author was convinced that any regular military establishment "must always be composed of people of the smallest property, and perhaps the least virtue among us." By close association in camp and barracks, these men soon lost the "gentleness and sobriety of citizens. The military spirit, by being transferred from the bulk of the country to a few mercenaries, is gradually monopolized by them, so that in a few years, from being our servants, we furnish them the means of becoming our masters. . . . History is dyed in blood when it speaks of the ravages which standing armies have committed upon the liberties of mankind: officers and soldiers of the best principles and characters have been converted into the instruments of tyranny. . . . In a word, had I the wings and tongue of an angel, I would fly from one end of the Continent to the other at the present juncture, and proclaim constantly in the ears of my countrymen, *Beware of standing armies!"*

Instead of an "army of mercenaries," "Caractacus" proposed the creation of a vigilant militia in each colony capable of responding at a moment's notice to any move of the enemy. To accomplish this, all men between the ages of 16 and 50 would be armed and trained, and one quarter of these, in rotation, would stand ready to march to any part of their own or a neighboring colony. Extolling the benefits to be derived from such a system, "Caractacus" pointed to the Republic of Switzerland which, he claimed, had "preserved its peace, as well as its freedom, longer than any country in Europe. The reason is plain: in Switzerland the soldier and the citizen are united in the same person."

At this point, the author indulged in a rather treasonous digression. Remarking upon the ancient republics of Greece and Rome, he observed that some felt their glory and success was due to their form of government rather than their dependence upon the citizen-soldier. "They tell us," he continued, "that in countries where every man has property, and an equal right to share in the legislation, to offer a soldier pay for his services is to offer a man a draught upon himself." This plug for republican government was only halfheartedly disavowed by "Caractacus" when he modestly concluded that he was "not prepared to answer these encomiums upon popular governments."[2]

Although the identity of "Caractacus" is unknown, it is possible to ascertain from the article that he was educated, familiar with both ancient and more recent history, and a sturdy republican. The faith he proclaimed in the militia was not echoed by his aristocratic contemporaries. George Washington and Philip Schuyler had little cause to speak well of the militia system, for men of their class were automatically viewed with mistrust and distaste by most militiamen. In contrast, officers such as Horatio Gates and Benedict Arnold found upon occasion that the militia could be used effectively against British regulars.

Whatever beliefs individual congressmen entertained concerning the merits of the militia as opposed to a regular army, a majority soon realized that the army gathered before Boston was desperately in need of reorganization. Washington sent numerous letters to the president and various members of Congress during July and August describing conditions in the army and pointing out needed changes. Also, many congressmen, following adjournment in August, hurried to the camp at Cambridge to view for themselves the state of the army.

Consequently, when Congress reconvened in September, it asked Washington to confer with his officers "upon the most prudent and effectual methods of accomplishing" the following: the continuation in the Continental service of the men under his command after the expiration of their present enlistments; the reduction of the provincial establishments into one, unified Continental force; and the number of men and quantity of supplies needed to maintain the army through the winter.

At the same time, the President of Congress thought it prudent to warn the commander in chief of some of the difficulties which would attend any change in the army. For the time being alteration of the mode of appointing officers or attempt to dispense with regiments which were not brought up to strength, he warned, "may create great jealousies and uneasiness." Hancock did hold out some hope that "a new modelling of the whole" army would soon occur and solve these thorny problems. The final question which the officers were requested to consider was rather novel: "whether the pay of the private men, which is considered very high, may not be reduced and how much?"[3]

The question of the pay and bounties to be given the soldiers was one which plagued Congress for the duration of the war. The basic problem was that, unlike the common soldier in Europe, the American enlistee often was a man of some property or occupied a position in the community which placed a high value upon his services. Thus, the army was forced to offer attractive inducements to prospective volunteers—especially for long enlistments. A further complicating factor was that privates were often from the same social and economic strata as the officers who led them, and, in the case of junior officers, often elected them to their position of rank. It was only natural, then, that there was no appreciable difference in pay between the private soldier and the officers.

While New Englanders found this arrangement not only acceptable but highly desirable, the class-conscious leaders of the Middle and Southern colonies thought it was shocking. Representatives from these colonies backed a proposal to reduce the common soldiers' pay. Washington was also quite emphatic about the need to differentiate sharply between the ranks with respect to pay. "I am of the opinion," he informed Hancock on September 21, "the allowance [of the officers] is inadequate to their rank and service and is one great source of that familiarity between the officers and men, which is incompatible with subordination and discipline." Charles Lee echoed this sentiment. While the pay "is indeed a fortune to the low wretches who live like the common soldiers and with the common soldiers," he observed, "men who choose to preserve the decent distance of officers must have a decent subsistence." Without it, he warned, "no authority or respect can be expected."[4]

On September 21, while Congress still debated reorganization of the army, Washington penned a fervent plea for immediate congressional action. If such action was not forthcoming, he warned, the army would simply melt away. Both the officers and men of the various provincial establishments which constituted his army had refused to sign the Continental Articles of War. To do so, they feared, would obligate them for a longer term of service. Discipline was difficult if not impossible, and Washington therefore recommended that the signing of the Articles be obligatory in all future enlistments.

The expiration of enlistments posed another problem for the commander in chief. Troops from Connecticut and Rhode Island were obligated only to December first, while none of the men in the camp had agreed to serve past January 1, 1776. He therefore urged Congress to act immediately to raise a new army or face the prospect of completely abandoning the siege of Boston. On the brighter side, he reported that his officers were of the opinion that most of the present army would reenlist, if allowed a furlough and if provision was made for adequate shelter and winter clothing. Nonetheless, Washington was far from optimistic. The pay chest was empty, rations skimpy, and "winter fast approaching upon a naked army." Consequently, the bulk of the army was "in a state not far from mutiny." A final complication was that although the men presently manning the lines had to be clothed and equipped for the winter, if they chose not to reenlist, the Continent would be put to the double expense of clothing and equipping their replacements as well.

On a related matter Washington did not wait for congressional action. He ordered extra rations to be given to officers at the following rate: major general, 15; brigadier general, 12; colonel, 6; lieutenant colonel, 5; major, 4; captain, 3; subaltern, 2; and staff officers, 2. In this manner the officers' pay was supplemented, since they could draw the cash equivalent in lieu of the actual rations.

The arrival of Washington's letter of the 21st served to stir Congress to action. Each section of the letter was carefully and extensively debated. Congress then appointed a committee of three to visit the camp and, in conference with civil and military officials, decide what measures should be adopted to reorganize and prepare the army for the winter. The three congressmen chosen for this assignment were Benjamin Franklin of Pennsylvania, Thomas Lynch, Sr., of South Carolina, and Benjamin Harrison of Virginia. Unaccountably—except in terms of provincial jealousy—not a single New Englander was chosen although the army was still composed almost exclusively of officers and men from the New England colonies.

Although the committee was primarily to consult with Washington concerning the needs of the army, the instructions given it by Congress were more inclusive. It was also directed to confer with the governors of Rhode Island and Connecticut, the council of Massachusetts Bay, and the president of the New Hampshire Convention on all matters touching upon the continuance, support, and regulation of a Continental army. The first duty of the committee, upon arriving in camp, was to persuade the Connecticut troops to remain with the army until the end of December. Next, it was to inform Washington that Congress would leave to his judgment any attack to be made upon the British in Boston. However, should such an attack take place before the end of December, and succeed, then the army should be reduced and the men's pay cut from an average of $6.66 to $5.00 a month. Finally, the committee was to consult with the commander in chief and others concerning the raising and regulating of a Continental army to serve for one year beginning January 1, 1776. The committeemen were to find out how many men were necessary for such an army, the organizational changes desirable, the proper pay differential between officers and enlisted men, the provisions and equipment needed (with an estimate of expense), and the best mode of selecting officers and men for the new army so as to destroy "all provincial distinctions."[5]

In appointing a committee to visit the army and confer with the commander in chief, Congress established the mode by which it would maintain contact with the various segments of the Continental army throughout the war. In addition, standing committees were appointed to deal with such matters as the letting of contracts for military supplies, the granting of commissions to foreign volunteers, and other matters touching upon military affairs. In 1777, overwhelmed by the amount of work involved in the regulation of the army, a Board of War was created consisting of men who were not members of Congress, and eventually, near the conclusion of the war, the office of secretary of war was created by Congress to handle military affairs. Despite these various shifts, Congress at all times retained ultimate authority over the regulation and direction of its armies. Thus, while certain administrative devices were experimented with between 1775 and 1783, special committees, similar to that appointed in September of 1775, continued to provide most of the information upon which Congress would shape its military policies.

The committee arrived in Cambridge during the second week of October and proceeded to fulfill its instructions. Agreement was quickly arrived at between the committee and Washington and the general officers concerning the size of the projected new army. They decided that an army of not less than 20,372 men was needed for the siege of Boston, while additional men would be recruited for the Northern army.[6] Acting realistically, the committee recognized the difficulties involved in inducing men to reenlist and at the same time reducing their pay and so agreed to continue the existing pay scale. However, men who reenlisted under this plan would be subject to discharge whenever their services were no longer required. On the other hand, if they agreed to accept a private's pay of $5.00 a month, then they could expect a full month's separation pay if discharged before the end of their term of enlistment.

In conference with the representatives of the New England governments, the committee was promised that by March 10, 1776, Congress could expect 20,000 volunteers from Massachusetts, 8,000 from Connecticut, 3,000 from New Hampshire, and 1,500 from Rhode Island. This would more than fill the expected needs of the army under Washington, but since the requirements of the Northern army were uncertain, the committee decided not to commit the Continental Congress to any definite quota assignments.[7]

Although not instructed to do so, the committee questioned the desirability of having Negroes in the army. A number of them were serving in the besieging army, and this had shocked the Southern congressmen who visited the camp during August. Indeed, Edward Rutledge of South Carolina introduced a resolution in Congress on September 26 directing Washington to discharge all Negroes, freemen as well as slaves. However, although strongly supported by the Southern members, this resolution failed because of the determined opposition of New England

and Pennsylvania. Despite this clear indication of Northern disapproval, the committee, presumably at the instigation of the two Southern members, raised the question of dismissal in conference with Washington and the general officers. While it was impractical to dismiss those already serving, it was decided that Negroes would not be enlisted in the new army.

The committee realized that it would take time to recruit the army to full strength, and, even then, it might not be large enough to meet certain emergencies. One such emergency envisioned by the committee and the general officers was a landing in force by the British at New York while Gage still held Boston. Washington felt that the proposed army would not be large enough to deal with both threats and the committeemen agreed. Therefore, Washington was authorized to call forth the militia of Massachusetts or the neighboring colonies should the necessities of the service require such action. Since this grant of power was unqualified, it was certain to raise the ire of the provincial authorities involved. At the same time, the committee assured Washington that he was under no compulsion to send part of his army to New York or anywhere else unless he thought it necessary for the common safety.[8]

Eventually the committee raised the question of how long Gage was to be allowed to occupy Boston without an effort by the colonists to oust him. The events which had culminated in the Battle of Bunker Hill had been the last effort in this direction, and, while Washington was willing to make another attempt, his council of war was not. Only a few days before the committee arrived in camp, the council had again rejected plans for assaulting the city.

There were more than military considerations involved in such an attack. Washington told the committee that he could capture the city if he waited for the harbor to freeze (thus removing the British men-of-war from contention), and then bombarded and stormed the town. However, in doing so, much of Boston would be destroyed and the property of Patriot and Tory alike would go up in smoke. When asked for its advice, the committee decided to refer the matter to Congress. In the meantime, no attack was to be made.

By October 24, 1775, the committee had nearly finished its work at camp, but it had yet to carry out the first article of its instructions— to convince the Connecticut troops to remain with the army to the end of December. Having enlisted to the first of December, the Connecticut soldiers persisted in their determination to start for home on that date. There was little the committee could do in such a situation, but the presence of the two Southerners certainly did not help. The ingrained dislike of Connecticut Yankees for Southern aristocrats only made them more obstinate.

Unable to count upon the presence of the Connecticut troops after December first, the committee agreed with Washington that the recruiting of the new army had to begin at once. In urging Congress to initiate recruitment, the committeemen shrewdly pointed out that it would be far easier to enlist men *before* they had experienced the hardships of winter campaigning. The pleasant days of Indian summer would soon give way to the rigors of a New England winter, so haste was in order.[9]

Its work finally completed, the committee returned to Philadelphia at the end of October. Congress, which had been kept informed of the proceedings at Cambridge, endorsed the committee's actions and proceeded to implement its recommendations. By November 13, Thomas Lynch could write Washington that all of their suggestions had been agreed to by Congress, and, in addition, it had voted a pay increase for line officers. However, he confidently reported, the new army might be superfluous before it was fully recruited! He had it on good authority that the destruction of the army in Boston or the capture of Quebec that winter would produce overtures of peace from Parliament by the spring. Lynch had complete faith in Washington's ability to accomplish the former, and although there was some opposition within Congress to the proposed attack upon Boston, he assured the general that he would "try to pave the way for it, and wait for the season as you do."[10]

Even while Lynch wrote optimistically of the future, the seeds of future discord were being sown in Congress. For in the month of October, the first major political clash occurred between the emerging nationalist and federalist factions in Congress. The issue that sparked the conflict was the question of who should appoint the field officers in the new Continental army—Congress or the colonies in which the regiments were raised?

Without awaiting the return of the committee from camp, Congress called for the raising of new Continental battalions in Pennsylvania and New Jersey. On October 9, 1775, Congress recommended to the New Jersey Congress that it raise two battalions of eight companies each for the Continental service. As part of the new army, the battalions were to enlist men for one year with the privates being paid at the new rate of $5.00 a month.[11] In the official resolution there was little to indicate any basic shift in policy. True, the new battalions would be "Continental" in a way that no others were as yet—with the possible exception of the rifle companies. The men's pay was in conformance with the new Continental pay scale as opposed to the 50 shillings per month allowed most of the privates then serving under Washington. But these were minor points and would not by themselves have caused any concern.

An indication of the new and disruptive element first appeared on October 9 in a letter from the New Jersey delegates, James Kinsey and

William Livingston, to the President of the New Jersey Congress, Samuel Tucker. "We have had a considerable debate," they informed him, "whether the provincial congresses should have the appointment of the field officers of the regiment or only the captains and the officers downward." At the time they wrote, the question of whether Congress or the provincial governments should make such appointments was still undecided. However, at the end of the letter was a passage, incompletely erased, which indicated the trend of events. "From what has already past [sic] in Congress we believe the majority of the Congress will incline to take the appointment of the field officers of the regiment into their own hands. Whether the New England colonies will submit to that inclination we doubt."[12]

The next day, October 10, a full debate on the question was initiated with the introduction of a motion "relative to the appointment of officers." The question put to the house was who would appoint the officers for the two New Jersey battalions authorized the day before? As the delegates from that colony predicted, the New England delegates were firmly against giving that power to Congress.[13]

The Connecticut delegation was most outspoken in its opposition. Roger Sherman was sure that it would be best to leave the appointments in the hands of the individual colonies, while Eliphalet Dyer believed that men would not enlist to serve under men they did not know. But Samuel Chase of Maryland declared that to leave the appointments with the colonies was to persist in error despite experience. "We have seen that giving the choice of officers to the people is attended with bad consequences," he pointed out. "Appointing persons because of personal friendship does not put suitable men in the positions." Edward Rutledge of South Carolina attempted to smooth ruffled feelings by assuring the New Englanders that there was no intention to alter what had already been done—only to reserve to Congress the right to reward merit in the future. Samuel Ward of Rhode Island was not convinced. "The motion is intended for a precedent," he prophesied. Anyway, he added, since the men would not serve under total strangers, New Jersey men must be found for the commissions, and he did not know a single man in the Jerseys. How then could he and his colleagues be better judges of whom should be appointed than the New Jersey Congress?

At this juncture, James Duane rose and delivered a speech in favor of congressional appointment which went to the heart of the issue. He recognized that making such appointments was a "matter of delicacy," but Congress was faced with the task of laying the foundation for an American army. In so doing, general regulations would have to be established and the whole army placed on the same footing. As to the question of precedent—well, the precedent had already been established. Colonels Campbell, Allen, and Warner had received their promotions from Congress. Let Schuyler and Montgomery in the North and Washington with the main army decide whom they wanted to appoint or promote, and Congress would confirm the appointments. Certainly, Duane observed, he would sooner trust the judgment of those gentlemen than he would that of any convention. In conclusion, Duane reminded his fellow delegates that the burden of supporting the army rested upon Congress—did this not entitle Congress to appoint its own officers?[14]

The precedent was not nearly as clear as Duane thought. Ethan Allen and Seth Warner had appeared before Congress on June 23, 1775, and requested that their Green Mountain Boys be enrolled in the Continental service. Congress agreed to do so and allowed the "Boys" to elect the field officers for the newly organized regiment. To his chagrin, Allen was not elected colonel. Warner was elected lieutenant colonel and received his commission from Congress, but the colonelcy was left vacant. Allen rejoined the Northern army as a volunteer, and then was granted a Continental commission as a colonel to raise a regiment of Canadians. Finally, Duane's reference to Col. Donald Campbell was somewhat irrelevant. Campbell was not a field officer at all, but rather, a deputy quartermaster general in the Northern department.[15]

John Langdon of New Hampshire was appalled by Duane's suggestions and warned Congress that they were "extraordinary and big with mischief." Silas Deane seconded Langdon's argument and contended that it was not Congress' money which supported the army, but the people's. The people should then retain the appointment of officers. The debate now became rather heated. George Ross of Pennsylvania announced that he was willing to go even further and give Congress the appointment of all officers—even ensigns! Until this was done, he declared, Congress would have no effective control over its own army. John Jay warmly supported Ross's position, and by way of showing the inequities of the present system, pointed out that the whole army had recently refused to be mustered by the Continental mustermasters! And then, perhaps unintentionally, Jay laid bare the real issue at dispute. "The Union," he proclaimed, "depends much upon breaking down provincial conventions."[16]

Not all those in favor of giving the appointment of field-grade officers to Congress were motivated by a desire to strengthen the Union at the expense of the individual colonies—nor is the reverse necessarily true of those who opposed such a move. Many Southern delegates favored the move simply because it was the only way they could obtain commissions for deserving men in their own colonies. If the war continued to be centered in the North, and if the army continued to be made up of regiments raised for the most part in New England and the Middle colonies (as seemed likely at the time), then leaving the appointment of officers to the colonies supplying the troops would exclude many able and ambitious Southerners. However, in the case of men like John Jay, James Duane, and George Ross, it seems likely that they were motivated by a desire to augment the power of the central government at the expense of the conventions and assemblies. Both Duane and Jay had been associated with the conservative faction in the First Congress, and in the years ahead they would press for the creation of a strong national government.

The opposition to congressional appointment of officers can be identified more closely with a particular faction—the former "republicans" or federalists. To such men, a strong central government, whether located in London or Philadelphia, represented a threat to the individual colonies' right of self-government. Moreover, the creation of an army solely responsible to the central government would not only strengthen such a government, but also bring all of the dangers associated with a standing army. The wisest—and safest—policy, these men insisted, was to maintain a small Continental army and augment it, when necessary, with militia.

On the very day the question of appointments was being debated in Congress, October 9, Elbridge Gerry wrote to Samuel Adams informing him of the action taken by the Massachusetts government to strengthen its militia. A militia bill was then before both houses, he reported, and he hoped that the militia would be formed not only into battalions but also into brigades, with a brigadier general appointed for every county. Such a system, if adopted throughout America, Gerry believed, would prove capable of repulsing aggression wherever it occurred.[17]

Adams agreed that a strong militia was desirable, but, he asked Gerry, "should we not be cautious of putting them under the direction of the generals of the Continent?" Samuel Adams was apprehensive about the ultimate nature of the central government as represented by Congress, and until his doubts were satisfied he felt "that the militia of each colony should remain under the sole direction of its own legislature *which* is and ought to be the sovereign and uncontrollable power within its own limits or territory." A more succinct expression of the federalist viewpoint would be difficult to find.

Even Adams, however, had to admit the necessity of having the Continental army present in Massachusetts since it was "evidently for our immediate security. But it should be remembered," he cautioned Gerry, "that history affords abundant instances of established armies making themselves the masters of those countries which they were designed to protect. There may be no danger of this at present, but it should be a caution not to trust the whole military strength of a colony in the hands of commanders independent of its established legislative."[18] The similarity between this argument and that put forward by "Caractacus" is suggestive.

Despite the adamant opposition of the New England delegates, the motion giving Congress the appointment of field-grade officers could have passed. However, after a short continuation of the debate on October 11, the matter was deferred until the return of the committee from camp. The obvious reason for such a move was that although New England was in a minority in Congress, it had supplied almost all of the officers and men comprising the army and must be heavily relied upon to supply the majority of those enlisted for the new army. Consequently, when New Jersey requested permission to appoint officers for its two regiments, it was informed that it should continue to recruit men "with all possible expedition but as the Congress are waiting the return of their committee from camp in order to establish permanent regulations for all the Continental forces, they for the present incline to suspend determination on the question about the appointment of regimental field officers."

Following the report of its committee, Congress adopted a policy with regard to field-scale appointments which constituted a compromise. On November 7, Congress selected colonels, lieutenant colonels, and majors for the two New Jersey battalions. However, the men chosen were the same as those nominated by the New Jersey Congress, a list of whom had been forwarded to Congress. In the same fashion, field officers for the new battalions raised in Pennsylvania were elected by Congress on November 25. Finally, on December 8, a standing committee was created consisting of one member from each colony, "to take into consideration the application of the several persons applying to be officers in the American army, to examine their qualifications, and report to Congress."[19]

Under this new arrangement, Congress had unquestioned authority to appoint all officers in the Continental army above the rank of captain. Accordingly, promotions above this rank also rested with Congress. While this represented a victory in theory for the nationalists, the federalists were somewhat mollified by Congress' practice of respecting the recommendations made by the provincial conventions.[20] It was soon clear, however, that Congress was not inalterably bound by such recommendations. In the election of officers for four new Pennsylvania battalions on January 3 and 4, 1776, it exercised a considerable degree of independence.

The Pennsylvania Committee of Safety recommended eight men

for the positions of colonel in an order which most likely indicated its preference Anthony Wayne, Samuel Atlee, John Shee, Arthur St. Clair, Daniel Broadhead, Robert Magaw, Lambert Cadwalader, and Francis Johnston. Nevertheless, Congress elected the colonels in the following order: St. Clair, Shee, Wayne, and Magaw. To remove any doubt concerning the importance of the order of election, Congress, the next day, resolved, "that in all elections of officers by Congress, where more than one are elected on the same day, to commands of the same rank, they shall take rank of each other according to their election, and the entry of their names in the minutes, and their commissions shall be numbered to show their priority." In the election of lieutenant colonels for the same battalions, Congress also changed the order of priority submitted by the committee of safety. More importantly, although the men finally selected were from the list of eight drawn up by the committee, the balloting in Congress was on a slate of 21 names! The additional 13 names were put in nomination by members of Congress.[21]

Thus, by the beginning of the new year, Congress had gone far toward creating a truly "Continental" army. In so doing, it followed closely the recommendations made by its committee of conference with the commander in chief. The size of the army surrounding Boston was to be in excess of 20,000 men, while the Northern army was to be enlarged. The size and make-up of companies and regiments was regularized. Despite the urging of the New England delegates, Congress refused to offer a bounty as an inducement to enlist in the new army—although the enlistees were to be provided with a new set of clothes. And finally, the most important step taken was to place the appointment and promotion of field-grade officers in the hands of Congress.[22]

While these alterations were applauded by the army's high command and a majority in Congress, grumbling was heard from the lower ranks and from some congressmen. A fundamental shift of power had taken place, and it was to be expected that some would disapprove. Samuel Ward of Rhode Island was one of the most vociferous opponents of the new system. Nathanael Greene, the Continental brigadier in command of the Rhode Island troops serving under Washington, valiantly— but futilely—attempted to reconcile Ward to the changes. While he recognized that "it is next to impossible to unhinge the prejudice that people have for places and things they have had a long connection with," he informed Ward that Washington intended "to bannish [sic] every idea of local attachments" within the army. Practically, Greene saw the necessity for this since it appeared to be the only way to bring many Southerners to support the war. Personally, he deplored the necessity, for he felt for "the cause and not the place."

Ward remained unconvinced, and in his next letter he also expressed his disappointment that Greene and the other general officers had not more strongly urged the need for a bounty to encourage both enlistment and reenlistment. Greene informed him that the generals were in favor of giving a bounty, but Washington had assured them that Congress would sooner give up the whole dispute with England. "What reason have you to think that a proposition of that sort if it came recommended by the general officers would be acceded to by the Congress? Most of the generals," he pointed out, "belong to the Northern governments. If Congress refuse to hear their delegates, I apprehend they would the generals also."

Greene, exasperated by Ward's attempts to shift responsibility for the changes to the army, indicated where, from the viewpoint of the New England officers and men, the real blame lay.

> You complain and say the New England colonies are treated ill, why are they treated so? You think there ought to have been a bounty given. The Congress always had it in their power to give a bounty if they pleased. Why were not the New England delegates sent to establish the plan for the constitution of the new army, why were strangers sent at so critical a period? History don't afford so dangerous a manoeuver as that of disbanding an old army and forming a new one within [point] blank shot of the enemy the whole time.[23]

Samuel Ward, however, could be neither consoled nor forced to accept any responsibility for the changes. The reports he received from the army of "infinite difficulty in reenlisting the army" bore out his greatest fears. The "new modelling" would prove the destruction of the army, all because "Southern gentlemen wish to remove that attachment injurious to the common cause," he declared, "but the strongest inducement to people to risk everything in the defense of the whole, upon the preservation of which must depend the safety of each colony."[24] Again the unmistakable hallmark of federalism was present—the Union existed for the protection and preservation of the individual colonies.

The federalists did win a small victory at this time. They succeeded in modifying the broad powers granted Washington to call forth and take command of the New England militia. A new resolution, probably the work of Samuel Adams, required Washington to receive permission from the executive branch of the colony involved before calling up its militia.[25] However, with this exception, it appears that federalism and the New England colonies suffered a number of setbacks in Congress during the fall and winter of 1775–76. One might well echo Greene's query: "Why were they treated so?"

Certainly during the First Congress, New England had played a dominant role. Indeed, one observer had accused Adams and his "crew" of "juggling the whole conclave." During the first session of the Second Congress they also achieved most of their objectives. The army was adopted by Congress and the entire Continent pledged to defend American liberties by force of arms. True, they had made some concessions, but at the time these seemed of no importance. What had happened between August and September to weaken New England in Congress?

The primary check to the ambitions of New Englanders was simply that, by the end of July 1775, they had achieved all they could hope for within the existing framework of the conflict with Britain. They had achieved Continental opposition to British aggression, but in return they were forced to accept a policy of defensive war and to give tacit support to further attempts at a reconciliation with the mother country. Hitherto, much of the influence of New England had rested in its ability to initiate aggressive action and then force a reluctant Congress to accept the *fait accompli*. Now, having placed the army under the direction of Congress, the New Englanders discovered that their most potent weapon was in the hands of more conservative men. Those interested in seeking a reconciliation with England proceeded to strengthen congressional control over the army in an effort to check the further spread of the conflict.

Thus, the only way that New England and the federalists could regain the initiative was to change the terms of the conflict from one in defense of colonial rights to one for American independence. Both factions in Congress were acutely aware of this, and although they never uttered the dread word "independence" it was central to the debates concerning the opening of American ports and the formulation of military policy which occupied Congress in the fall of 1775. In each case, it was those who favored reconciliation who emerged victorious. They succeeded in delaying the opening of American ports to all nations (which would have constituted a *de facto* declaration of independence), and they proceeded very cautiously in exploiting the military advantage then enjoyed over Generals Gage and Carleton.

This refusal to vigorously prosecute the war against the British had incalculable results. John Adams firmly believed that the continued attempts at reconciliation by John Dickinson, James Duane, and others in Congress was responsible for the failure to capture Quebec and to destroy the British army in Boston.[26] While this charge may seem harsh, it contained a good deal of truth. By adopting an ambiguous attitude toward the invasion of Canada, positive action in that theater was delayed until the fall. By that time it was almost certain to fail with the nearness of winter and the imminent expiration of enlistments. With regard to Boston, approval of an assault on that town was not forthcoming until late December, by which time Washington could not act until the new army was recruited.[27] Consequently, Howe was able to evacuate Boston in March without opposition.

The first day of the new year of 1776 marked the birth of the first truly Continental army. But it also witnessed the violent death of part of the old army in Canada and the steady disintegration of the remainder at Cambridge. On that cold January morning the Union Jack still flew over Quebec and Boston, and hopes of a decisive American victory, which might bring Britain to terms, vanished. Although most did not realize it—and some never would—that New Year's Day was a turning point. The United Colonies were now fully committed to a war which would drag on for another seven and a half years. And despite the continued attempts of many conservatives, the cause of reconciliation had also perished in the snowy streets of Quebec. The colonies, having failed to achieve a decisive victory, could expect to feel the full weight of British retaliation in the spring of 1776. Then the theoretical arguments over the nature of the Empire and the colonies' place in or out of it would cease to be important. Soon the only concern of the American colonies would be survival.

Charles Lee

New Candidate for the Canadian Command

T HE CURTAILMENT of active campaigning by the onset of winter afforded Americans in and out of uniform time to consider problems they would have to face in the new year of 1776. The lack of response to Congress' conciliatory overtures to England forced many to consider seriously the prospect of independence. If the colonies were forced to take this irretrievable step, the nature of the conflict would be drastically altered. All hopes of a short, limited war would disappear. Britain would exert all the force she could bring to bear to prevent the dissolution of her empire, and America would face the prospect of a long, arduous war whose outcome no man could know.

At the same time, consideration of America's political future raised the question of what was to be done about that considerable number of colonists who preferred to remain loyal to their sovereign, George III. One man who gave a great deal of thought to both of these pressing problems was General Charles Lee. To one degree or another, all of the Continental general officers (and indeed men of lesser rank) failed to confine themselves to purely military matters, and Charles Lee was outstanding in this respect if in no other. He freely commented on both internal and external political affairs, and urged his opinions upon various members of Congress—particularly those whom he knew disagreed with him. He was probably the first major American leader (military or civil) to commit himself in writing to independence. As early as July of 1775, he denounced the reconciliation efforts as an indication of weakness on the part of Congress, and urged a more dynamic policy of "talking high and acting decisively." Instead of sending humble petitions to the king, he asserted that Congress should send a declaration stating:

"Sir, if you do not withdraw your troops upon the receipt of this, we will absolve ourselves of all allegiance to you, and we will divorce ourselves forever from Britain."[1]

When it was learned that King George III had declared on October 26, 1775,[2] that the American colonies were seeking independence and pledged the use of whatever force was necessary to subdue them, Lee became even more outspoken—as did many other patriots. In January of 1776 he turned all of his persuasive powers on the two staunchest foes of independence in Congress, Robert Morris and John Dickinson. To the former, on January 3, Lee declared that "the king's speech absolutely destroys all hope of reunion. . . . We must be independent or slaves." Later in the month Lee expanded his thoughts on the subject, pointing out not only the illogicality of not declaring independence, but also the advantages to be reaped from such an act. After chiding Morris about Pennsylvania's positive instructions forbidding its delegates to vote for independence, he pointed out how ridiculous it was to fight British regulars and still profess loyalty to the Crown. "By the Heavenly God if you do not act more decisively we shall be ruined, *decision, decision* ought to be our word. Are we at war or are we not? Are we not at war with the King? or with whom are we at war? do not the people of England tho' not from zeal, but from want of spirit support the tyrant? Why are we to eternity whining about a connexion with these depraved people?" "[I]n short," he concluded, "as they now suffer their Parliament without tearing them to pieces to support the Tyrant, they cannot be considered as able or worthy of remaining the presiding part of the Empire."

When Robert Morris expressed some surprise that Lee "should join in the cry for independence," Lee replied on January 30 that until the king's speech he had not been convinced of its propriety, but it now appeared the only solution. He expressed similar views to Dickinson, and went even further to proclaim that even if the two countries might in some way be returned to their former, happy relationship, "I cannot help shuddering at some consequences." For, "every engine of corruption will be set at work," he prophesied, "your morals will be in a short time contaminated . . . [and] attachment to the person of and trappings of a diabolical tyrant will be substituted in the room of honest industry and a reverence for equal laws."[3]

Lee was perhaps more outspoken than most on the subject of independence, but it is noteworthy that a growing number of officers shared his convictions. Horatio Gates believed such a step was inevitable as early as the fall of 1775,[4] and on January 4 Nathanael Greene expressed to Samuel Ward his belief that "we have consulted our wishes rather than our reason in the indulgence of an idea of accommodation. Heaven hath decreed that Tottering Empire Britain to irretrievable ruin —thanks to God since Providence hath so determined America must raise an Empire of permanent duration."

Charles Lee differed from his fellow officers in that once he was convinced that something was right and necessary, he would let nothing stand in the way of its attainment. The ends, to him, justified any means necessary to secure them. Some of his contemporaries recognized this. Lady Sarah Lennox Bunbury, his cousin's wife, once remarked that Lee could be as tyrannical, given excuse and opportunity as George III himself.[5] This facet of his personality, combined with a conviction that independence was imperative, resulted in a critical conflict between Lee and the civil authorities of New York.

Beginning in July of 1775, Lee urged upon Congress the necessity of putting New York City and its environs in a proper state of defense. One of the first steps that he recommended was the arrest of Royal Governor William Tryon, who, because of his popularity, Lee believed was particularly dangerous to the American cause. Congress demurred. There were British men-of-war in New York harbor and Tryon's arrest could lead to the bombardment of the city. Lee was not impressed, and informed Benjamin Rush on October 10 that Tryon should not be allowed to remain at liberty.

Despairing of action by Congress, Lee, on October 26, took the extraordinary step of urging Colonel Alexander McDougall of the New York regiment (and a former leader of the New York Sons of Liberty) to use his influence with the city's committee of safety to have Tryon and his supporters taken into custody. People were beginning to wonder about New York's attachment to the cause, he warned McDougall, and such action would serve to allay suspicion. He pooh-poohed the danger of retaliation and advised that the senior naval officer should be warned that if he cannonaded the town, the first house set ablaze would be Tryon's "funeral pile." Moreover, this was to be no idle threat—should the navy disregard the warning, he urged the governor's prompt execution.

The opportunity for Lee to put some of his ideas concerning the treatment of Tories into action was soon provided. In December of 1775, Governor Nicholas Cooke and other patriot leaders in Rhode Island requested Washington's assistance in putting their colony in a state of defense. The request was prompted by a rumor that the British in Boston planned an expedition against their colony, but equally disturbing were the large numbers of reputed Tories within the colony who could give aid to the enemy. Washington responded by sending Lee and a small detachment to Rhode Island. Lee threw himself into the job with great vigor, touring the colony in five days, inspecting harbors, and making recommendations concerning fortifications. In addition, he frightened the local Tories, exacting a solemn oath from them not to give aid or information to the British and to support the Continental Congress. Those who refused to take the oath were arrested and jailed in Providence.[6]

Lee boasted of these accomplishments to Robert Morris on January 3, 1776, expressing the hope that "our sovereign, for such now must the Congress be esteemed" would approve of his actions. It was quite unnecessary for Congress to venture an opinion since Lee's actions were endorsed by the civil authorities in Rhode Island. However, in view of later developments, it is quite likely that Lee was looking for an indication that Congress would approve similar measures in New York. Indeed, in this same letter, he confided to Morris that he wished "the same step was taken with New York as I thought indispensable at Newport." But neither approval nor disapproval was forthcoming.

Undeterred, Lee, having failed to enlist the support of either Congress or Alexander McDougall, now turned to the commander in chief. "The consequences of the enemy possessing themselves of New York have appeared to me so terrible," he dramatically informed Washington, "that I have scarcely been able to sleep from apprehensions on the subject." Something had to be done, and done quickly. To Lee, the only man with the authority to act was Washington. He was certain Congress would approve of any action the commander in chief took to safeguard New York and so there was no need to first obtain that body's approval. Indeed, he assured his chief, "I have the greatest reason to believe, from the most authentic intelligence, that the best members of Congress expect that you would take much upon yourself; as referring every matter of importance to them is, in fact, defeating the whole project." Ultimately, he warned, "the salvation of the whole depends on your striking, at certain crises, vigorous strokes, without previously communicating your intention."

Having justified action by Washington, at least to his own satisfaction, Lee proceeded to outline his plan to secure New York. He knew that Washington could not spare him men from the main army for this purpose, but if "you detach me to Connecticut, and lend your name for collecting a body of volunteers, I am assured that I shall find no difficulty in assembling a sufficient number for the purposes wanted. This body, in conjunction (if there should appear occasion to summon them) with the Jersey regiment under the command of Lord Stirling . . . will effect the security of New York, and the expulsion or suppression of that dangerous banditti of Tories, who have appeared in Long Island, with the professed intention of acting against the authority of the Congress. Not to crush these serpents, before their rattles are grown," he concluded, "would be ruinous." As a clincher, he added that the Connecticut volunteers would serve without pay.

This last point must have aroused Washington's suspicion. Yankees who volunteered to serve without pay would certainly bear watching! Nevertheless, he had long been concerned about leaving New York undefended. Also, his spies reported that Sir William Howe was embarking a large body of troops aboard the fleet in Boston harbor and a southern expedition was almost a certainty with New York as the most likely objective. On the other hand, despite Lee's assurances, the commander in chief was not at all sure that he had authority to act independently of Congress in ordering the occupation of Manhattan and Long Island without the consent of the New York authorities. Fortunately, he did not have to make the decision entirely alone. John Adams, temporarily absent from Congress, was at hand to give advice on the political consequences of such a move. Adams, like most New Englanders, had strong reservations concerning the New York "patriots," and he unhesitatingly endorsed Lee's plan.

On the question of Washington's authority, Adams believed the situation was quite clear. "Your commission constitutes you commander of all the forces now raised, or to be raised, and of all others who shall voluntarily offer their services." There was much more involved than this, however, and Adams well knew it. For one thing, the New York authorities were sure to resent the intervention of Connecticut troops in their province—and the authority of Congress (to say nothing of its generals) to act in such a manner without the request of the New York authorities was highly questionable. For his own reasons, Adams chose to ignore this fact.

Instead, Adams addressed himself to the question of whether Washington's command extended to New York. Since the previous summer it had become customary for Congress to issue intructions directly to the generals in the Northern department, thus making it virtually a separate command. The Northern department embraced the upper parts of New York, but did it also include the city and its environs? If so, orders pertaining to that area would normally issue from Congress to the general commanding the Northern department, Philip Schuyler, and not from George Washington. Adams, however, expressed the opinion that sending instructions directly to Schuyler had been merely a matter of convenience and had not in any way limited the scope of Washington's command. Consequently, he assured the commander in chief, "New York is within your command, as much as the Massachusetts."[7]

Washington was now convinced, and on January 8, 1776, he approved Lee's plan. Lee was authorized to raise volunteers and call upon the commanding officer in New Jersey for any assistance needed to "put that city [New York] into the best posture of defense, which the season and circumstances will admit, disarming all such persons upon Long Island and elsewhere, (and if necessary otherwise securing them), whose conduct or declarations have rendered them justly suspected of designs unfriendly to the views of Congress. . . . In all other matters relative to the execution of the general plan you are going upon," Lee was assured, "your own judgment (as it is impossible with propriety to give particular directions) and the advice of those whom you have reason to believe are hearty in the cause, must direct you; keeping always in view the declared intentions of Congress."

These instructions gave Lee carte blanche to put New York in a state of defense. An adequate force of Connecticut volunteers and New Jersey Continentals was put at his disposal, and he was specifically authorized to disarm the Tories and "if necessary otherwise secure them." Thus, the commander in chief tacitly endorsed the administration of test oaths and the jailing of dangerous Tories. Finally, and in view of later developments, most importantly, Lee was responsible only to Washington for his actions—not to the New York Congress or Committee of Safety, nor even to the Continental Congress, except that he was to "keep in view the declared intentions" of that body—whatever that meant.

By January 15 Lee was in New Haven, where he took command of 1,200 militiamen before proceeding westward to Stamford.[8] Here, six days later, Lee received the first intimation of resistance to his plans in the form of a letter from the New York Committee of Safety. There was a rumor that Lee was on his way to New York with a considerable body of troops, he was informed, but the committee refused to believe it. Surely, if there was any truth in it, the civil authorities would have been advised of such a move by Congress, General Washington, or himself. The committee therefore apologized for bothering Lee with such a ridiculous report—but would he send assurances that it was ridiculous?

Then, setting aside its feigned disbelief, the committee expostulated against Lee's occupation of the city. While assuring him that it, and the New York Congress which it represented, was "as unanimously zealous in the cause of America as any representative body on the Continent," the committee believed that such a move would provoke a naval bombardment and the needless destruction of the city. If Lee was still determined to proceed, it requested that he leave his troops at the border of Connecticut until he had provided the New York authorities "with such an explanation on this important subject, as you conceive your duty may permit you to enter into with us."

Lee promptly informed the Committee of Safety that its fears were exaggerated. The British would be foolish to destroy New York, or any seaport city for that matter, since they were valuable hostages which could be continually *threatened* with destruction. Also, if the navy was foolish enough to bombard the city, and thus destroy its value as a hostage, then "the first house set in flames by their guns shall be the funeral pile of some of their best friends." As a concession to the committee's fears, however, Lee agreed to leave the main body of his troops at the border and bring into the city only a force strong enough to secure it.

At this juncture, on January 22, Lee took time to inform Congress of his expedition and its objectives, the New York Committee of Safety's objections, and his determination to proceed with all haste to occupy the city with a portion of his command. He did not feel compelled to minimize the danger of British retaliation in his letter to Congress. For, "if they [the British] are to prescribe what number of troops, and what number not, are to enter the city, all I can say is that New York must be considered the Ministers' place, and not the Continent's.":

Although Lee had scorned the committee's response as "the spirit of procrastination, which is the characteristic of timidity," the opposition of the New York civil authorities posed a serious threat to his plans. In a recent resolve, Congress had declared that troops operating in a province other than their own would be under the direction of the executive of that province. When this was brought to his attention, Washington had favored abandoning the New York project. Lee was unwilling to do so, although he admitted that the resolve was "fraught with difficulties and evils," and that it would be impossible to accomplish anything worthwhile if he were to be responsible to Washington, Congress, *and* the New York Committee of Safety.[9]

This situation was not without elements of irony and humor. The New York delegates in Congress had led the fight to strengthen the authority of the Continent by granting more discretionary powers to the commanders of the Continental army. At the same time, however, New York was leery of its neighbor, Connecticut. There had been friction between the two from the beginning of the war, with the New York leaders fearful that power might be wrested from them by the popular elements in New York backed by military units from Connecticut. Thus, the delegates now found it expedient to demand that

Lee and his Connecticut volunteers should be answerable to the province of New York despite the fact that Lee's commission and his instructions from Washington clearly made him responsible only to the Continent.

A showdown between Lee and the New York committee was averted, however, when Lee was incapacitated by an attack of gout. While he recuperated in Stamford, Congress sought a solution to the ticklish problem his mission posed. The method, if not the object, of Lee's and Washington's plan to occupy New York touched upon the sensitive issue of the proper relationship between the individual colonies and Congress. It was further complicated by the specter of raising the military above the civil authority. Thus, the question was now raised "on the one side as to the propriety of an armed force from one province entering another without the permission of the civil power of that province, or without express orders from Congress. It was alleged that this was setting up the military above the civil. On the other side was urged the absolute necessity of securing that province, the loss of which would cut off all communication between the northern and southern colonies and which if effected would ruin America." After many hours of debate, it was finally decided that a committee consisting of Benjamin Harrison, Thomas Lynch, and Andrew Allen of Pennsylvania would go to New York and consult with both the committee and General Lee upon the proper measures of defense. The New York delegates informed the committee of safety of this most recent development, expressed their unqualified approval of the men chosen, and urged that the congressional delegation be shown every courtesy and mark of respect, since "the safety and preservation of the capital of our own colony" depended upon it.[10]

On the afternoon of Sunday, February 4, 1776, General Lee (still too ill to ride) entered New York in a litter at the head of one regiment of Connecticut volunteers, and expressed pleasure at the presence of the congressional committee. "I consider it as a piece of the greatest good fortune," he wrote Washington, "that Congress have detached a committee to this place; otherwise I should have made a most ridiculous figure, besides bringing upon myself the enmity of the whole province." Strangely enough, the arrival of British General Sir Henry Clinton aboard a man-of-war the same afternoon also afforded him some pleasure.

The appearance of General Clinton, instead of heralding the imminent invasion of the city, lent an air of unreality and the bizarre to the tense atmosphere in New York. He had brought only two light infantry companies with him from Boston, and pledged his word to Lee that no more troops were on the way. He had stopped at New York to pay a social call on "his friend Tryon," he informed Lee, and then would proceed to North Carolina where, meeting five fresh regiments from England, he would undertake the subjugation of the South. "This is certainly a droll way of proceeding," Lee skeptically observed to Washington on February 5, "to communicate his full plan to the enemy is too novel to be credited. Lee had no intimation of how droll it really was. Clinton was telling the truth, which revealed both a whimsical nature and an utter contempt for American military power. Ironically, it was Lee, commanding the Continental forces at Charleston, who would deal Clinton's campaign its decisive defeat only a few months after their chance meeting in New York.

Meanwhile, the conferences between Lee and the congressional and provincial authorities went surprisingly well. All parties readily agreed that it was impossible to protect the city against naval bombardment, but nevertheless decided to garrison Manhattan with 2,000 troops, keep 3,000 more on Long Island, and station a battalion in the Highland fortification. Lee's aggressiveness for the moment seems to have abated. His gout probably had something to do with it, but he was also diverted by the prospect of greener pastures in the way of military glory. For it now appeared likely that he would be given the command of the army in Canada.

News of Montgomery's defeat and death at Quebec reached Congress on January 17. It was a terrible shock. The last communication from Montgomery, dated December 5, 1775, had been optimistic about the chances of carrying Quebec by storm. Assuming that Canada was as good as won, Congress had adopted measures to defend it against any future British counterattack. Nine new battalions were authorized for this purpose, and the increase in the size of the Northern army justified promotions for some of its deserving officers. Foremost among these was Colonel Benedict Arnold, but opposition to his elevation to brigadier general developed. Although Arnold had distinguished himself in the Canadian campaign, he was far from the most senior colonel, and provincial jealousies once more precipitated a lengthy debate. Congress finally promoted Arnold on January 10, but not before the same honor was bestowed upon a far less distinguished colonel from Massachusetts, Joseph Fry.

News of the debacle at Quebec shattered the complacency which made possible lengthy debates on such trivial matters. Congress immediately directed New Hampshire to raise and send a regiment into Canada. To speed recruitment, it offered a bounty of 40 shillings and an advance of one month's pay. Regiments already raised in Pennsylvania and New Jersey were put under orders to march northward within 10 days, while New York and Connecticut were to raise additional regiments to augment the Northern army.[11]

Finding a new commanding officer for the army posed a far more serious problem. With Montgomery dead and Arnold seriously wounded, the command devolved upon General Wooster as the senior officer in Canada. However, Wooster could not be named Montgomery's successor. He was a junior brigadier, a bitter enemy of Philip Schuyler, and simply too old and infirm for the task. A major general of ability and stature was needed, and it was not long before Charles Lee was being talked about "out of doors" as the most likely candidate. Horatio Gates was one of the first to discern this possibility, and on January 22 he wrote Lee that "the hard fate of poor Montgomery will, if I have any foresight, immediately induce the Congress to cast their eyes on you." Gates also passed on an interesting piece of gossip: "Knox tells me, he is convinced from Schuyler's conversation that he wished to be excused acting as general." It would appear that Congress had also heard that rumor.

While Lee lay at Stamford nursing his gouty leg, Washington informed him at the end of January that Congress was anxious to have an "active general" appointed for Canada. "Should they not approve of the New York expedition, and think another general necessary for the Northern department," he confided, "it is probable they will fix on you to take the command there." However, while the commander in chief thought Lee's "admirable talents" well suited him for such a command, he foresaw certain complications. Congress seemed to think that Philip Schuyler wished to retire, while the letters the Northern commander wrote to Washington indicated nothing of the kind. Under the existing arrangement, the officer commanding the army in Canada was subordinate to the commander of the Northern department. Lee, however, was Schuyler's superior, and therefore could not serve under him. Lee had been commissioned as a Continental major general on June 17, 1775, while Schuyler was not named to that rank until June 19. In addition, it was generally understood that Lee was the second in command after Washington. Clearly, then, an organizational change was necessary before Lee could accept the Canadian command.

Developments in the Northern department seemed to lend weight to Washington's forebodings. General Wooster, as the senior officer in Canada, was issuing orders affecting the regulation of the army in that province. This, Schuyler complained to Congress, was insubordination. As commander of the Northern department, he insisted that all orders should be first cleared by him. Wooster, for his part, was becoming increasingly indignant over Schuyler's carping. "You will give me leave to inform you," he wrote the Northern commander, "that the commanding officer who is with this army is to give out orders & is the only competent judge of what is proper & what not for the internal regulation of the army & for the immediate safety of this country. Since the death of the worthy and brave General Montgomery (with whom I had the happiness to serve in the strictest harmony & friendship & who even treated me like a gentleman) the command devolves upon me & I shall give out such orders as appear necessary for the public good."¹² Technically, Wooster's words and actions were the quintessence of insubordination, but with Schuyler in Albany and the army in Canada, Wooster, while he might have been more tactful, was the only officer who could issue such orders. Congress realized that as long as Schuyler remained as head of the Northern department, any officer it sent to command in Canada would face the same dilemma.

Aware of the many difficulties attendant upon the Canadian command, Lee at first exhibited a marked lack of enthusiasm when several congressmen intimated that it was his for the asking. Robert Morris, who, with his recent appointment to the powerful Committee of Secret Correspondence, was a man of growing influence in Congress, informed Lee that he was almost certain to be appointed Montgomery's successor. Although flattered, and expressing a willingness to serve in any capacity Congress desired, Lee penned Morris a note on Feb. 9 revealing his fear that the rigors of the northern climate might bring on a renewed attack of gout and rheumatism which would totally incapacitate him. Lee also felt that Congress was putting the cart before the horse, for, he wrote Washington on February 14, "unless they expedite an army, and some heavy artillery, it will be in vain to trouble their heads about a general."

Congress did not "trouble their heads about a general," for long. On February 17, 1776, it unanimously elected Lee to the command in Canada. The members considered the threat posed to Lee's health, but decided to discount it since the winter would be nearly over before he could reach Canada. Many congressmen felt that the first, and biggest, step toward recouping American fortunes in Canada now had been taken. On February 17, Morris, informing Lee of his appointment, expressed the hope of many "that it will not be long before we are happy enough to hail you the Conqueror of Quebec."

Congress had still to decide the command relationship between Generals Lee and Schuyler. It was a matter of considerable delicacy, and if improperly handled might doom to failure all efforts to secure

Canada. Nevertheless, Congress at first did little to clarify the situation. It did decide that Schuyler should assume responsibility for the command in lower New York which Lee would vacate. By implication, this would give Lee a free hand in upper New York and Canada. President Hancock wrote Schuyler of this decision on February 20, informing him that it was not intended as a slight on his abilities. On the contrary, Congress would have been happy to make use of his talents in Canada, but "being apprehensive should you be sent on so fatiguing a service as that of Canada must be, especially at this inclement season, your country might be deprived of the advantage of your services . . . it was thought best to send General Lee to Canada, reserving for you the command of the forces and the conduct of military operations in the colony of New York."[13]

Hancock certainly did little to clarify the command situation in the North by confirming Schuyler's control of troops and operations throughout the province of New York. Schuyler still commanded the Northern department, and the letters from Congress to both Schuyler and Lee stressed the need for cooperation between the two—apparently on the basis of equality. Thus, Lee was directed to confer with Schuyler on the best way to secure the northern lakes and to supply the army in Canada, and "as far as in your power give mutual aid in supporting the cause of freedom and liberty." In turn, Congress directed Schuyler to give Lee "all the aid and assistance in your power" to facilitate the support of the army in Canada.[14]

Faith in Schuyler's cooperative propensities, however, received a sharp setback with the arrival of a letter written by him on February 20. In it Schuyler took issue with Wooster's contention that the officer commanding the army in Canada could consider himself in any way independent of the superior command of the Northern department. Congress had never given any indication that it constituted a separate command, he pointed out, and Montgomery had always acted in the capacity of a subordinate officer.[15] With Schuyler's view of the relationship between the army in Canada and the Northern department, it seemed folly to appoint an officer to command the army who was superior in rank to the head of that department. Congress concluded that the creation of a separate Canadian department was the only logical solution. However, at the same time that Congress arrived at this conclusion, it was forced to face the need for the creation of a military department to embrace the Southern colonies.

By late February the British threat in the South had assumed major proportions. Lord Dunmore, with the aid of the Royal Navy, continued to harrass the coasts of Virginia and Maryland, while in North and

South Carolina large numbers of armed Tories sought to wrest power from the Patriot faction. To make matters worse, it now appeared that Sir Henry Clinton had been candid with Lee concerning his plans, and that a major British offensive in the South was contemplated with Charleston as its first objective. In response to this threat, Congress authorized the raising of some 14 Continental battalions in the South.[16] The coordination and direction of this force necessitated the creation of a Southern department.

Thus, on February 27, Congress divided the colonies into four military districts: an Eastern department embracing the New England colonies; a Middle department including New York, Pennsylvania, New Jersey, Delaware, and Maryland; a Southern department for Virginia, North and South Carolina, and Georgia; and finally determined to make Canada a separate department. Under this new arrangement, General Washington would command the Eastern department in addition to his duties as commander in chief, Schuyler would head the new Middle department, and Lee would have the Canadian command.

The major problem posed by the new arrangement was that it made no provision for the command of the Southern department. The man chosen for that post would have to have outstanding abilities, for the South would not only be the scene of major campaigning during the coming year, but, because of the distance from both Congress and the commander in chief, it would constitute a virtually independent command. To complicate matters, the only two major generals not holding a department command were Ward and Putnam, and, the question of ability aside, being New Englanders, they were unacceptable to the Southerners.

There was never any doubt as to whom the Southern delegates preferred. Indeed, on the very day the Southern department was created, Edward Rutledge nominated Charles Lee to be its commander. Lee's abilities were highly rated, and, in addition, he was a Southerner— at least by adoption. So, except for the fact that he had already been appointed to the Canadian command, Lee was the perfect choice for the South. The importance of Canada made Congress reluctant to change the appointment, and this was reinforced by the conviction that Lee was the only man in whom New England, the commander in chief, and even Schuyler could place unreserved confidence. Consequently, Congress directed Lee to delay his departure for Canada until the matter could be settled.[17]

While Congress debated the question of the Southern command, the brief period of cooperation between Lee and the New York authorities came to an end. Almost recovered from the gout, Lee again evinced a disquieting aggressiveness. The ambivalent attitude of the New York toward Governor Tryon continued to bother Lee. Although the governor now resided aboard a British man-of-war in the harbor, he maintained contact with many of the city's citizens. In addition, the British squadron continued to draw provisions from New York and at the same time menace the supply lines of the American forces at Manhattan. Lee viewed such policy as foolish and dangerous, and when the British seized several vessels laden with provisions for the troops in Manhattan, he promptly clamped down an embargo on all goods and provisions destined for the British fleet. At the same time, he forbade any further communication between people in the city and Governor Tryon. His action, he informed Washington on February 29, "has thrown the mayor, council, and Tories into agonies. The propensity or rather rage for paying court to this great man, is inconceivable." In fact, they appeared infantile in their devotion to the governor. "They cannot be weaned from him," he warned. "We must put wormwood on his paps or they will cry to suck, as they are in their second childhood."

The "wormwood" Lee proposed was a test oath similar to the one he administered in Rhode Island. Those who refused to take an oath of allegiance to the Continental Congress would not be allowed merely to post bond for their good behavior (a method favored by the New York Provincial Congress) for, he asserted, "the first body of [British] troops that arrive will cancel these bonds." More direct and decisive measures were needed in view of the exposed and threatened position of New York. All those whom the oath revealed to be enemies of the cause, Lee informed the president of the New York Congress on March 4, 1776, must be immediately removed from Manhattan and Long Island where they were in a position "to co-operate with those without in working your destruction."

Lee chose Isaac Sears to administer the oaths, and he could not have found a better man for the job. As a result of his years as a leader of the New York Sons of Liberty, Sears knew most, if not all, of the leading Tories in the area. A refusal to take the oath, Lee instructed him "must be construed as no more or less than an avowal of their hostile intentions, you are therefore to seize their persons and send 'em up without loss of time to Connecticut where they can be no longer dangerous." A copy of the oath given in New York is not extant. However, the following oath which Lee used in Rhode Island is presumed to be nearly identical:

I, ———, here, in the presence of Almighty God, as I hope for ease, honor, and comfort in this world, and happiness in the world to come, most earnestly, devoutly, and religiously do swear, that I will neither directly nor indirectly assist the wicked instruments of ministerial tyranny and villany, commonly called the king's troops and navy, by furnishing them with provisions and refreshments of any kind, unless authorized by the Continental Congress or legislature, at present established in this particular colony of Rhode Island.

I do also swear, by the tremendous and Almighty God, that I will neither directly nor indirectly convey any intelligence, nor give any advice to the aforesaid enemies described; and that I pledge myself, if I should by any accident get knowledge of such treasons, to inform immediately the committee of safety.

And, as it is justly allowed that when the rights and sacred liberties of a nation or community are invaded, neutrality is not less base and criminal than open and avowed hostility, I do further swear and pledge myself, as I hope for eternal salvation, that I will, whenever called upon by the voice of the Continental Congress, or by the legislature of this particular colony under their direction, take up arms, and subject myself to military discipline in defense of the common rights and liberties of America. So help me God.

Lee realized that the administration of such an oath might be interpreted as overstepping his authority as military commander. He justified himself to Congress by declaring that in his judgment it was the only step which could secure the colony against "our gracious sovereign's cut throats." The New York Congress indignantly disagreed. Hearing of the arrest of Samuel Gale by the military, and his deportation and imprisonment in Fairfield, Connecticut, the provincial congress on March 6 demanded an explanation from Lee. What were the charges against Gale? Why had he been sent to Connecticut? Full details were required so that he could be either punished or released. In addition, Lee was accused of usurping powers belonging exclusively to the provincial civil authorities. "It may not be improper to remind you," the congress informed Lee, "that the right of apprehending, trying, and punishing citizens who violate the resolutions of Congress, or act inimical to the liberties of America, is by the Continental Congress, delegated to the provincial conventions in the respective colonies. This right we think is our duty to insist upon, as essential to the security of our constituents."

Lee wisely did not contest the provincial congress's authority. "I agree . . . entirely with you," he replied the same day, "that the apprehension, trial, and punishment of citizens is not my province, but of the Provincial Congress. But, irregular as it was, I had the assurance of many respected men that he [Gale] was a most dangerous man, and ought not to be suffered to remain on Long Island. . . . However, their assurances and my opinion form no excuse, and I heartily repent that I did not refer him to you, his proper judges."

Lee may have been repentant, but he was not reformed. "I must now inform you," he continued, "that in consequence of the last instructions from the Continental Congress, to put this city and its environs in a state of defense, I have ordered Colonel Ward . . . to secure the whole body of professed Tories in Long Island. When the enemy is at our door, forms must be dispensed with; my duty to you, and the Continental Congress, and to my conscience, have dictated the necessity of the measure." He fully realized the impropriety of his actions, and should his fears prove unfounded, he knew he would be considered "foolish, rash, and precipitate," but his duty appeared clear, and he was ready to risk his reputation in pursuance of it.

The New York delegates in Congress were also indignant when they learned of Lee's actions. Without waiting for instructions from the provincial congress, they immediately protested this encroachment on the rights of "representatives of a free people" by the military. However, they were cautious because of Lee's popularity, and thought it expedient to take up the subject on general principles. Their basic contention was "that there can be no liberty where the military is not subordinate to the civil power, in everything not immediately connected with their operations." A number of circumstances made Lee's present actions appear particularly reprehensible. Both Congress and the New York convention were in session, easily accessible to Lee, and "ready to enforce every reasonable proposition for the public safety." Therefore, his failure to seek endorsement for his extraordinary actions from one or the other was inexcusable.

In addition, Lee had already taken similar steps in Rhode Island, and, declared the New York delegates, "reiterated precedents must become dangerous; we therefore conceived it to be our unquestionable duty to assert the independence and superiority of the civil power, and to call the attention of Congress to this unwarrantable invasion of its rights by one of their [sic] officers." The majority in Congress, agreed, and on March 8 passed a resolution stating that "no oath, by way of test, be imposed upon, exacted or required of, any inhabitants of these colonies by any military officer."[18]

The resolution was tantamount to a public censure, and it cut Lee to the quick. He freely admitted that his actions were extraordinary, but since he had acted from the purest motives, he did not think he deserved "such a thundering stigma." "I confess that I expected a reprimand," he informed John Hancock in a personal letter dated March 21, "but flattered myself it might have been conveyed to me in a less severe manner than by a public resolve." Nevertheless, what was done could not be undone, "and I sincerely wish that a natural warmth of temper and (if I may so express it) an immoderate zeal for the rights and safety of this country may never hurry me a second time into a measure which may so justly merit reprehension."

The general's friend, Richard Henry Lee, attempted in a note on March 25 to take the sting out of the congressional censure by confiding that in Congress "every gentleman acknowledged the necessity under which you acted, and approved the measure." It was only the precedent they feared and what could happen if a man of less judgment than Lee took upon himself such authority. "They endeavored therefore to guard against pointing at you by directing their resolve to future occasions." This, for all practical purposes, ended the test oath episode.

The zealous Isaac Sears, however, continued his oath-giving activities on Long Island, apparently in defiance of the congressional resolve, and gloatingly reported his successes to Lee even after the latter had left New York. At Newton, he "tendered the oath to four of the great Tories, which they swallowed hard as if it was a four pound shot, that they were trying to get down." At Jamaica he encountered some difficulty in running the Tories to earth, but he finally managed to catch and administer the oath to five suspects. The more he saw of things on the Island, the more he was convinced that Lee's actions were justified. "I can assure your honor," he reported to Lee, "they are a set of villains in this country, and [I] believe the better half of them are waiting for support and intend to take up arms against us. And it is my opinion that nothing else will do but removing the ringleaders to a place of security."

Sear's endorsement of Lee's actions must have been gratifying, but by the time he received it he was well on his way to assume his new command in the South. On March 1 Congress finally decided that Lee's services would be more valuable in that quarter than in Canada. Consequently, on March 6, Congress promoted Brigadier General John Thomas to the rank of major general and entrusted him with the Canadian command. At the same time it raised William Alexander—or Lord Sterling, as he preferred to be called—to the rank of brigadier general and gave him the command of the troops in New York City.[19]

Despite his initial reluctance to go to Canada, Lee did not approve of this new disposition of commands. "As I am the only general officer on the Continent who can speak and think in French," he protested to Washington on March 3, "I confess it would have been more prudent to have sent me to Canada." Washington agreed. "I was just about to congratulate you on your appointment to the command in Canada," he replied on the 14th, "when I received the account that your destination was altered. As a Virginian I must rejoice at the change; but as an American, I think you would have done more essential service to the common cause in Canada. For, besides the advantage of speaking and thinking in French, an officer who is acquainted with their manners and customs and has travelled in their country must certainly take the strongest hold of their affection and confidence." A good deal stronger, Washington might have added, than General Thomas who had served against the French in both King George's War and the French and Indian War! Like most New England officers, Thomas was probably a Francophobe and thus unlikely to win much support for the American cause among the French Canadians.

The change in the Canadian command had other disturbing ramifications. The appointment of Thomas, without the advice or approval of Washington, established a clear precedent by which the Northern commander was to be directly responsible to Congress rather than the commander in chief. Also, the command relationship between Thomas and Schuyler posed a difficult problem. Schuyler had accepted Lee's appointment to the Canadian command with good grace. However, Lee was Schuyler's senior in rank while Thomas was the most junior major general in the army. With Schuyler's touchiness about such matters, the new arrangement was potentially explosive.

The danger of a clash between the two generals was heightened when Schuyler refused to leave northern New York. Although Congress had ordered him to repair to New York City as soon as his health permitted, Schuyler believed "that if that obstacle was immediately removed, I should not be able to leave this [Albany] until the batteaus [sic] now building at Fort George were finished, and everything got into such a train, as that [the] army in Canada may not suffer for want of provisions." Congress saw the wisdom of this, and countermanded its order. Instead, Schuyler was to fix his headquarters at Albany and continue to make arrangements for the supply of the army in Canada in addition to performing his duties as commander of the Middle department. Since nothing was said to the contrary, it must be assumed that Thomas was to enjoy the same independence in his command as Congress had intended Lee to have. However, on March 25, Richard Smith made a note in his diary of a question which was to have grave consequences in the near future: "An incidental question was debated whether Schuyler or Thomas was to have the chief command and whether Canada was a distinct department."[20]

Canada Lost

O<small>N</small> March 17, 1776, Sir William Howe began the evacuation of Boston, and a few days later the fleet departed, taking with it not only British troops but a considerable number of Tories as well. Boston's long ordeal as an occupied city was over and its citizens welcomed as liberators the tatterdemalion American army. Whatever satisfaction George Washington and his staff may have felt upon the occasion, it was soon overshadowed by the concern they felt for Howe's future intentions. With reinforcements on the way from Britain, Howe would certainly secure a new base somewhere in the colonies from which he would attempt to crush the rebellion. And there was little doubt in anyone's mind that Howe's objective would be any other than New York City. Securely based on Manhattan, Long Island, and Staten Island, the British army—in conjunction with the Royal Navy—could strike at will in every direction; northward, up the Hudson River; across Long Island Sound into Connecticut and Rhode Island; southward to the Chesapeake; or across the bay to New Jersey and Pennsylvania. In addition, New York's sizable loyalist population would afford more congenial surroundings for the British than they could expect to find anywhere else on the continent.

So even before the sails of Howe's transports had dipped below the horizon, Washington detached General William Heath's Massachusetts brigade, along with the Virginia and Pennsylvania rifle companies, and sent them posthaste to New York. Sullivan's brigade followed on March 29, and then Greene's and Spencer's brigades with Colonel Henry Knox and the artillery train. By April 13 Washington and his staff established headquarters on Manhattan and began preparations to defend the city.

The departmental command assignments which Congress had made in February had to be altered when Washington moved with his army into the Middle department. A new commander was needed for the Eastern department and with the commander in chief personally directing operations in the Middle department, a new command designation for Schuyler was called for. To discuss these changes and lay plans for the coming year's campaign, Congress summoned Washington to Philadelphia.

At the same time, Congress was increasingly concerned with the problems faced by the Northern army in Canada. In spite of the repulse at Quebec, hopes were still alive that Canada could be secured before the expected British reinforcements arrived. Indeed, if it were not, many feared the British would "soon raise a nest of hornets on our backs that will sting us to the quick."[1] Throughout the late winter and early spring, regiments from New England and the Middle colonies were rushed northward to give new substance to the wasted and dispirited Northern army. In addition, a special committee was dispatched to investigate the causes of the previous year's failure and attempt to win over the Canadians and enlist their active support for the American cause.

To execute this important trust, Congress chose Benjamin Franklin, Samuel Chase, Charles Carroll of Carrollton, and Charles' brother, Father John Carroll. Franklin's acknowledged gifts as a diplomat and his knowledge of French made him a logical choice. The two Carrolls were Roman Catholics—John a priest and future bishop—and it was hoped they would be able to allay the suspicions and latent hostility borne by the French Canadians toward the New Englanders who still composed the bulk of the Northern army. Chase was chosen because of the strong interest he had evinced in the Canadian venture and his friendship with Philip Schuyler—the man with whom the committee would have to deal extensively.[2]

By early May the committee was hard at work in Montreal, and the new commander of the Northern army, General John Thomas, was busily taking stock of the military situation. He found the army reduced by the expiration of enlistments, sickness, and desertion to barely 1,900 men—of whom no more than 1,000 were fit for duty. It must have been obvious to Thomas from the beginning that his task was hopeless. Quebec was the most heavily fortified city in North America and it had a garrison of 1,600 men. In addition, on May 2 a British fleet entered the St. Lawrence carrying General John Burgoyne with eight regiments of regulars and 2,000 German mercenaries. With reinforcements in the offing, General Guy Carleton sallied forth from Quebec on May 7 and easily routed the force of 250 Americans Thomas was able to muster.

The disorganized remnants of the American army halted briefly at Deschambault, 40 miles upriver from Quebec, and held a hurried council of war. When Thomas put the question: "Is it prudent for the army in its present situation to attempt to make a stand at this place?" the officers voted 12 to 3 to continue the retreat to Sorel at the mouth of the Richelieu.[3] Conditions at Sorel did not bear a promising aspect either. The army, almost completely demoralized, was little better than a mob. But even Thomas, knowing he must bear the blame for the retreat, could not find it in his heart to blame the men. As he described them, they were "disheartened by unavoidable misfortunes, destitute of almost every necessity to render their lives comfortable or even tolerable, sick and (as they think) wholly neglected and [with] no prospect of speedy relief." Smallpox was the bane of the Northern army, and Thomas was stricken with it at Sorel. On June 2, barely a month after he assumed command of the Northern army, John Thomas died, and the again leaderless army continued its retreat up the Richelieu toward Chambly.[4]

Meanwhile, Brigadier General William Thompson, at the head of more than 2,000 fresh troops, reached St. Johns on May 13, 1776. Thompson, the commander of the battalion of Pennsylvania riflemen sent to Boston after the Battle of Bunker Hill, had received his promotion to brigadier general on March 1 and reassigned to the Northern army. Displaying his ignorance of the situation in Canada, he complained bitterly to Schuyler that he was "surprised at the confused manner in which our army retreated from before Quebec, and still more to hear that it is intended to abandon the country as far north as the mouth of the Sorrel [sic]." While he admitted that "the confused state of this country is past description," he confidently asserted that "matters will be soon settled."[5] Thompson's notion about getting things "settled" did not include reporting to Thomas, his commanding officer. Instead, he wrote to the congressional committee (then at Montreal conferring with General Wooster) and told it what he thought should be done. The committee, in turn, embodied his ideas in a set of instructions to his superior. Before this farce on military protocol could be fully acted out, Thomas was dead and the army in headlong retreat toward Lake Champlain.[6]

In mid-May, before he knew the full extent of the Canadian debacle, Schuyler attempted to lay blame for it far from his own doorstep. "The misfortunes we experience," he informed Washington, "would in all probability have been prevented had the Connecticut troops not quitted Canada as early as they did last year." But while Schuyler bemoaned the fact that Canada was certainly lost, hopes reawakened as a brigade of 3,300 New Yorkers under Brigadier General John Sullivan moved down the lakes to meet Thompson at St. Johns.[7]

With Thomas dead, Sullivan, as the senior brigadier, assumed command of the army, strengthened now by some 6,000 fresh troops. In hopes that he might garner the "laurels to be acquired in Canada" which had eluded Montgomery, Arnold, and Thomas, Sullivan boldly took the offensive and struck the British at Trois Rivières, halfway between Quebec and Montreal. The assault delivered by General Thompson and 2,000 picked men was an unqualified disaster. For hours the American force floundered about in a swamp, and then, utterly exhausted, it was routed by the combined forces of British regulars, Canadian irregulars, Indians, and "musketoes of a monstrous size." The Americans suffered 400 casualties—236 of whom were captured, including General Thompson—while the British counted only a dozen lost.

With a third of his force exhausted and demoralized by the defeat at Trois Rivières, and threatened by the advance of Carleton and Burgoyne with more than 8,000 fresh, confident, British regulars, Sullivan decided he could no longer maintain the American foothold in Canada. Withdrawing the garrison under the command of Wooster from Montreal, he retreated with the entire army to Ile aux Noix in Lake Champlain. Low, flat, and only a mile long by a quarter mile wide, the island was a brush-covered waste dotted with swamps. Disease, always the most remorseless enemy of the Northern army, now exacted a staggering toll. Of the 8,000 troops evacuated to the island, some 2,000 were already down with smallpox and it spread rapidly through the ranks of the uninfected. In addition, dysentery and malaria broke out in the camp two days after the army landed. Without shelter, medicine, or firewood, and with only salt pork and a little flour to eat, the sick suffered horribly. To add to their torments, swarms of black flies engulfed the island by day and a myriad of mosquitoes by night. Day after day the dead were rolled into shallow grave pits and added their stench to the miseries of the living. To escape the horror which surrounded them, many of the officers drank themselves into insensibility. Finally, when not a well or able-bodied man remained, someone realized that the army must perish to the last man if it lingered on that island. In early July of 1776, the pitiful wreckage of a once proud army stumbled into Crown Point. The Northern army had returned to the spot from which it had set out 10 months earlier to conquer Canada.

Bitterly disappointed with the performance of the Northern army,

Congress sought scapegoats. Schuyler, in his frequent letters to President Hancock, consistently blamed the New England officers and men in his command for American reverses in Canada. Increasingly, congressmen from the Southern and Middle colonies echoed these sentiments. They castigated New England for its failure to raise and forward to Canada the regiments requested by Congress during the previous winter. New Hampshire was singled out for particular blame, and her delegates to Congress ruefully admitted that if the New Hampshire regiment had marched when it was supposed to, the collapse of the Northern army might have been prevented. To make matters worse, those New Hampshire men who were in Canada appeared to have acted badly. The reports reaching Congress averred that they panicked at Quebec and ran from the enemy, "leaving their cannon and sick and everything behind them without firing one musket."[8]

The return of Franklin, Chase, and the two Carrolls from Canada and their report to Congress did nothing to dispel the growing conviction that the New Englanders were alone to blame for the American reverses. "General Wooster is, in our opinion, unfit, totally unfit, to command your army and conduct the war," the commissioners asserted. "His stay in this colony [Canada] is unnecessary and even prejudicial to our affairs; we would therefore humbly advise his recall."[9]

Their report on the conduct of junior officers and the common soldier was equally unflattering. "Their account of the behavior of our New England officers and soldiers touches me to the quick," wrote Josiah Bartlett of New Hampshire. "By their account, never [have] men behaved so badly. . . . Stealing and plundering arms, ammunition, military stores, etc. and taking the battoes [sic] and running off. One man it is said stole six guns and to conceal them broke the stocks to the pieces, cut up a tent, to make a knapsack to carry off the barrels, locks, etc.—and all is said to be owing to the officers. Unless our men behave better," he sadly concluded, "we shall lose all our former credit and be despised by the whole Continent. This is the account here. I pray to God it may not be so bad as it is represented."[10]

The attempt to make New England the scapegoat for the Canadian disaster was unjust. New York, Pennsylvania, and New Jersey also had been tardy in sending reinforcements to the Northern army, and, as we have seen, troops from those colonies, when they did arrive, proved no more capable of stemming the British advance than had the New Englanders. Indeed, the officers and men involved in the defeat at Trois Rivières, were all from Pennsylvania and New Jersey.

The first formal protest against this injustice came from General Wooster. Protesting "the unjust severity, and unmerited abuse, with which my character has been treated in the colonies," he demanded, on June 26, a full congressional investigation of his conduct so that he might be "acquitted or condemned upon just grounds and sufficient proof." In Congress, John Adams led the defense of the New England soldiers and vented most of his anger on Samuel Chase. Since his return from Canada, Chase had repeatedly asserted in Congress that the blame for the failure of the Northern army must be borne by the New England officers and men. Finally, exasperated by his allegations, Adams lashed back, denouncing Chase's "imprudence" while with the army in fomenting "jealousies and quarrels between the troops from the New England and Southern states." If Chase were now "penetrated, as he ought to be, with a sense of his improper and wicked conduct," Adams continued, "he would fall down upon his knees, on this floor, and ask our forgiveness. He would afterwards retire with shame, and spend the remainder of his life in sackcloth and ashes, deploring the mischief he had done to his country."[11]

Neither begging Congress' forgiveness nor retiring in sackcloth and ashes, Chase became an even more outspoken critic of the New Englanders and a steadfast supporter of General Schuyler. However, the ferocity of Adams' personal attack on Chase indicated the growing intensity of feeling over affairs in the Northern department.

Stung by the criticism directed at them, some New Englanders retaliated by spreading rumors questioning Schuyler's loyalty. On June 7 the committees of safety of several towns in Berkshire County, Massachusetts, wrote Washington and warned him that Schuyler and his close supporters were secret Tories. The allegation was untrue, but because of the animosity toward Schuyler, many New Englanders believed it. The Reverend Cotton Mather Smith, chaplain of Colonel Benjamin Hinman's Connecticut regiment, believed that Schuyler was "as earnest a patriot as any in our land, and he has few superiors in any respect." Smith, however, admittedly did not speak for most of the men in his regiment. "Full one-third of my time," he complained, "is taken up in trying to make them see that we have no warrant for suspicions of him and every reason for the greatest confidence."[12]

The rumors caused Schuyler so much concern that he wrote Walter Livingston and the other members of the New York Secret Committee and warned that "we must watch with care and circumspection, and convince our countrymen by our actions that we are true Sons of Liberty." In the meantime, he advised, they should resign themselves to "bear with the caprice, jealousy, and envy of our misguided friends and pity them." Schuyler, however, had no intention of bearing such slanders silently, no matter how misguided their perpetrators might be. "A deluded set of people have branded me with a character, which my soul abhors," he wrote the President of Congress on May 31, "which I trust my conduct from early youth has given the lie to & which it will continue to do in the future." Therefore, he requested a full inquiry into his conduct so that "my innocence should be made as public as the charge against me."[13]

While charge and countercharge were hurled by Schuyler and his Yankee detractors, the victorious British army, having liberated Canada, embarked upon the second phase of its northern campaign. Ship construction was begun at St. John's to regain mastery of Lake Champlain and open the way for the recapture of Crown Point and Ticonderoga. If this could be achieved before the end of the campaign season, the British would have a base from which a massive invasion could be launched against New York in 1777. Fully aware of the stakes involved, American civil and military leaders agreed that the northern posts must be held at all costs. The question was, how?

Defeated, demoralized, and without effective leadership, the Northern army was at best a poor and unreliable weapon with which to check the British advance. To make matters worse, New Englanders still constituted the bulk of the army. Even the most optimistic congressmen no longer expected New England troops to fight well under Schuyler's command, while the pessimists were convinced they would not fight at all. The only hope of stopping Carleton and Burgoyne lay in finding a major general who would command the respect of the New England officers and men, and have the talent to use them to their best advantage. Only one officer filled these requirements—Horatio Gates.

On May 16 Gates had been promoted to major general to fill the vacancy made by the resignation of Artemas Ward. Gates was the senior brigadier in the Continental service, and by right of seniority he should have been given the rank of major general in March, instead of John Thomas. The value placed upon his services as adjutant general probably induced Congress to delay his promotion. However, many in Congress were growing impatient. "I wish you were a major general," John Adams had written Gates in April. "What say you to it?"[14] Ward's resignation offered the friends of Gates their opportunity. There was no question of his ability and, furthermore, the New England delegates saw in him a friend of republicanism, a kindred spirit, and were anxious to have him command the Eastern department.

Gates's promotion, then, is readily understandable and by itself of little significance. Nevertheless, it was destined to have an incalculable impact upon future events—both military and political. Looking back on the event in his autobiography, John Adams testified to its historical import:

> I take notice of this appointment of Gates, because it had great influence on my future fortunes. It soon occasioned a competition between him and Schuyler, in which I always contended for Gates, and as the rivalry occasioned great animosities among the friends of the two generals, the consequences of which are not yet spent. Indeed they have affected the essential interests of the United States and will influence their ultimate destiny. They affected an enmity between Gates and Mr. Jay who always supported Schuyler, and a dislike in Gates of Hamilton who married Schuyler's daughter . . . and whatever Hamilton may have pretended, I am persuaded that the decided part I had acted and the free speeches I had made in Congress against Schuyler and in favor of Gates, had been rankling in Hamilton's heart from 1776 till he wrote his libel against me in 1799.

Adams always maintained that he had no personal prejudice or dislike for Schuyler, but opposed him simply because "the New England soldiers would not enlist to serve under him and the militia would not turn out," and they would for Gates.[15] Of course, little of what was to come could be foreseen in 1776, and initially everyone seemed pleased by Gates's promotion.

Although Gates's appointment to the Northern command was inevitable, some of the New England delegates resisted it almost to the last. These men believed that it was more essential for New England's interests to have Gates command the Eastern department. However, the steady deterioration of the American position in Canada, the blame heaped upon New England, and the death of General Thomas combined to reconcile the New England delegates to Gates's reassignment.

"The rumor you have heard of General Gates [being assigned to command the Eastern department] will prove premature," John Adams informed his wife on June 16. "I have endeavored both here and with the General to have it so, and should have succeeded, if had not been for the loss of General Thomas. Cruel smallpox! Worse than the sword! But now I fear we must part with Gates for the sake of Canada."

Actually, as early as June 13 a majority in Congress was convinced of the necessity of sending Gates to Canada. "It is more than probable that Congress will order our friend Gates to Canada," Richard Henry Lee informed Washington. "His great abilities and virtue will be absolutely necessary to restore things there, and his recommendations will be readily complied with." And, William Whipple reported the next day, "it is expected that General Thomas is dead before this. If so, the command devolves on Sullivan, but there will be another general officer sent there—believe Gates will be the man.[16]

Finally, after considerable debate over measures to be adopted relative to Canada, Congress resolved on June 17 "that General Washington be directed to send Major General Gates into Canada, to take the command of the forces in that province." Congress realized that distance and difficult communications made Canada virtually an independent command, and it therefore realistically granted Gates discretionary powers in excess of even those given to the commander in chief. The appointment of staff and line officers without prior congressional approval was the most important of these powers. "We have ordered you to the post of honor, and made you dictator for six months," John Adams informed his friend, and added humorously, "or at least until the first of October. . . . We don't trust you generals, with too much power, for too long Time." Although much was made of this "extraordinary" grant of power, it was extraordinary only in the sense that Congress had not seen fit to bestow formally such power upon the previous commanders in Canada. In practice, however, Montgomery, Wooster, and Sullivan exercised such authority, and it is certain that Congress had determined to make a similar grant to Charles Lee before he was sent to the Southern department.[17]

On June 24 Washington informed Gates of his appointment and gave him his instructions, paraphrasing the resolves of Congress. Although anxious to leave for his new post, Gates waited in New York for additional congressional instructions. For all the powers presumably bestowed upon him, Congress had been vague about a number of major points. Most significantly, it had failed to indicate the command relationship between Gates and Schuyler. By implication, it appeared they were to be equals, although Gates was clearly junior in rank. By congressional decree, Gates was to have complete command of the Northern army in Canada, while Schuyler continued in command of the Northern department, embracing the northern portions of the province of New York. On this point, Congress was explicit. However, if the army retreated into New York, which by mid-June appeared a definite possibility, a serious question would be posed over the relationship between the army's commander and the head of the Northern department. Gates naturally wished to know what his position would be in such a situation, but Congress refused to commit itself, and Gates finally departed for Albany with the question unresolved.

To add to Gates's apprehensions, Samuel Chase emphasized the necessity of maintaining cordial relations with Schuyler. "I cannot but recommend to you the most unreserved, and unlimited confidence in General Schuyler," the former Canadian commissioner wrote. "Be assured of his integrity, diligence, abilities, and address. I know him well, and will be answerable for that gentleman as for myself." However, it appeared that "unlimited confidence" was not enough. "If you have not a constant and friendly intercourse with General Schuyler," Chase prophesied, "you will fail in Canada. . . . Be attentive to this advice—more depends on it than I can explain in a letter." Chase's emphasis on maintaining constant and friendly communications with Schuyler implied that Gates's Canadian command would not be as independent as his instructions indicated.[18]

The pretensions of General Sullivan posed a more immediate problem for Gates. That worthy, after a few weeks with the Northern army, considered himself an "expert" on Canadian affairs. With the unexpected devolution of command upon him, his ambition and vanity led him to hope that Congress would confirm him as Thomas' successor. In a private letter to George Washington, Sullivan declared that he wished either the commander in chief or General Lee would assume the command in Canada, "but in case neither of you can come to take command, I beg that, if any other officer is sent to take it, I may have leave to return, as I am well convinced that the same disorder and confusion which has almost ruined our army here would again take place, and complete its destruction, which I should not wish to see."[19]

Washington realized immediately what Sullivan was immodestly hinting at, and on June 17 passed the letter on to Congress with suitable comments. That Sullivan "is aiming at the command in Canada," he observed, "is obvious. Whether he merits it or not, is a matter to be considered." The commander in chief admitted that Sullivan was "active, spirited, and zealously attached to the cause. . . . But he has his wants, and he has his foibles. The latter are manifested in a little tincture of vanity, and in an over desire of being popular, which now and then leads him into some embarrassments. His wants are common to us all," Washington concluded magnanimously, "the want of experience to move upon a large scale; for the limited, and contracted knowledge which any of us have in military matters stands in very little stead."

While Washington had reservations concerning Sullivan's ability to cope with the command problems in Canada, he was more concerned with his refusal to serve under anyone but the commander in chief or General Lee; for by this time Washington knew that Gates was slated for the northern command. He therefore questioned the wisdom of leaving Sullivan in the Northern army.

Although leaving the final decision to Congress, Washington pointed out that two questions were of the utmost importance. When

Sullivan wrote his letter, did he know that Gates had been promoted to major general, and did he know that Gates was no longer adjutant general? If Sullivan was unaware of these developments, then perhaps he would consent to add Gates to the rather exclusive list of men under whom he would serve. On the other hand, if Sullivan knew of Gates's promotion, the letter had to be interpreted as a declaration of his unwillingness to serve under Gates.

With all of the problems attendant upon the Canadian command—exclusive of the purely military one of checking the advance of a powerful British army—Gates may be forgiven if he had qualms about his new assignment. Despite the warning that success depended upon close cooperation with Schuyler, Congress failed to clarify the command relationship between the two generals. Nor, could he count upon the support of his principal subordinate, for despite Washington's warning, Congress failed to take any action with regard to General Sullivan. Worst of all, before Gates left New York City, the Northern army had retreated out of Canada, and, technically, his command no longer existed.

☰ ☰ ☰ ☰ ☰ ☰ ☰ ☰

The Clash of Commands

THE distressing news of the Northern army's withdrawal from the Ile aux Noix to Crown Point greeted Major General Horatio Gates when he arrived in Albany at the end of June, 1776. The departure of the last American soldier from Canadian soil made a fiction of the Canadian department. Since Congress had failed to make allowances for such a contingency in its instructions to Gates, he was now without a command. Unwilling to accept this fact, Gates insisted that Congress intended him to command the Northern army regardless of its geographic location. General Philip Schuyler, whom he met in Albany, viewed matters quite differently.

The appointment of two staff officers served to bring matters to a head. Using the authority granted him by Congress, Gates, before he left New York, named Morgan Lewis deputy quartermaster general for the Northern army. (Morgan Lewis was the son of Francis Lewis, an influential New York politician and member of Congress from 1774 to 1779.) At the same time, the commissary general, Joseph Trumbull, apparently with Gates's approval, appointed Elisha Avery to replace Walter Livingston as deputy commissary for the Northern army. Both appointments were predicated on the belief that the army was in Canada. However, since the army was now in New York, Schuyler claimed that its command and direction automatically reverted to him as commander of the Northern department, and he therefore informed Gates that the appointments were no longer valid.

The confrontation between Schuyler and Gates came on June 30. Walter Livingston was present and kept an official record of the conversation. The two officers' divergent views of the command situation ap-

107

peared when Schuyler refused to recognize Lewis' and Avery's appointments, and Gates replied that although he had no authority in Albany, as soon as he reached the army he would see that the two young men were employed. Asked for a clarification of his remark, Gates asserted that he was empowered by Congress to make any appointments in the Northern army he saw fit. Schuyler rejoined that while he would be happy to appoint anyone Gates recommended, "the army being now out of Canada he conceived that it was under his command and he could suffer no appointment to be made by General Gates." Furthermore, to clarify the command relationship as he saw it, Schuyler declared "that he conceived the army to be altogether under his command *when on this side of Canada* subject however to the control of General Washington; that in his absence General Gates commanded the army in the same manner as General Sullivan did now and only as eldest officer."

Schuyler admitted that his health did not permit him to spend much time with the army, and that the senior officer, in his absence, would have considerable discretionary power, but that was all. If Congress did intend Gates to command the army in the Northern department, then Schuyler would acquiesce, "but they could not after imagine that he would remain in it." "He was a creature of theirs," Schuyler admitted, "and they had a right to move him wherever they pleased, but they could not put him under the command of a younger officer, nor oblige him to be a suicide and stab his own honor." Recognizing that matters were at an impasse, Schuyler terminated the conversation by magnanimously observing that "if he was superseded it would give him great pleasure to be superseded by a gentleman of General Gates's character and reputation." By mutual consent, Schuyler sent a transcript of the conversation to General Washington.[1]

Thus far, despite their disagreements, Schuyler and Gates were on cordial terms. Each respected the other, and intended to be perfectly frank on the command question so as to avoid any misunderstanding. "As both General Gates and myself mean to be candid, and wish to have the matter settled without any of that chicane which would disgrace us as officers and men," Schuyler informed Washington on July 1, "we have agreed to speak plain, and to show each other what we have written to you upon the occasion, and he has accordingly read the whole of what I have above said." Before the letter was dispatched, Gates showed Schuyler the resolutions of June 17 which Schuyler believed confirmed his contention that Gates was "only to command the army in Canada."

The incipient command crisis in the Northern army caused Washington great concern. He forwarded Schuyler's letter and a copy of the enclosed transcript to Congress with a warning of "the evils which must inevitably follow a disrupted command." While the commander in chief did not "presume to advise in a matter now of this delicacy," yet it appeared to him that the Northern army could now act only defensively from posts in northern New York and "one of the major generals in that quarter would be more usefully employed" with the main army. Although he did not specify which major general, Washington obviously meant Gates whose services as adjutant general he had reluctantly parted with a few weeks before. With a major British thrust at New York City expected, Gates would be of far greater utility if he were with Washington than he could ever be as a supernumerary major general in the Northern department.[2]

Joseph Trumbull agreed. While there was a need for Gates's talents in the north, they would be wasted if he was forced to serve under Schuyler. "General Schuyler is willing to let anybody fight the battles that will, under him," he contemptuously wrote on July 5 to his friend in Congress, Elbridge Gerry, "but let him command the chest, the commissary and quartermaster departments and he is pleased." Would Gates serve under Schuyler on those terms? "I think he will not," Trumbull declared, "I am sure I would not—for God's sake let this matter be set right, or I shall give up all our affairs to the Northward as lost." It was fortunate that the lakes were "between Burgoyne and us at this juncture," but this was a temporary respite at best. "Let the command be properly settled, or let Gen. Gates come back to us, we want him, we wish for him; he is necessary there, but if you keep him there, don't keep him in shakles [sic], let him be able to act, and then if he doesn't act, blame him. This half way doing business," he disgustedly concluded, "everlastingly comes to nothing."

Under pressure from Schuyler, Gates, and Washington to decide who commanded the Northern army, Congress resolved on July 8, 1776: "That Major General Gates be informed, that it was the intention of Congress to give him the command of the troops whilst in Canada, but had no design to vest him with a superior command to General Schuyler, whilst the troops should be on this side of Canada; that the president write to Major General Schuyler and Major General Gates, stating this matter, and recommending to them to carry on the military operations with harmony, and in such manner as shall best promote the public service."[3]

In fairness to Congress, it should be remembered that throughout May, June, and early July the delegates had been preoccupied with the question of independence. The meetings, debates, and consultations which had culminated in the acceptance of the final draft of the Declaration of Independence on July 4 had, understandably, left little time for mature consideration of other problems. Even so, it is difficult to imagine how Congress believed that the resolution of July 8 could clarify the command situation in the Northern department. Neither the resolution nor the letters to the two generals said who commanded the Northern army.

According to the resolution, Gates had "command of the troops whilst in Canada." Now that the army was "on this side of Canada," however, it declared that Gates did not enjoy "a superior command to General Schuyler." Since Congress did not say Gates was subordinate to Schuyler, it appears that it intended the two generals to *share* the command. President Hancock's letters to Schuyler and Gates confirm, absurd as it may seem, that this was Congress' wish. "As they think it expedient he should still continue to act with you," he informed Schuyler on July 8, "I am earnestly to recommend to you to cultivate a harmony in your military operations." Furthermore, "a mutual confidence and good understanding are at this time so essentially necessary, that I am persuaded they will take place on all occasions between yourself and General Gates, and that by your joint exertions in the cause of freedom, your country will receive the most essential benefits." Similarly, Hancock informed Gates that Congress approved his resolution to avoid any disagreements that would injure the public service, and "it is their most earnest desire, you will go on to act in the same manner, and cultivate harmony in all your military operations."[4]

A few in Congress realized that such a quixotic disposition of the Northern command was doomed to failure. "Admitting both these generals to have the military accomplishments of Marlborough and Eugene," Samuel Adams observed, "I cannot conceive that such a disposition of them can be attended with any happy effects, unless harmony subsists between them. Alas! I fear this is not the case—already disputes have arisen, which they have referred to Congress! And though they appear to treat each other with a politeness becoming their rank, in my mind, altercations between commanders who have pretensions so nearly equal, I mean in point of *command*, forbode a repetition of misfortunes."[5]

There was one aspect of the situation which no one in Congress apparently appreciated. Command carried with it the concomitant of responsibility. Both Schuyler and Gates would be acutely aware that a mistake by one could ruin the reputation and career of the other. The joint command, therefore, demanded a complete selflessness on the part of the two generals—a quality which neither Gates nor Schuyler ever had in abundance.

It appeared at first that the fears expressed by those who viewed the divided command with alarm would prove groundless. The two generals accepted Congress' decree with surprisingly good grace and attempted to abide by it. Gates acknowledged the limitation of his command to Canada and, in company with Schuyler and Arnold, proceeded to Crown Point to see what could be salvaged from the wreckage of the Northern army. For his part, Schuyler was well pleased by the "perfect harmony" which subsisted between him and his subordinate. The differences which had threatened to divide them had been openly and frankly dealt with and now should be forgotten. Both men seemed inclined for their own well-being as well as the public good, to let matters rest at that.[6]

In any event, there was little time for airing personal differences. Reports indicated that the British were constructing a sizable naval force at St. Johns with which they hoped to regain control of Lake Champlain. To meet this challenge, Schuyler and Gates initiated a naval building program of their own at Skenesboro and took steps to strengthen the fortifications at Ticonderoga. While no one questioned the propriety of this course of action, the concomitant decision to abandon Crown Point aroused opposition within the army and brought unprecedented rebukes from George Washington and the Continental Congress.

The ruined condition of the old British works at Crown Point convinced both Schuyler and Gates that the position was indefensible. Brigadier Generals Sullivan, Arnold, and Baron de Woedtke agreed. (Baron Friedrick Wilhelm de Woedtke, a major in the Prussian army, was appointed a brigadier general by Congress on March 16, 1776.) Consequently, a council of general officers voted unanimously on July 7 to abandon Crown Point and concentrate all effort on the enlargement and strengthening of the fortifications at Ticonderoga. This included the erection of works to the east of Ticonderoga which were named Mount Independence.

Angry protest greeted the announcement of the generals' decision. Twenty-one junior officers, led by Colonels John Stark, Enoch Poor, and William Maxwell drew up a petition to contest formally the council's action. The army was expected to contest every inch of ground with the enemy, they declared, and abandoning Crown Point without a fight would not only give the enemy a strong position from which to attack Ticonderoga, but also make it impossible for an American naval force to operate north of the Point. More specifically, the officers, most of whom were New Englanders, expressed their fear that the British would use Crown Point as a base from which their Indian allies would burn and pillage the New England frontier. Finally, they complained that Ticonderoga was notoriously unhealthy and concentrating the army there would greatly increase the sickness which continually plagued the Northern troops.

Schuyler countered by informing the dissatisfied officers that the abandonment of Crown Point was "indispensably necessary for a variety of reasons," and, from his point of view, the arguments they had put forth against the proposed action did not "bear sufficient weight to alter it." The officers were unhappy with this reply, and more so because Schuyler refused to inform them of the reasons which had induced the general officers to arrive at their decision. At least one disgruntled officer wrote a colleague in the main army informing him of the situation and representing the council's decision in a most unfavorable light. In this manner it came to the attention of General Washington.[7]

The first indication that something of the sort had occurred appeared in a letter from Washington to Schuyler on July 17. The commander in chief acknowledged that his personal ignorance of the terrain and situation of the Northern army made it impossible for him to judge the propriety of giving up Crown Point. "However," he continued, "I cannot but observe, tho' I do not mean to encourage, in the smallest degree, or to give the least sanction to inferior officers, to set up their opinions against the proceedings and councils of their superiors, . . . that the reasons assigned by the officers in their remonstrance appear to me forcible and of great weight. They coincide with my own ideas. I have ever understood Crown Point to be an important post, and from its situation, of the utmost consequence to us, especially if we mean to keep the superiority and mastery of the lake."

It was clear that Washington doubted the wisdom of evacuating Crown Point, and in his eyes the responsibility for the decision ultimately rested with Schuyler as the commanding officer. However, while he rebuked Schuyler, he did not reveal the full extent of his displeasure and misgivings. Such was not the case when he took up pen two days later to write his former adjutant, Horatio Gates.

Washington had been on fairly intimate terms with Gates since the beginning of the war, and this prompted a candor which was absent in the purely formal communication he had just dispatched to Schuyler. One thing that puzzled him, he informed Gates, was the reason given by the council for abandoning the post: that it could not be held with the present force. All of the field officers apparently believed otherwise, and this cast suspicion on the motives of the general officers.

Washington also detailed the evil consequences of giving up the post to the enemy—in terms identical with the colonels' memorial— and then, in a manner which would probably have caused Schuyler to resign had the letter been addressed to him, the commander in chief declared that he would have overridden and reversed the council's decision were it not too late. "Nothing but a belief that you have actually removed the army from the Point to Ticonderoga, and demolished the works at the former; and a fear of creating dissensions, and encouraging a spirit of remonstrating against the conduct of superior officers by inferiors, have prevented me, by the advice of the general officers here, from directing the post at Crown Point to be held till Congress should decide upon the propriety of its evacuation. I can give no order in the matter, least between two opinions, and places, neither are put into such a posture of defense, as to resist an advancing enemy. I must however express my sorrow at the resolution of your council, and wish, that it had never happened, as every body who speaks of it also does; and that the measure could yet be changed with propriety." ~

Unquestionably, Washington's assessment of the council's decision owed much to the advice of his New England subordinates. General Nathanael Greene, one of his most trusted officers, wrote Governor Cooke of Rhode Island on July 22 that Schuyler had "come to one of the most mad resolutions I ever heard of, that is to quit Crown Point. There never could be [madder] a piece of policy; we lose all the advantage upon the lake; we have no such supremity there that the enemy could not injure us this summer. We lay all the back parts of New England open." This seems to have been the consensus of the officers in the main army, and it is therefore little wonder that Washington reacted as he did.

General Gates responded to Washington's criticism with a spirited defense of the council's decision. The general officers had unanimously endorsed Schuyler's recommendation to abandon the post, and in Gates's opinion, Schuyler's arguments were "founded in reason and good sense." "As to the field officers being all of a contrary opinion," he chided the commander in chief, "who ever gave your Excellency that intelligence, was the author of an assertion contrary to fact." Gates insisted that only two field-grade officers actually objected to the decision, while most, including "those whose long service and distinguished characters deservedly gives their opinions a preference," fully concurred with the general officers. While Gates did not presume to question Washington's right to criticize, or even reverse, decisions made by the generals with the Northern army, he did express resentment that his and Schuyler's actions had been subjected to review by the council of general officers in New York. With one exception—Israel Putnam—those officers were junior to Schuyler and Gates and knew nothing of conditions in the Northern army.[8]

In retrospect, Gates's reply seems fair and even restrained when compared with Washington's highly critical letter to him. However, Washington was offended. Refusing to comment on the fact that not all of the field officers had opposed the move—as he had been led to believe—Washington informed Gates on August 14 that although his subordinates were critical of the decision, yet "there was no council called upon the occasion, nor court of enquiry, nor court martial, as has been suggested by some. I will not take up more time upon the subject," he concluded brusquely, "or make it a matter of further discussion."

Washington was equally brisk when he dealt with General Schuyler. Schuyler had informed the commander in chief on August 6 that he considered the censure of his actions by a council of officers in New York an outrage, and he threatened to resign unless the council was in turn censured by either Washington or Congress. Washington told Schuyler essentially the same thing he had told Gates, and advised him to forget the whole matter. However, should he persist, then Washington was prepared to pass his letter, which threatened resignation, on to Congress. While Gates heeded Washington's advice and let the matter drop, Schuyler felt he could not follow suit. He viewed the whole affair as proof that there were men in Congress and in the army eager to discredit him.

Events in Congress tended to strengthen Schuyler's conviction that his enemies were making the most of the opportunity afforded by his unpopular decision. On July 17 Washington had informed Congress of his dissatisfaction with Schuyler's abandonment of Crown Point, and President Hancock promptly replied that the commander in chief could dispose of all Continental forces, including those in the Northern department, as he saw fit. Thus, he was empowered to reverse Schuyler's decision. "I am sory [sic] to find how egregiously you have been represented to the members of Congress," Samuel Chase commiserated with Schuyler. "You have enemies."[9]

General Arnold added fuel to the fire by voicing his opinion that Schuyler's enemies played a major part in the criticism of the relinquishment of Crown Point, and that they would attempt to "attribute our misfortunes in Canada to [Schuyler's] misconduct. . . . A base and envious world are ever aiming their envenomed shafts at those in elevated stations," he warned his superior on August 23; "they cannot bear to see any soar above their own level." These warnings from men whom he trusted, whetted Schuyler's suspicion. Increasingly, he viewed all criticism and challenges to his authority as part of a plot to drive him in disgrace from the army.

While perhaps exaggerated, Schuyler's fears were not unfounded. Most of the New England congressmen wished to drive him from the Northern command, and they grasped at every opportunity to discredit him in the eyes of their colleagues from other states. After months of aspersing his command abilities, loyalty, and personal bravery without much effect, Schuyler's enemies elicited a strong reaction by calling into question the operation of the commissary in the Northern department. Schuyler was unusually sensitive to such criticism for three reasons: first, he considered the supplying of the Northern army his greatest contribution as departmental commander; second, he rationalized his absence from the army by pleading the need to personally supervise the commissary and quartermaster operations; and third, he considered charges of irregularities in the supply departments as a reflection upon his personal honesty.

Until July of 1776 there was some doubt concerning the extent of the commissary general's power. When Congress created that office on June 16, 1775, there was only one army to be provisioned—the recently adopted army before Boston. However, with the enlargement of the war, a new army came into existence in northern New York. Thereupon, Congress appointed a deputy commissary general to supply the Northern army, and for the remainder of 1775 and the early part of 1776 the deputy, Walter Livingston, operated virtually independently of the commissary general, Joseph Trumbull. The preoccupation of the latter with the organization of an effective supply system for the main army, combined with the relative isolation of the Northern army in Canada, accounts for the freedom of action enjoyed by Livingston. However, with the retreat of the Northern army from Canada and the removal of the main army to New York, Trumbull attempted to bring the affairs of the Northern commissary under his direct control.

Much to his surprise, he discovered that Livingston denied his authority. Trumbull considered his deputy insubordinate and determined to remove him at the earliest opportunity. The New York delegates, one of whom, James Duane, was Livingston's brother-in-law, rallied congressional support to thwart Trumbull. They argued that the Northern commissary was independent and that Livingston was responsible only to Congress.[10]

The New Yorkers' argument was spurious and was probably intended only as a gambit in their attempt to obtain the commissary generalcy for Livingston. In early June of 1776, Trumbull's friends in Congress attempted to obtain for him the office of quartermaster general; a position generally considered superior to that of commissary general.

Livingston's friends quickly saw an opportunity to advance him to the latter office—a move which would be made easier if Livingston's pretensions as Trumbull's equal could be established.

Both groups were disappointed when Congress elected Stephen Moylan quartermaster general. However, Elbridge Gerry assured Trumbull, Congress had not intended its action to be a reflection on his merit. On the contrary, his outstanding service as commissary general had determined Congress to keep him in that post. In any event, Gerry concluded, Trumbull's promotion to quartermaster general would have opened the way for Livingston's advancement to the commissary generalcy, "which I should have considered as an unfortunate exchange."[11]

Trumbull was not convinced. He viewed the congressional action as either an indication of displeasure with his present services or an intentional slight to force him from the service so that others (Livingston?) might gain control of the commissary. Resignation seemed the only honorable course. Trumbull's reaction alarmed Gerry and he hastened to reassure his friend. "You are greatly misinformed with respect to your being ill used *in* Congress and out, by some who want to transfer the office to other hands. What is done out of doors I know not, but your conduct in Congress has been highly approved as any officer's in the service. With respect to Mr. L[ivingston] perhaps he is stung with disapointment [*sic*], but I assure you whatever may be his desires relative to supplanting you it will never be effected; and by your *own resignation,* which he may hope to bring about by such detestable conduct as you mention, can he alone effect his purpose."[12]

Temporarily dissuaded from his intention to resign, Joseph Trumbull turned to the problem of ridding himself of Livingston. Since he had not appointed Livingston, he did not feel he could simply remove him from office. However, the creation of the Canadian department made it possible to make Livingston superfluous. He appointed Elisha Avery deputy commissary general, gave him exclusive authority to supply the army in Canada, and sent him northward with General Gates. In this manner, he hoped, the entire supply of the Northern army would pass from Livingston to Avery.

Upon his arrival in Albany, Avery found himself in much the same predicament as General Gates. The retreat of the army from Canada effectively voided his commission. Undaunted, Avery approached Schuyler and requested money with which to buy commissary stores for the Northern army. Schuyler seemed surprised and asked if Walter Livingston had been superseded. Avery responded by showing his commission. Schuyler pointed out that Avery's appointment was as deputy commissary in Canada and he therefore in no way superseded Livingston in the

Northern department. Avery could not deny this, but he asserted in the strongest terms that it was Trumbull's intention "that he should have the whole management [of the Northern commissariat], and that Mr. Livingston was only to be considered as a contractor."

At this juncture Schuyler called in Livingston who declared, among other things, that Trumbull had no authority to remove him—only Congress could do that. Avery, seeing that nothing further could be gained in the face of the joint opposition of Schuyler and Livingston, proceeded to Crown Point with Gates who promised to find him some employment with the army.

Thoroughly put out by this turn of events, Trumbull informed Washington that he would assume no responsibility for the supply of the Northern army as long as a man not of his appointment (and not enjoying his confidence) remained as its deputy commissary. Washington sympathized with Trumbull, and urged upon Congress the necessity of having *all* commissary affairs under the direction of the commissary general.[13]

With the commander in chief's support, Trumbull's friends in Congress now pressed for and received a ruling on July 8 "That the commissary general have full power to supply both armies, that upon the lakes as well as that at New York; and also to appoint and employ such persons under him, and to remove any deputy commissary, as he shall judge proper and expedient; it being absolutely necessary, that the supply of both armies should be under one direction."[14]

Armed with this authorization, Trumbull was free to dispose of Livingston when and as he saw fit. However, Livingston's position was not the only one compromised by the congressional resolve. Schuyler, not Livingston, had in fact superintended the commissary in the Northern department, and with the interposition of the commissary general's authority he would no longer be able to do so. Thus, having successfully coped with the challenge to his command posed by General Gates, Schuyler found himself outflanked by Joseph Trumbull.

The Battle for the
Northern Commissary

PHILIP Schuyler and Walter Livingston must have realized that they could not hope to retain control over the Northern commissary in the face of Congress' resolve of July 8. Nevertheless, they refused to surrender without a fight. On July 17, immediately upon receipt of the resolve, Schuyler informed Washington that "he should be under great apprehensions that the service will not be carried on so well as I wish" if Livingston was forced from the commissary. In an attempt to enlist the commander in chief's services in his and Livingston's cause, Schuyler asked him to bring the matter to Trumbull's attention.[1]

Whether or not Washington informed Trumbull of Schuyler's plea is uncertain. However, he did show him the part of Schuyler's letter which reported that "the incredible waste of provisions has been such, that we have but 600 bbl. of pork. . . . Fresh beef is not to be had." Trumbull quickly turned this admission to his advantage. Holding Livingston personally responsible for the "incredible waste of provisions," he ordered him to launch an immediate investigation and discharge "the unfaithful and negligent people" he had employed. In addition, Trumbull ordered fresh beef sent to the Northern army and instructed Livingston to pay for it out of the Northern department's chest. Livingston took offense at Trumbull's orders and promptly tendered his resignation to Schuyler—with the condition that before it took effect "the aspersions thrown on my conduct may be wiped off . . . that I may stand clear and unimpeached with either negligence or male-conduct [sic]." Livingston concluded by reiterating his denial of Trumbull's authority in the Northern department, and remarking that the words "deputy commissary" were hardly adequate to describe the only deputy commissary general commissioned directly by Congress.

118

Nevertheless, pursuant to Trumbull's order, Livingston directed an investigation of commissary affairs at the various northern posts. No corruption was uncovered—or at least none was reported—but a situation came to light which directly involved General Gates in the commissary squabble. At Ticonderoga, Mr. Bleecker, Livingston's investigator, discovered that Elisha Avery had received charge of the public stores by Gates's order. In addition, Gates authorized Avery to purchase cattle for the Northern army. In effect, Avery was functioning as commissary for the major part of the Northern army without the consent, or even the knowledge, of the deputy commissary general.

Livingston considered Avery's presence intolerable. After seeking and receiving advice from his father, Robert Livingston (the third Lord of Livingston Manor), and James Duane, his brother-in-law, he once again informed Schuyler on August 5 that he was determined to resign. "It is a question with me whether you wont very soon resign yourself," he concluded.

Schuyler considered Avery's activity as much a reflection upon his authority as it was on Livingston's, and promptly registered a protest with Washington. Although he professed acknowledgment of Trumbull's authority in the Northern department, he maintained that Avery's commission applied only to the Canadian department.[2] No mention was made of Gates's part in this new incident. However, it must have been the most disturbing fact to Schuyler. In Schuyler's presence, Gates had promised Avery employment with the Northern army when he had first arrived in Albany. Now, despite his apparent acceptance of Schuyler's superior authorilty to make appointments in the Northern department, Gates had kept his promise.

Reports filtering back to Congress from the Northern department stirred growing impatience with Schuyler. Although the invasion from Canada loomed ever larger, Congress heard little of preparations to meet the threat and much of petty bickering and jealousy. To make matters worse, affairs to the northward compared unfavorably with American successes in the Southern department. On June 28 General Charles Lee's troops repulsed a combined naval and land attack on Charleston led by Admiral Parker and General Clinton. Although the numbers involved were small, decisive and resolute action had thwarted the British invasion of the South. Inevitably, unfavorable comparisons were made with the officers and men in the Northern army. "Some of the Southern gentlemen say that America must be saved by the Southern, not the Northern, troops," Josiah Bartlett angrily informed John Langdon. "However, I hope it will yet appear that the New England troops are not behind any in the Continent in point of bravery."[3]

Chided by their Southern colleagues, New England congressmen were more determined than ever to make Schuyler the scapegoat for the failures of the Northern army. Fortune seemed to smile on their efforts. The decision to abandon Crown Point led Congress to question Schuyler's military ability, and the dispute over the Northern commissary revealed how petty and quarrelsome he could be. At the same time, Gates, the man Congress had intended to command the Northern army in Canada, was rising in the esteem of men in Congress and in the army. "Generalship is now dealt out to the army by our worthy and well-esteemed General Gates," reported a New Jersey officer in the Northern army, "who is putting the most disordered army that ever bore the name into a state of regularity and defence."[4] New Englanders missed few opportunities to compare Gates's achievements with Schuyler's failures.

In July of 1776 a fresh opportunity to discredit Schuyler was provided with the leveling of charges which alleged gross mismanagement of funds in the Northern commissary and quartermaster departments. Jonathan Trumbull, Jr., who was the deputy paymaster general for the Northern department, complained bitterly to his brother Joseph of "his and the Northern army's unjust treatment," and hinted darkly at fiscal irregularities in the supply services. The commissary general received this letter in late July, and immediately forwarded it to William Williams, the Connecticut congressman. Williams lost no time in showing the letter "to many members whom I could trust" as well as certain members of the Board of War. Although the deputy paymaster's allegations were vague, Congress was sufficiently suspicious of the management of the Northern department to pass a series of resolutions designed to uncover any irregularities in the handling of public funds.[5]

Congress sent $200,000 to Jonathan Trumbull, Jr., and ordered him to make a complete report on his disposal of "all the monies which have passed through his hands since his appointment to . . . office." In addition, the commissary general and all of his deputies, the quartermaster general and all of his deputies, and the commanding officer of each department, were to make monthly returns of funds received and disbursed by them.[6]

Although seemingly innocuous, Williams claimed that the sole purpose of the resolutions was "to find out what Schuyler has done with his money." Still, he pessimistically informed Joseph Trumbull, "I dont see at present that it would be possible to remove him, if the utter ruin of the Continent was to be the known consequence of his continuence in office." Nevertheless, he promised, "endeavors will not be wanting."

Samuel Adams was more sanguine. "These resolutions perhaps may not please *everybody*," he declared, "but if they are duly executed they may detect mistakes, or *frauds* if any should happen. As to what has passed in Canada and near it, some person has in my opinion been most egregiously to blame, and, to use a homely proverb, the saddle has been laid, or attempted to be laid on the wrong horse." In Adams' mind, it was not Wooster but Schuyler who should bear the burden of failure in the North.

Adams also turned up information concerning Livingston's pretensions that he was answerable only to Congress. Examining the printed Journals of Congress, Adams found that in July of 1775, Livingston had been appointed deputy commissary "for the New York department during the *present* campaign." Since that campaign was now long over, Livingston technically had no authority to act as deputy commissary and, in Adams opinion, Trumbull was free to dispose of his troublesome subordinate as he saw fit. Furthermore, if Schuyler intervened on Livingston's behalf, he advised Trumbull to lodge formal protests with Congress and General Washington.[7]

It would appear, however, that Trumbull was more influenced by the pessimistic Williams than he was by Adams. Certain that no solution to the problems besetting the Northern department would be found until its commander was removed, Trumbull recommended to Adams that Schuyler be made head of the Eastern department where "he can do no harm . . . , & the Massachusetts gentlemen, will keep him in order."

Trumbull may not have been serious when he recommended Schuyler for the Eastern command. It is more likely that he was simply driven to desperation by his most recent clash with Schuyler and Livingston. He had received a number of complaints from officers in the Northern army that the issuing commissaries showed favoritism in the allowance of extra rations. It was customary to allot an officer a certain number of extra rations according to his rank, a cash equivalent of which could be accepted to supplement his pay. Understandably, the Northern officers objected when they discovered that some of their number were receiving more for their rations than others. Trumbull therefore ordered Livingston to secure from Schuyler a general order establishing the value of a ration.

When Livingston informed Schuyler of Trumbull's request, he immediately declined to issue the order, pleading ignorance of the price of provisions. On the other hand, even if he did know the price of rations, Schuyler asserted that it was not his business to decide what should be allowed to the officers in lieu of their extra rations. To do so would "risk incurring either the blame of the officers or the disapprobation of Congress."[8] Refusing to act for fear of disapproval by the officers or

Congress was irresponsible, and, for a man of Schuyler's experience in the supplying of the Northern army, the plea of ignorance as to the price of provisions was certainly something less than candid.

Nevertheless, Trumbull was effectively stymied. Schuyler would not issue the general order, and a uniform system of reimbursement for extra rations could not be established. "It will be extremely difficult for me to act, or send any person to act, where we shall surely meet every opposition from the commanding officer," he bitterly complained to Samuel Adams on August 12; "it's rowing against wind & tide."

As Schuyler's enemies began to despair, he gave them new hope. Stung by real and imagined slights, he began, confidentially at first, to intimate his intention to resign. For months, New Englanders—both in the army and in Congress—had imputed the loss of Canada to his failings as a commander. Now, they were casting doubt upon his honesty as well, and many were beginning to listen. His obstinate refusal to allow anyone to intrude in the commissary department or to investigate those responsible for the purchase of supplies tended to sharpen suspicions. Even Robert Morris, who was not among Schuyler's enemies, had misgivings about his continuance in command. "Certainly there has been great mismanagement in that department," he wrote General Gates on July 25, "and I find some people attributing this to a source I never should have suspected. Is it possible that a man who writes so well & expresses such anxiety for the cause of his country as Gen. S[chuyler] does, I say is it possible that he can be sacrificing the interest of that country to his ambition or avarice[?] I sincerely hope it is not so—but such insinuations are dropped."[9]

Although Congress did not officially endorse any of the allegations made against Schuyler's conduct, it did something which he thought was just as bad. A committee appointed to investigate the reasons for the miscarriages in Canada, finally made its report on July 30. No one found fault with what the report said—but Schuyler objected vigorously to what it failed to say. In short, the report imputed the Canadian debacle to a wide assortment of difficulties: short enlistments, disobedience of the troops, lack of money, and disease—especially smallpox. However, no mention was made of General Wooster, whom Schuyler blamed for the American failure in Canada.[10]

Indeed, Congress, on August 17, 1776, committed an unforgivable sin (in Schuyler's eyes) of formally exonerating Wooster of any misconduct in the performance of his duties. Although the commander of the Northern department did not learn of this until October 22, he suspected that the committee's report was intended to exculpate Wooster and place the blame for American reversals on his shoulders. "I am confident the misfortunes in Canada, are to be imputed to more causes, than those mentioned in the resolutions of the 30th ulto," he caustically informed the President of Congress, "and as I wish my conduct should undergo the strictest scrutiny, Congress will therefore permit me to entreat them, to charge the committee above mentioned, or to appoint another, minutely to enquire how far, if at all, any of the miscarriages in Canada are to be imputed to myself. . . . I shall court the most ordeal trial, nay altho' conscious of the mediocrity of my talents & that I am vastly inadequate to the important command I am honored with. Yet on this occasion I may be allowed to say that I do not believe that I shall be even convicted of an error of judgment."[11]

Perhaps as well as anything, this letter reveals the side of Philip Schuyler that alienated so many of his contemporaries. There was nothing contained in the committee's report to justify his outburst of self-righteousness. He patently fished for a complimentary denial when he pleaded that he was inadequate to his command. Surely, to claim—after the series of disasters which had overtaken the army he commanded—that he had not been guilty of even one error of judgment was a piece of arrogance which might well have staggered his closest friends.

Two days later, on August 18, Schuyler expressed to Washington his displeasure with Congress's action, and complained that artful and jealous men were plotting against him. Suspicion and envy had followed him ever since he "reluctantly" accepted his command. The investigation he requested of Congress, he was sure, would not only honorably acquit him, "but . . . judicious men will discover in me the honest man and the faithful American. But as envy even in that case will not cease, nor malevolence without its slander, I am determined to quit the army as soon as my conduct has been enquired into and [envince] myself in private life what I have strove to do in public, the friend of my injured country."[12]

It is significant that Schuyler had not notified Congress that he intended to resign. Indeed, in his letter to Congress of the 16th, he declared that if his name was cleared by a formal inquiry, "that confidence will be established, which is so indispensably necessary that an army have in the general." The implication was that he would continue as commander of the Northern department.[13]

At this point, the impasse over the control of the Northern commissary was finally broken in a manner which convinced Schuyler that his enemies were firmly in control of Congress. Probably at the urging of Walter Livingston, Schuyler, on August 20, directed General Gates to order Avery to make weekly returns of his transactions at Ticonderoga to Livingston. Avery indignantly refused, and informed

Schuyler on September 5 that he was not in any way subordinate to Livingston, and that his instructions ordered him to make returns directly to Commissary General Trumbull and to Schuyler as commander of the department. This he would continue to do, but he would resign before he subordinated himself to Livingston.

When Trumbull heard of this new attempt to challenge his authority, he directed Avery to leave Ticonderoga immediately, and wrote a stinging letter to Schuyler. "I find he [Avery] nor any other person, can have anything to do in the commissary department, in the Northern district, without a continual clashing with Mr. Livingston." Since Livingston was supported by the departmental commander, "all must give way to him."

While it appeared that Trumbull was giving way, appearances were deceiving. The recall of Avery was a dramatic gesture .designed to impress upon Congress the degree to which Trumbull's authority was still thwarted by Schuyler and Livingston. Trumbull's tactic succeeded, and Congress expressed its amazement that anyone could be in doubt concerning his authority after the adoption of the resolution of July 8. It therefore voted that a copy of the resolution be "immediately transmitted to the commanding officer in the northern department, and to the commissary general, as the full sense of Congress on the commissary general's right to direct the operations of his department, both as contractor and issuer of provisions; and that Mr. Trumbull be informed, Congress expect this will remove his difficulties, and induce his continuance in the office of commissary for both armies, at New York, and on the lakes."

On the same day, September 12, Congress dealt Schuyler's authority in the Northern department another blow. In July, General Gates had dispatched Morgan Lewis (his deputy quartermaster general–designate) to Congress to report the problem faced by Lewis and John Trumbull (the adjutant general–designate) as a result of the Northern army's retreat from Canada. Both men had been put to considerable expense in equipping themselves for their new posts, and they were keenly disappointed when Schuyler informed them that they lacked authority to act in the Northern department. Congress sympathized with their plight, and voted without dissent on September 12 to appoint John Trumbull deputy adjutant general of the army in the Northern department, and Morgan Lewis deputy quartermaster general.[14]

The next day, William Williams gloatingly informed Joseph Trumbull of these developments, and speculated about Schuyler's future. "Many of them," he confided, referring to his fellow congressmen, "greatly resent the conduct of the gentleman [Schuyler] who has so interfered with you and there are appearances of many other things against him, which begin to work, and will I believe prove his downfall, but these things are not fully ripe yet, nor can they possibly be attended to now. He had lately written a very long epistle to enforce the necessity and expedience the bestness and the cheapness etc. of supplying the northern army by a contract with somebody there. It was hastily read through in the House, and not the least further notice taken of it. I presume he will not interpose in your department again, tho' I know he has paid but little attention to his orders in many things."[15]

Walter Livingston must have known that Congress would never support his defiance of Trumbull's authority, for, on September 12, his letter of resignation was laid before the house. Trumbull had finally won his battle for control of the Northern commissary, and he could not resist the temptation of rubbing it in when he informed Schuyler of Livingston's replacement on September 20. "This will be delivered to you by Mr. Avery who succeeds Mr. Livingston, as deputy commissary, in the Northern department. Your aid to, & support of him, shall be gratefully acknowledged by me. And whatever sums of money [he] has occasion [for], & applys for, & you give him warrants on the paymaster for, I shall hold myself accountable to the continent for the disposition of, in supplying their army and that district with provisions & necessities."

Close on the heels of Livingston's resignation, Schuyler dramatically tendered his own. "I do therefore now, hereby resign my commission as major general in the army of the American States," he informed Congress on September 14, "and all & every other appointment of office, which I have been honored with by the honorable Continental Congress." Congress must immediately select a new commander for the Northern department, and, in the meantime, Schuyler promised to "continue to act as usual, until such a reasonable time has elapsed, in which one could be sent, which I should suppose need not exceed a fortnight."[16] If Congress accepted his resignation, Schuyler must have known that Horatio Gates would be his successor. Was that what he wanted, or did he expect Congress to reject his resignation, declare its unqualified approval of his conduct, and "convince" him to remain as head of the Northern department? In view of subsequent events, the latter seems more likely.

Whatever Schuyler's motive, his friends in Congress applauded his action. Foremost among these was Edward Rutledge of South Carolina who informed Robert R. Livingston of Schuyler's intention to resume the seat in Congress to which he was still entitled. "I wish he was now here. You know as well as I do, that the rascals who took much liberty with the character of that gentleman would not venture to look him in the face. I admire his wisdom; it was the only step which he could take to recover and establish his reputation."

Schuyler, however, was not content to await a face-to-face encounter with his enemies, and a week and a half after offering his resignation, he lashed out at Congress as a whole in a letter which fairly dripped with venomous sarcasm and righteous indignation. "I thank Congress with a sincerity equal to the attention they have evinced in the resolution of the 14th of September whereby I am made acquainted that my letter 'of the 16th of August was duly received and referred to the committee appointed to enquire into the miscarriages in Canada'. . . . permit me to entreat the favor of a further resolution that I may be permitted to defend my conduct, and if possible point out other causes of the miscarriages in Canada beside those taken notice of in the resolution of the 30th July—causes which are so obvious that I could not but wonder that they passed unnoticed." He bitterly complained that Congress had failed to answer numerous letters which he had written in July, August, and September (including that containing his resignation!), "one or other of which I humbly conceive contain matters of some moment to the weal of the American States."

Schuyler was incensed at another congressional action which also served to prod his growing suspicion and jealousy of Gates. "Congress will pardon me if I presume to hint," he bristled, "that there appears to me a little impropriety in resolving that the powder &c. 'be immediately sent to *General Gates for the use of the army in the Northern department.*' as I believe *my* resignation had not yet reached Congress on the date that resolution was made [September 14]."[17] He also complained to Washington of this congressional impropriety.

Washington, desperately trying to maintain a foothold on Manhattan in the face of General Howe's triumphant army, nonetheless found time on September 30 to patiently reassure his northern subordinate. He was certain that the resolution was not "calculated or designed in the smallest degree" to give offense. He also pointed out to Schuyler that "the application for stores had been made as a requisition from Genl. Gates, which I presume occasioned the resolve, ordering 'em to be sent to him. Also the words 'for the use of the Northern army' nothing is to be inferred from them," he concluded. "Whenever stores are sent to any department, it is said always for the use of the army there."

There was therefore nothing unusual about the resolution nor did it reflect upon Schuyler's authority. Passed on September 14, nine days before Congress received Schuyler's resignation, the resolution simply consigned 15 tons of powder, 20,000 flints, and 100 reams of cartridge paper to General Gates "for the use of the army in the northern department."[18] The use of the words "northern department" was perhaps unfortunate; however, it was not the calculated insult that Schuyler thought. In this, as in many things, he had become unduly sensitive and suspicious. Nevertheless, it terminated the spirit of cooperation and mutual respect which had existed between Schuyler and Gates since early July. In Schuyler's mind, the offensive resolution provided a link between Gates and Schuyler's enemies in Congress. Was it not possible that Gates, disappointed in his Canadian command, coveted the Northern department and was conniving with the New Englanders to obtain it?

It is rather remarkable that such a suspicion had not occurred to Schuyler long before mid-September. That it did not, considering the northern commander's disposition, is a tribute to Gates's tact and circumspection. Also, the two generals had remained physically separated for most of the time. As Francis Lewis commented in late August, "General Gates commands at Ticonderoga. General Schuyler is treating with the Indians at the German Flatts. They will always be on separate commands."[19] This optimism was perhaps naive, but physical separation undoubtedly was a factor in delaying the appearance of suspicion and in staving off the final break between the two until the spring of 1777.

Increasingly convinced of Gates's ambition, Schuyler may well have regretted his letter of resignation. Needless to say, there was no such regret evinced by the New England congressmen. Elated by Schuyler's resignation, Elbridge Gerry predicted that "harmony will ensue" in the Northern department.[20] There was another reason to rejoice. "We have obtained Col. Moylan's resignation and General Mifflin comes again into the office of quartermaster general," he jubilantly informed Gates on September 27. Thus the Lee–Adams junto—the powerful congressional faction led by the Lees of Virginia and the Adamses of Massachusetts—of which Gerry was a member, could be well satisfied. Bound together by the common conviction that reconciliation was now hopeless, the junto sought to advance those who shared that belief. Men of their choosing controlled the commissary and quartermaster generalcies, and, in the Northern department, after a long struggle, Livingston had been disposed of, Schuyler was on his way out, and Gates would almost certainly succeed to the command. But Gerry and his friends seriously underestimated the political finesse of Philip Schuyler.

By September 28, the politically astute realized that Congress would not accept Schuyler's resignation, and, further, that he had never intended that it should. Shorly after the arrival of the letter of resignation, Congress received a "spirited remonstrance" from the New York Convention warning that "fatal and total destruction" would attend Schuyler's removal. Observing the perfect timing, one delegate speculated that Schuyler himself might have written the convention and procured the remonstrance. Be that as it may, the delegate continued, "his friends here blaze away on the same side, and have got a committee to consider the remonstrance and to report, and no doubt what the report will be. His friends are so many and fierce, that I doubt not those who would willingly accept it [the resignation] must give way to such a torrent in his favor for the sake of peace here."[21]

Philip Livingston, of the New York delegation, confirmed this assessment of the situation. "The committee is to our wishes," he informed the president of the New York Convention, "viz: Mr. [Edward] Rutledge, Mr. [William] Hooper, and Mr. [Thomas] McKean. As soon as this report is agreed to, it shall be forwarded for your information. It will, without question, be satisfactory."[22]

Livingston's confidence was justified. On September 27 the President of Congress, John Hancock, apologized to Schuyler for not having the time to answer several of his letters, but promised to rectify this neglect in the near future. Then, on October 2, Congress resolved:

> That the president be desired to write to General Schuyler, and inform him, that the Congress cannot consent, during the present situation of their affairs, to accept his resignation, but request, that he continue the command which he now holds; that he be assured, that the aspertions [sic], which his enemies have thrown out against his character, have had no influence upon the minds of the members of this house, who are fully satisfied of his attachment to the cause of freedom, and are willing to bear their testimony of the many services which he has rendered to his country; and that, in order effectually to put calumny to silence, they will, at an early date, appoint a committee of their body, to enquire fully into his conduct, which, they trust, will establish his reputation in the opinion of all good men.[23]

It was now the turn of Schuyler's friends to be jubilant. Edward Rutledge, who composed the above resolution, declared to Robert R. Livingston that "when some of us took the opportunity of applauding his (Schuyler's) conduct in high terms, no man could be found to say anything against him." However, he cautioned, "Let him not imagine from this, that the members are all his friends. This is not to be expected nor do I know that it is to be desired."

THE NORTHERN COMMISSARY 129

Whether intentional or not, Schuyler's timing of his resignation made it virtually impossible for Congress to accept it. The British had finally begun their long expected counteroffensive in August of 1776. The result had been the defeat of the main army under Washington on Long Island (August 27), and its retreat to Manhattan, where, after checking the British advance at Harlem Heights (September 16), Washington was forced to abandon the island and the city of New York to General Howe. Desertion was rampant, and for a while it appeared that the main army would simply disappear.

Instead of pressing his advantage, Sir William Howe paused to make conciliatory overtures, and thereby afforded Washington a much needed respite in which to regroup his forces. Since Howe's terms for a reconciliation called for a renunciation of the Declaration of Independence and submission to British authority, they were not taken seriously by the representatives Congress sent to confer with him. Indeed, as one of the conferees (Edward Rutledge) confided, delay was their sole object in agreeing to the conference, and he only wished "we could have procrastinated matters until we could have procured more assistance from the southward." As it was, from the time Howe first proposed the meeting until it broke up, some 4,000 Maryland and Virginia troops were brought up to reinforce Washington's army. Nevertheless, the future was none too bright.

American prospects to the northward were no better. When Schuyler tendered his resignation, the British were putting the finishing touches to a fleet designed to reclaim mastery of Lake Champlain and enable Carleton to capture Ticonderoga before the close of the campaign season. Although a hastily constructed American fleet under the command of Benedict Arnold badly mauled the British at Valcour Island (October 11), in the running battle which followed the American withdrawal, Arnold's modest armada was destroyed and the lake opened to the advancing enemy.

This was hardly the moment for the commander of the Northern department to resign. With the enemy fleet triumphant, and many patriots gloomily predicting that the British would winter in Albany, Congress simply could not accept his resignation. If Schuyler had any idea of the seriousness of the northern situation, his action could have been interpreted as cowardice. It was tantamount to desertion in the face of the enemy, and while his friends would not place this construction on his resignation, his enemies would not hesitate to do so. The rejection of his resignation had avoided such a charge; however, Schuyler showed no gratitude toward his supporters in Congress.

When Congress refused Philip Schuyler's resignation and agreed to hold an inquiry into his conduct as commander of the Northern department, it assumed that his injured pride would be salved. Such was not the case, for before he received word of these actions, he found new cause for complaint. In a letter dated September 27, the President of Congress had informed Schuyler that a committee was on its way to confer with him on matters relating to the department. "I apprehend this mistake crept into your letter by the variety of business which claims your attention," he replied on October 6, "for I find by the resolution of Congress of the 25th ult. that the commissioners are to confer with General Gates. My name is not so much as mentioned in any of the resolutions of that day, except in the second, and by that it would seem as if I acted under General Gates. Indeed from the resolutions of that day it seemed unnecessary to have sent me any of the other papers, as it strongly implied that I do not any longer command in this department."[24]

On the same day he indignantly informed Washington of this latest insult. The resolutions of September 25 represented proof to Schuyler that the resolution of September 14, directing supplies to Gates, had been an intentional slight. But the latest resolutions were much worse. "Without advising me that I am no longer in command," he complained, "they resolve that 'Mr. Stockton and Mr. Clymer' are 'appointed a committee to proceed to Ticonderoga to confer with General Gates with respect to the army under his command.' "[25]

Schuyler grossly misrepresented the content and intent of the resolutions of September 25. Contrary to his assertion, they referred to him, by name, *twice,* but made *no mention of General Gates!* There was, to be sure, some vagueness concerning the men with whom the committee would confer. Schuyler's letter of resignation had been received, but not yet acted upon. Therefore, the resolutions simply instructed the commissioners to "consult with the commanding officer in the northern department, and such other of the general officers as may be thought proper." The quotation Schuyler included in his letter to Washington was pure invention. Indeed, Richard Stockton and George Clymer were not named members of the committee until September 26, and they were then given no additional instructions.[26] While it is possible that Schuyler was the victim of misinformation, it is more likely that, convinced that he was being persecuted by Congress, he managed to distort reality to fit the imaginings of an overly suspicious mind. Significantly, Washington, having failed to calm Schuyler's agitation over the resolution of September 14, chose to ignore his latest complaint.

Schuyler also informed Robert R Livingston of the alleged insult, and Livingston, in turn, on October 10, castigated Edward Rutledge and his congressional colleagues for "ordering a committee to confer with *General Gates.*" Furthermore, a few days later, on October 13, Schuyler wrote Livingston of his displeasure with the resolutions of October 2, refusing his resignation and calling for a formal inquiry into his conduct. He conceded that Rutledge and his other friends in Congress undoubtedly meant well in securing those resolves, but he was "resolved severly to animadvert not only on that but on the ungentlemanly conduct of Congress."

Apparently Schuyler found the rigors of superintending the affairs of the department from Albany too much for him. For, when he again took pen in hand, to dress Congress down for *its* inattention to business and abuse of his character, he was at his comfortable country estate at Saratoga. "The calumny of my enemies has risen to its height," he informed President Hancock, "their malice is incapable of heightening the injury. I wish for the sake of human nature they had not succeeded so well, I wish they had not been countenanced by the transactions of those whose duty it was to have supported me. In the alarming situation of our affairs, I shall continue to act some time longer, but Congress must prepare to put the care of this department into other hands; I shall be able to render my country better services in another line, less exposed to the repetition of the injuries I have sustained. . . . I have not heard a word from the fleet or Ticonderoga."[27]

This new letter of resignation, dated October 16, did little to enhance Schuyler's reputation in Congress. He not only rejected congressional efforts to soothe his pride by granting the inquiry he had requested, but he also made the serious allegation that Congress was aiding and abetting his enemies. It was also difficult for the congressmen to be impressed by his noble offer to remain in "command" of the Northern department, whose administrative offices were in Albany, some miles to the southward of Saratoga, and whose army was at Ticonderoga.

However, the allegations made in the letter of October 16 were mild compared with the accusations Schuyler hurled at Congress one week later. "I was greatly at a loss to what cause to impute that very rapid increase of calumny which I experienced after my return from the Indian treaty [August 5]," he wrote the president of Congress. "I did not know that I was principally indebted to Congress for this misfortune, until yesterday, when, and never before, did I see the resolution of the 17th of August last, which whilst it exculpates General Wooster from any mal-conduct in Canada, is couched in such terms as to leave even to the candid & judicious no alternative but that of supposing that Canada was not properly supplied either by Congress or me. Judge on whom the public censure would fall and let every *gentleman* in

Congress for a moment fancy himself in my situation. . . . Is it sir, consistent with that dignity which should be inseparable from the most respectable body on the earth, thus partially and precipitately to enter into a resolution which leaves so much room for the public to consider me as a faithless servant? Deeply sensible of the injury I have sustained from the hand which ought to have supported me, I shall endeavor yet to be patient [and] do my duty in this critical juncture with zeal, alacrity and firmness."[28] While Schuyler indulged himself in self-pity, Carleton occupied Crown Point after the battle at Valcour Island, and British scouts probed the defenses of Ticonderoga.

With this latest vituperative attack on Congress, Schuyler finally went too far. As Congressman Abraham Clark of New Jersey pointed out, "when they [Congress] cleared General Wooster of misconduct, [they] never thought of laying it on General Schuyler, but imputed the miscarriage there to the short time the soldiers had enlisted for, the small-pox getting into the army, the want of hard money to purchase provisions in Canada, and the almost impossibility of transporting any quantity there in the winter." He might also have added that these were the very causes listed by Montgomery, Arnold, and Schuyler during the previous winter.

Even Robert R. Livingston, one of Schuyler's closest friends, was distressed. He did not believe that the construction Schuyler put upon the resolutions obtained by Rutledge to clear his name was either just or politic. "It was intended by Rutledge & your other friends as an ample justification of your conduct," he admonished Schuyler on October 27, "and such I must own it appears to me. If so, your censure of it would naturally excite their resentment, & render those who now wish to serve you cool to your interest." Even more ill-advised, Livingston warned, were Schuyler's continued attacks upon the dignity and honor of Congress, for, should it ever come to a choice of supporting either him or Congress, "your very friends must take part against you, or contribute to lessen the influence of a body on whose power their very salvation depends. Should any unfortunate accident happen," he concluded, "it would be charged and perhaps justly, to your precipitate conduct (for such it would be called) & God knows whether you could escape the blind resentments of the people."

Despite Livingston's fears, Edward Rutledge took no offense at the general's seeming ingratitude. "That you have sustained for a length of time an uncommon load of calumny is alas! too true," he commiserated. However, he was certain that Schuyler would soon appear in his "true character; I mean the character of a firm and disinterested patriot."[29]

Rutledge soon revealed to Livingston and John Jay his plan for restoring Schuyler's reputation. He urged Livingston on November 23 to "immediately prevail upon Schuyler to come down to Congress. After improving the first opportunity which may offer to clear up his character, he will proceed to explain to the House the steps which are necessary for preventing Carleton from making any impression from Canada; and having obtained full powers for that purpose, let him return to his command to carry those measures into execution." Rutledge conveniently ignored the fact that Carleton had already made quite "an impression from Canada," and that Schuyler had ample authority to take any steps he thought necessary to block the British invasion. It is more than likely that Rutledge simply thought that Schuyler's physical presence in Congress would embarrass his critics into silence.

Rutledge recommended the same plan to Jay, but in doing so he added some observations which revealed rather starkly one of the principal bonds which tied him to the Livingston–Jay–Schuyler faction— his distaste for democracy or the "popular spirit." When Schuyler returned from his projected encounter with Congress to the northern command, he assured Jay, "your country I think, will be safe, provided you establish a good government, with a strong executive. A pure democracy may possibly do, when patriotism is the ruling passion but when the state abounds with rascals, as is the case with too many at this day, you must suppress a little of that popular spirit."[30]

Military developments in the Middle States made it impossible for Schuyler to comply with Rutledge's suggestions. In mid-November Sir William Howe, after a month of relative inactivity, again pressed the offensive against Washington's army. On the 16th, the last American foothold on Manhattan, Fort Washington, fell to the British. Although the fort was itself of little strategic importance, its capture was a crushing blow. In addition to 154 men killed or wounded in the fort's defense, the British captured 2,818 members of the garrison!

Howe now proceeded with more alacrity than was usually his wont, and two days later took Fort Lee on the Jersey shore opposite Fort Washington. This time, in addition to more than 100 prisoners, the British seized large quantities of cannon, arms, shot, cartridges, tents, and other equipment and stores sorely needed by the American army. Then, with Cornwallis in the van, Howe set in motion the pursuit of Washington across New Jersey to the banks of the Delaware. Although the American army managed to escape destruction by crossing to the Pennsylvania side of the river on December 8, the future looked bleak to the commander in chief. With barely 3,000 men, he knew he could not stop a determined British effort to cross the river and capture

Philadelphia. Indeed, he wrote his brother Lund on December 17, if reinforcements did not quickly arrive, "I think the game will be pretty well up."

Congress, well aware of the approaching danger, issued desperate calls for the New Jersey and Pennsylvania militiamen to rally to Washington's support. The result was so disappointing that it was called treasonous. Then, as a last resort, Congress resolved on November 23 "That General Washington be directed forthwith to order, under his immediate command, such of the forces, now in the Northern department, as have been raised in the states of Pennsylvania and New Jersey."[31] Earlier in the month Carleton had withdrawn his forces into Canada for the winter, thus ending the immediate danger of a British invasion from that quarter. Veterans from the Northern army could be safely drawn southward to reinforce the main army, and Washington quickly directed Schuyler to have the Jersey and Pennsylvania troops march to his relief.

Therefore, by the end of November the core of the Northern army under the command of Generals Gates and Arnold was on the march to join Washington—which it did on December 20 in time to take part in the successful attack at Trenton on Christmas Day. Although the number of men in the Northern department was thereby drastically reduced, Schuyler complained that it only increased his burdens. It left him, he informed Robert R. Livingston on December 20, without a single general officer in the department. In addition, the quartermaster Congress had imposed upon him (Morgan Lewis) had no qualifications for the job, and so he had to act as quartermaster in addition to his other duties. If he was to do what Livingston urged and go to Congress, the department would collapse into hopeless confusion.

Thus, Philip Schuyler absorbed himself in the administrative details of maintaining his depleted forces through the winter. However, the suspicion, jealousy and bitterness that had prompted his acrimonious letters to Congress were not forgotten—they merely slumbered and would awaken when spring once again quickened military activity in the north.

The Politics of Command

In December of 1776, as the British army advanced through the Jerseys, Congress moved to the comparative safety of Baltimore. Attendance, poor before the move, now was barely sufficient to transact the public business. To make matters worse, those present were for the most part new men who lacked the experience—and in some cases the political acumen—of their predecessors. "I have the mellancholly [sic] prospect before me of a Congress continually changing, until very few faces remain, that I saw in the first Congress," John Adams lamented to James Warren. The two Adamses, Roger Sherman, Richard Henry Lee, Samuel Chase, and William Paca were the only ones left. "The rest are dead, resigned, deserted, or cut up into governors, etc."[1]

Nonetheless, Congress had much work to attend to if the young nation was to survive the coming year. It must enlarge the army, reorganize the supply system, and name officers to lead the Continental forces during the approaching campaign season. On all of these points there was disagreement and jealousy, and perhaps it was worse in regard to the promotion of officers. Indeed, feelings were to run so high on this subject that the very existence of the army was threatened.

George Washington initiated the selection of new officers in February 1777 by informing Congress that the army required the appointment of three major generals and 10 brigadiers. The mode of election and the individuals to be selected the commander in chief discreetly left for Congress to decide. The result was a display of provincial jealousy similar to that which had attended the selection of the first general officers in June 1775. "Notwithstanding many declarations to the contrary," reported Francis Lewis, "colonial prejudices

135

sway the minds of individuals." From the standpoint of New York this was particularly reprehensible since Lewis was the only representative attending Congress from that state, and unless others soon arrived, it would be deprived of having any voice in the promotions.[2]

Provincial jealousy was not the only complication in the promotion of officers. Congress had to determine the extent of its authority as opposed to that of the states, in shaping and controlling the Continental army. If Congress was merely a forum for the individual states, then the appointment of officers and their promotions should rest ultimately with the states. If, on the other hand, Congress was something more than the sum of its parts, then it should exercise the final authority in all matters touching upon the Continental army—including the promotion of its officers.

Many of the Continental officers believed that the only way the war could be won was by raising a large regular army. This would enable them to move quickly to counter any British moves, or take advantage of favorable opportunities to press offensive operations. This was simply not possible under the existing system in which provincial troops and militia formed the bulk of the army for any given campaign. When the campaign was over—and many times when it was not—these troops returned to their homes. Short-term enlistments made even the small regular army unstable. One-year enlistments were still the rule, and rare indeed were the three-year enlistees. The attitude of the prospective enlistee was perhaps best summed up by Josiah Bartlett who observed that "many who would be very willing to serve for one year look on the enlistment for three years as selling themselves for slavery for life."[3] One suggested remedy was that men be offered land grants if they would enlist for the duration of the war. However, while the military in general favored this, the civil authorities could not as yet be brought to agree to it.

As early as the summer of 1776 John Adams observed that a majority in Congress opposed the idea of giving money and land to encourage enlistments for the war, but most of them seemed to show little concern over the dangers of a regular army. He, on the other hand, would vote for the bounty and land grants, but was very apprehensive of the consequences should the regular army become too strong and be corrupted. "Although it may cost us more, and we may put now and then a battle to hazard by the methods we are in," he observed, "yet we shall be less in danger of corruption and violence from a standing army, and our militia will acquire courage, experience, discipline, and hardiness in actual service."

Quixotically, Adams wrote a few days later to Henry Knox that he was "a constant advocate for a regular army, and the most masterly discipline, because I know, that without these, we cannot reasonably hope to be a powerful, a prosperous, or a free people, and therefore, I have been constantly laboring to obtain an handsome encouragement for enlisting a permanent body of troops." There is no real contradiction here. Adams, while always acutely aware of the risks involved, consistently favored the formation of a regular army.[4]

The Board of War recommended in early September of 1776 that a regular establishment of 84 regiments should be raised to serve for the duration of the war, and that all who enlisted should be granted 100 acres of land and given a $20 bounty. After several days of debate, Congress accepted the Board's recommendation on September 16, with a few minor amendments. However, for some reason, the appointment of all officers below the rank of general was left to the states in which the regiments were raised. This was contrary to the practice Congress had been following—and was not strictly adhered to after the adoption of these resolves. But it did cause some confusion and much concern.[5]

Some members of Congress feared that leaving the appointment of regimental officers in the hands of the state legislatures would foist on the army "officers of the quality that they now suffer under." In an attempt to avoid this, Congress wrote Washington and requested a list of officers whom he wished to see kept in the army. The intention was then to "send the list with a member of Congress to their respective states who have been ordered to stress the necessity of appointing men of education to military offices if the country is to be saved."[6] The criticism of the present group of officers was echoed by William Ellery of Rhode Island who commented that "the officers of the army in general are not equal to their appointments, and from hence it is that our soldiery is disorderly and undisciplined. . . . It is agreed on all hands that our men will make good soldiers when they have good officers."[7]

By February of 1777 the question of appointments was acute. With the increase in the size of the army—it was estimated that it would number 60,000 men—more general officers were needed. The appointment of general officers, of course, remained with Congress, but it had never established a rule governing the mode of selecting brigadiers from the ranks of the colonels, nor the criteria to be used in promoting brigadiers to the rank of major general. Thus, when the necessity of promoting new general officers arose in February 1777, there was some doubt as to how Congress should proceed. In the words of Thomas Burke of North Carolina: "The debates were perplexed, inconclusive and irksome."

Some of the congressmen wanted to adopt definite rules for promotion, and several were proposed. The delegates from Maryland, Virginia, and North Carolina suggested "that each state should recommend officers in proportion to the men they furnish: three battalions, one brigadier, nine [battalions], one major general. This was rejected." Another proposal was to simply promote general officers on the basis of seniority. This too failed. The only thing everyone apparently agreed upon was that no matter what mode was adopted, Congress must reserve to itself the right to deviate from it to reward outstanding merit.

Burke was deeply disturbed by this inability to reach an agreement on a rule to govern promotions, for, as he pointed out to his fellow members, unless such a rule was adopted, "Congress would be an object of very jealous apprehension, unchecked and unlimited as it is, if the officers of the army held their honor at the precarious leisure of a majority. Officers hold their honor the most dear of anything," he warned. "Setting them aside when they were entitled to promotion would wound that honor very sorely. Their attention would therefore be entirely to that authority which had so much power to wound it, or cherish it. This policy was always observed by monarchs, and the end was to keep the army dependent on them." Burke believed such a policy unbecoming to Congress. He admitted that the rule of succession by seniority was more familiar to the officers (and therefore more agreeable, but he still believed that the apportionment of general officers according to the number of battalions raised by the states would give more satisfaction to the states, "and the satisfying them was of greatest importance and ought to be adopted."

Dr. Benjamin Rush disagreed with Burke. "It is to no purpose to talk of the practice of despotic princes," he declared on February 19. "They promote according to seniority it is true, but they possess an absolute power of recalling, disgracing or breaking their general officers as soon as they make them, and we find they are fond of exercising this power. . . . The case is different with us. A general may lose a battle or a province, and we possess no power to recall or displace him."

Although the debate was carried on in rather general terms, no one could escape the underlying dissatisfaction of many of the members with certain of the general officers. As John Adams observed to his wife on the 21st, "Schuyler, Putnam, Spencer, Heath, are thought by very few to be capable of the great commands they hold. . . . I wish they would all resign." Adams also had a rather novel suggestion on the mode of promotion. "For my part I will vote upon the general principles of a republic for a new election of general officers annually, and every man shall have my consent to be left out, who does not give sufficient proof of his qualifications."[8]

In the end, a compromise was struck which included all of the suggestions. On February 19, Congress resolved "That in voting for general officers, a due regard shall be had to the line of succession, the merit of the persons proposed, and the quota of the troops raised, and to be raised, by each state." By trying to please everyone, Congress only succeeded in passing a meaningless resolve. As Burke rather bitterly pointed out: "it was agreed to, but no notice was taken of it in the nomination or appointments. N. Carolina did not vote for major-generals; because the delegate [Burke] found, no rule was observed, and he knew nothing of the merit of any officers in nomination, and did not choose to give a vote in Congress, for which he could give no reason."[9]

Nevertheless, it appears that Congress laid heavy emphasis on the number of troops contributed by the several states when it made the final selection of general officers. Inevitably, many of the officers who were passed over felt grievously injured. Two hopeful aspirants for a major generalcy—David Wooster and Benedict Arnold—were not promoted despite strong efforts on their behalf by the Connecticut congressmen. Two other Connecticut officers whom Washington had recommended for promotion to brigadier general—Jedediah Huntington and Jeremiah Wadsworth—were similarly ignored. The reason given in both instances was that Connecticut already had more general officers than the troops contributed by that state justified. There was an element of truth in this. Although Connecticut had provided a substantial percentage of the manpower for the armies commanded by Washington and Schuyler during the first year and a half of the rebellion, by 1777 most had long since returned to their homes.

Such considerations aside, merit alone should have induced Congress to promote Arnold—and Connecticut congressmen were not alone in this opinion. The snub given Arnold was particularly galling since Massachusetts, which certainly did not lack for general officers, succeeded in having Benjamin Lincoln appointed major general direct from the Massachusetts line, thus passing over all of the Continental brigadiers!

New Jersey found itself in a position similar to that of Connecticut. Elias Dayton was passed over because the state already had two generals—William Maxwell and Lord Stirling—and this it was claimed was more than its quota. To make matters worse, Abraham Clark informed Dayton that he should have received the promotion to general that went to Maxwell in the fall, but was prevented because "General Schuyler had never mentioned you as having done anything good or bad, he is always sparing of praise."

The importance of good recommendation from a superior officer had been pointed out to Col. Anthony Wayne by Benjamin Rush the previous September. He had suggested that Wayne carefully cultivate Gates's good opinion of him and see to it that he was mentioned in Gates's reports to Congress. Wayne apparently heeded Rush's advice, for he was among those promoted to brigadier general on February 21.[10]

The final promotion (which appeared unfair to many) was that of Col. Enoch Poor to brigadier over the head of Col. John Stark, his superior in the New Hampshire line. As expected, Stark resigned, and this left two regiments without senior colonels. Reluctantly, the New Hampshire representatives concluded that the simplest method of filling the vacancies was to promote the lieutenant colonels in each regiment.[11]

The overall effect of the promotions was to breed dissatisfaction among many of the officers who felt they were unjustly passed over, and to pose a dilemma for Congress. Many of the present high-ranking officers were apparently unfit for command; however, if Congress superseded these men by promoting abler junior officers it was subjected to insults and threats of resignation. In addition, if it attempted to promote men purely on the basis of seniority, it was opposed by those states whose tardy support of the war had deprived them of general officers, while the present quotas of troops they were contributing entitled them to positions of high rank. But if Congress chose to take this into consideration, and thereby passed over able senior officers from states which had their "quota" of generals, then they did these men an injustice and risked their resignations. Little wonder that tempers in Congress grew short and the members became particularly sensitive to any criticism by the military. It was in this unfavorable atmosphere that the Gates–Schuyler controversy was revived and thrust upon a resentful Congress.

The immediate cause of the renewal of the command problems in the Northern department was a complaint by John Trumbull, who had been appointed the deputy adjutant general in that department. His appointment was dated September 12, 1776, but he did not receive official notification of it until February 22, 1777! This, he informed President Hancock, was "an insuperable bar" to his accepting it. "I have served in that office since the 28th June last," he continued, "by the appointment of the honorable Major-General Gates. . . . I expect, sir, to be commissioned from that date (if at all)."[12]

Superficially, Trumbull's request seemed nothing more than a routine, and justified, plea for a correction which would give him the seniority he felt was his due. However, there were other complications, one of which was Hancock's apparent enmity for John and the rest of the Trumbulls. The following tale, related by John Trumbull, is revealing on this point:

While I was in General Washington's family, in 1775, Mr. Hancock made a passing visit to the General, and observing me, he enquired of Mr. Mifflin who I was, and when told that I was his fellow aid-de-camp, and son of Governor Trumbull, he made the unworthy observation, that 'that family was well provided for.' Mr. Mifflin did not tell me this until after he (Mr. Hancock) had left headquarters, but then observed that he deserved to be called to account for it. I answered 'No, he is right; my father and his three sons are doubtless well provided for; we are secure of four halters, if we do not succeed.' "[13]

Hancock's apparent hostility may have had something to do with the dating of the commission and its late arrival. However, there was also a strong possibility that Trumbull's only offense was being associated with Gates and that Schuyler and his supporters in Congress were responsible for his embarrassment. In a letter to James Lovell of March 3, 1777, in which he reviewed the muddle over the granting of commissions to Morgan Lewis and himself the previous summer, Trumbull made such an allegation. "I should have less reason to complain," he concluded, "did I not know, that, in the *Northern Army,* officers of inferior rank to myself, have been *advanced* and *commissioned* without the least difficulty [an allusion to Schuyler's aides, Philip Livingston and Richard Varick]. This prevents the hurry of business being alleged in excuse of my treatment. From this day, therefore, I lay aside my cockade and sword, with a determination, *fixed as fate."* Lovell attempted to dissuade Trumbull from resigning by expressing his belief that it was an accident that would be rectified. He added that he had shown the letter to Gates (who was then in Philadelphia) and that Gates advised against resignation.[14]

General Gates apparently believed that the dating of the commission was an oversight caused by the "multiplicity of business, by which Congress was then so entirely employed." He therefore asked Hancock to recommend to Congress "the colonel's being reinstated in his rank from the time of his embarking with me at New York, to join the Northern Army."[15]

Under normal circumstances, Gates's request would probably have sufficed to obtain the changes Trumbull desired. However, because of the new sensitivity of Congress concerning complaints from the military, Trumbull's letter met with unexpected opposition. The tempers of the congressmen had just been aroused by "insolent passages of the late letters of S[chuyle]r" when Trumbull's letter was opened and presented by his friends. Despite a favorable report on his request, and General Gates's recommendatory letter, no action was taken. "Congress are highly piqued at the style and manner of your demand," his friend Lovell reported to him on March 22. "Every member is entirely willing to accord you a commission agreeable to the date you expect; but they are determined on the other hand, to lose, *even your acknowledged abilities* if they do not receive a different request from what is now before them." This might seem somewhat extreme, but, Lovell cautioned Trumbull, "you are also unacquainted with the provocations which have been given Congress for attention to the style of the letters of their officers, prior to the receipt of yours." He therefore recommended that Trumbull immediately write a letter to Hancock in more polite and formal language and even included a sample letter which he might send. If this were done, he concluded, "you may be assured of an instant compliance here."

Elbridge Gerry further elucidated Congress' resentment, and, while he sympathized with John Trumbull's plight, he too could not "altogether approve of the style in which he addressed the legislative authority of the Continent. It is the fixed determination of Congress," he informed Joseph Trumbull, "to preserve the civil above the military, and the authority of that will not be surrendered should it be necessary to disband the army in preserving the same." This may have been a slight exaggeration of the extent to which Congress would go; however, it did point up the increasing jealousy with which that body was guarding its control over the military.[16]

John Trumbull was not to be deterred from his determination to resign. As to Congress' pique over the language he had used, well, they were becoming a little too arbitrary and uppity for his democratic tastes. He acknowledged that his letters had been written with freedom, but *"a freedom which it would illy become the representatives of a free state to discourage."* When Congress received this letter, it was moved that General Gates should be allowed to choose a replacement. At which point, Dr. John Witherspoon of New Jersey "rose and said he had no objection, in case he was restrained from reappointing Mr. Trumbull." Consequently, on April 29 Hancock requested Gates to fill the vacancy, but warned that "it is not the intention of Congress that Mr. Trumbull should be reappointed."[17]

While the affair of John Trumbull's commission served to revive the antagonism between the supporters of Gates and those of Schuyler, it was soon overshadowed by the revival of efforts to have Gates supersede Schuyler in the command of the Northern department. Schuyler continued to complain from Albany that Congress was countenancing injustices to him, and took the congressmen to task for doing so. Gates, meanwhile, was in Baltimore, renewing old friendships and making new

ones in Congress. His supporters felt the time to act had arrived. Samuel
Adams quite bluntly stated: "General Gates is here. How shall we make
him the head of that [Northern] army?"[18]

Most members of Congress were embarrassed to have the major
general they had appointed to command the army in Canada now sitting,
unemployed, on their doorstep. In an attempt to relieve themselves of
this problem, they directed President Hancock on February 23, 1777, to
offer Gates his old post as adjutant general. The president promptly
complied. "The good of the service, which is so essentially concerned in
your complying with the desire of Congress on this occasion, will, I
make no doubt, induce you to gratify their wishes," Hancock concluded,
on a somewhat wistful note. Gates very quickly indicated that he could
not be induced to gratify this congressional wish.

Gates expressed surprise at this offer—particularly since it had not
been preceded by a note from Washington with whom he would be
working very closely. If Washington did not himself make the request,
then, Gates opined, "I am certain all my endeavors as Adjutant General would be vain and fruitless. I had last year the honor to command
in the second post in America," he observed, getting to the real heart of
the matter, "and had the good fortune to prevent the enemy from making
their so much wished for junction with General Howe; after this, to be
expected to dwindle again into the Adjutant General requires some philosophy upon my side, & something more than words upon yours." Consequently, Gates, before he would give a definite answer, demanded the
following conditions: "That it is General Washington's desire I should
resume the office of Adjutant General—That my pay be established at
332 dollars a month—and that my aides-de-camp and appendages of
rank and office be continued as heretofore."[19]

One of these conditions was at least partially met shortly after
Gates completed his letter to Hancock. A letter arrived from Washington requesting him to resume the office of adjutant general. Gates now
revealed his extreme reluctance to take himself out of the line and again
assume a staff position. "Unless it is your earnest desire such a measure
should [directly?] take place," he informed the commander in chief, "I
would by no means consent to it." However, the final decision was with
Washington. Should he request him to accept the post, Gates declared
that he would "with cheerfulness and alacrity proceed to headquarters."[20]

Although Gates and Washington had apparently worked well together before, the former now had some apprehension concerning their
ability to do so. This may have been as a result of the rather sharp exchange between the two over the abandonment of Crown Point. At any
rate, Gates indicated his concern to Joseph Reed, the retiring adjutant

general, who in turn passed it on to Washington. "General Gates in conversation after mentioning some terms on which alone he should accept it went further and observed that as it was necessary the Commander-in-Chief and Adjutant General should perfectly understand each other, he should not accept it until your approbation was signified to him. From this I should suppose he expects to hear from you particularly before he decides."[21]

Gates soon had an unequivocal and highly complimentary reply from Washington. "Altho I often wished in secret, that you could be brought to resume the office of Adjutant General," Washington wrote on March 10, "I never even hinted it, because I thought it might be disagreeable to you for the reasons which you yourself mention. . . . Give me leave to return you my sincere thanks, for this mark of your attention to a request of mine, which, now you give me an opening, I make, and at the same time assure you that I look upon your resumption of the Office of Adjutant General, as the only means of giving form and regularity to our new army."

This letter convinced Gates of Washington's sincere desire to have him return to his former post, and he almost surely would have agreed had not events now moved rapidly to restore him to the more attractive Northern command. Congress moved back to Philadelphia from Baltimore during the first weeks of March 1777, and when it reconvened, it continually called in Gates for conferences concerning affairs in the Northern department. Significantly, at the same time that Congress was becoming convinced of Gates's grasp of affairs in that department, it was becoming increasingly vexed with Schuyler's continued complaints and accusations.

Congress was particularly irked by Schuyler's letter of February 4, in which he complained of "the odious suspicion contained in Mr. Commissary Trumbull's intercepted letter to the Hon. William Williams, Esq.," and took Congress to task for its failure to leap to the defense of his injured character.[22]

Finally, on March 15, Congress resolved, "That it is altogether improper and inconsistent with the dignity of this Congress, to interfere in the disputes subsisting among the officers of the army; which ought to be settled, unless they can be otherwise accommodated, in a court martial, agreeable to the rules of the army; and that the expressions in General Schuyler's letter of the 4th of February, 'that he confidently expected Congress would have done him that justice, which it was in their power to give, and which he humbly conceives that they ought to have done,' were, to say the least, ill-advised and highly indecent." President Hancock informed Schuyler of this resolve, and further advised him to "be more guarded for the future; and that you write in a stile [*sic*] better adapted to their [the members of Congress] rank and dignity, as well as your own character."

Schuyler chose to disregard this advice, and personally to carry the fight to the floor of Congress. On March 16 he informed Jonathan Trumbull, Jr. (the deputy paymaster general), that he would leave on the 24th for Congress and was unsure when he would return. "I am something more certain on another point—that is I shall not return a general. I find Congress will have no occasion for me. I am happy they have persons capable of advising them on everything to be done in this department so much so that it does not even appear necessary to consult me on any matter whatsoever." Should he be forced from the army, Schuyler apparently intended to resign as Indian commissioner as well and, as he put it, thus be "freed from the disagreeable importunity of their mightinesses the princes of the wilderness."[23]

Influenced no doubt by Gates's proximity and knowledge of affairs in the Northern department, and by Schuyler's insulting behavior, Congress shelved plans to have Gates resume his duties as adjutant general, and instead, directed him on March 25 to "immediately repair to Ticonderoga, and take command of the army there." In Hancock's letter to Gates informing him of the resolve, he underlined the last six words. The implication was that this time there would be no confusion over the command of the army—it was Gates's even if Schuyler remained as head of the department. Gates's position was further strengthened when he was allowed to pick Major General Arthur St. Clair as his second in command.[24]

For a man determined to resign, Schuyler exhibited a remarkable interest in the extent of Gates's new command. Hearing of Congress' action after he left Albany, Schuyler wrote his former aide and present deputy mustermaster in the Northern department, Richard Varick, and directed him to find out all he could about Gates's new appointment.

Following Schuyler's instructions, Varick first sought out Doctor Potts, a known friend of Gates, who had just returned from Philadelphia. He carefully avoided the subject he was interested in, and attempted to allay any suspicions the doctor might have. Then after dinner on the second day, he managed to bring the subject of Gates's command into the conversation. Whereupon, Potts declared that he had heard nothing of Schuyler being superseded nor of Gates being sent to the Northern department. Indeed, said Potts, Gates himself did not know where he would be sent.

This contradicted information Varick had been able to elicit from Morgan Lewis the day before, April 1. Lewis said that Potts had informed him in confidence that General Gates was to command in the Northern department and was to supersede Schuyler. However, Potts had not heard this from Gates, nor could Lewis discover by whom it was said—if anyone. "As Dr. Potts speaks positively the other way," Varick reported to Schuyler, "I have the greatest possible cause of suspicion, that there is more on the carpet, than either he [Potts] or Col. Lewis choose to have mentioned to any person who they are not *certain* of being equally prejudiced in General Gates's favor as themselves."

On April 17 Gates and his entourage arrived in Albany and conjecture over the command situation soared. John Pierce, Jr., deputy paymaster under Trumbull, wrote his superior informing him that Gates's aides were saying that he was *"commander in chief* in the *N. department."* At the same time, President Hancock was apparently confirming this by sending Gates "information as may be necessary for your future conduct in the department immediately under your care."[25]

Richard Varick's dismay at the rumors of Gates superseding Schuyler was soon turned into horror by the knowledge that his spying for Schuyler was known. Gates made it a point to inform Varick at their first meeting that he had opened a packet of his letters enroute to Schuyler. Gates explained that he thought "that as it was directed on the public service he had a right to do it. I am under the greatest concern on this account," Varick informed Schuyler on April 18, "as he must have seen the very letters I wrote in answer to yours. If he is to command here, I shall have a Hell upon earth with him." The general's great "coolness" seemed to confirm Varick's worst fear, and he believed that the only course now open was to resign before he was dishonorably dismissed, for, he reported, "It is rumored that he is to command in the department & that he has the appointment of all the staff for this army."

Meanwhile, in Congress, Schuyler had finally been granted his long-sought-after inquiry. Many had opposed it by claiming that since no charges or complaints had been made, nor anything said to his dishonor in the House, an inquiry would be an implied censure. However, the New York delegation silenced the opposition. "If the general had done his duty faithfully," it asked, "why was his authority pared away to nothing and the command of the army, in effect, transferred from him to General Gates, a junior officer?" Consequently, Congress, on April 17, appointed a committee of 13—a member from each of the states— to inquire into the conduct of Major General Schuyler since his appointment to command in the army of the United States.[26]

Neither Schuyler nor his friends had any doubt as to the outcome of this inquiry. However, while Congress would undoubtedly approve his past conduct, its appointment of Gates to command the army placed an obstacle in the way of Schuyler's continuance in the army. "They wish me to remain in the command," he confided to Varick on April 26, "but having already appointed (or at least implicitly so) Gen. Gates to the command of the Northern department, they do not know how to manage the matter. They wish to make Ticonderoga a separate command; that they have a right to do, but they know that I will not serve at Albany on those conditions. Indeed, not on any unless an absolute command is giving [sic] me over every part of the army in the Northern department. This they will not do, and therefore I shall return Mr. Schuyler only to Albany." In the same vein four days later, he wrote General Washington announcing his intention to resign his commission and return to private life.

With the active campaign season about to open, it appeared that the command in the North was finally to be shifted from Philip Schuyler to Horatio Gates. At such a moment, even Schuyler's enemies in Congress could afford to be magnanimous. He was assured of endorsement for his past actions, but with Gates appointed to the command of the Northern army Schuyler was effectively removed from the direction of military affairs.

Once more, however, Schuyler's enemies were to be disappointed. While his actions were still being reviewed by the committee, his friends in Congress undertook a counterattack designed to restore him to his full command. In doing so they cleverly used the suspicions of New York's loyalty to the American cause to their own advantage. Disaffection, they admitted, was prevalent. Indeed, it was only the leadership of Philip Schuyler which prevented wholesale defection to the enemy. If he now was removed at the very moment when the British were poised for an invasion of northern New York, then the state would certainly be lost and the cause of American independence seriously endangered. In addition, they pointed out the absurdity of making General Gates commander of the Northern army *at Ticonderoga*. Could the enemy then be expected to confine his activities to attacking that single post? Was the entire Northern army to be stationed in that one spot? If not, then who was to command the rest of the Northern army, and who was to decide how much of the army was to be at Ticonderoga and how much elsewhere?

While the contention that Schuyler was indispensable for the safety of New York was highly questionable, the observations concerning the logic of making Ticonderoga a separate command were telling ones in Lovell's opinion, and undoubtedly influenced many members. So much so, that Gates's staunchest supporters began to realize that the fight to remove Schuyler was far from over. "How this matter will be untangled

I cannot now exactly determine," James Lovell reported to Gates on May 1, "but I suspect not entirely agreeable to your sentiments."

These proceedings angered General Gates, and made him somewhat impatient with his friends in Congress. "Unhappy state! that has but one man in it, who can free the wavering minds of its inhabitants to the side of freedom," he chided Lovell on May 12, "how could you sit patiently and uncontradicted suffering such impertinence to be crammed down your throats?" Also, he saw nothing wrong with the commander of the army being stationed at Ticonderoga. The British had followed that practice in the French and Indian War and their reasons for doing so were still valid. It was the only major invasion route available to an enemy based in Canada. Thus, it was there the major contest would take place, and there that the commanding officer belonged! As to the possibility of his serving at Ticonderoga while Schuyler held the overall command at Albany, it was out of the question. "I shall ever be apprehensive of being commanded to make large detachments when perhaps my whole strength is most wanted upon the spot; or have the channel of information so obstructed, as never to have it flow pure, or regular; or the military chest so emptied, at Albany, as to cause desertion, and mutiny, at Ty." Consequently, he had already informed Congress that if Schuyler were returned to the command of the Northern department, he would have no other course but to ask for "an honorable dismission from their service."

Meanwhile, in Congress, James Duane and Philip Livingston were particularly active on Schuyler's behalf. They first made the acquaintance of the new members in order "to undeceive those who wished for conviction." Then, while the committee appointed to inquire into Schuyler's conduct was just beginning its work, the New York delegates succeeded in having the general cleared of any imputation of irregularity in the handling of the specie sent to him in 1775 for the use of the army while in Canada. Next, Schuyler was prompted to submit a memorial to Congress "stating such of their resolutions, as conveyed a censure upon him, justifying himself in every particular." Whereupon Congress adopted a resolution "That the memorial was satisfactory, and that the Congress entertained the same *favorable* opinion of the general as they entertained before the passing of those resolutions." Since "a complete and honorable vindication of the general's character and conduct" was implied by this action, Duane and Livingston reported, "we shall give ourselves no trouble about the proposed enquiry."[27]

The fondest hopes of Schuyler's friends (and the worst fears of Gates's) were amply realized when on May 15 the Board of War reported to Congress its recommendation:

That Major General Schuyler be directed forthwith to proceed to the Northern department, and take upon him the command there.

That a letter be written by the President to Major General Gates, informing him, that Major General Schuyler is ordered to take upon him the command of the Northern department; and that Congress are desirous that Major General Gates should make his own choice, either to continue in the command of the Northern department, under Major General Schuyler; or to take upon him the Office of Adjutant General in the Grand Army immediately under the Commander in chief, with the rank he now holds.[28]

This report, as Schuyler himself informed Washington, "occasioned a warm debate." Indeed, it must have come as a shock to Gates's supporters. The phrase "to continue in the command of the Northern department, under Major General Schuyler" was a fatuous play on words. This, then, was no choice at all, and the only course left open was to accept the position as adjutant general which had been considered a demotion in February—and would now be considered even more so.

James Lovell and a few others put up a determined opposition to the Board of War's recommendation and managed to prolong the debate for several days. The major point they attempted to drive home, was the futility of putting the commander of the army at Ticonderoga "under the absolute orders of another at 100 miles distance, in treaty with Indians or busied in the duties of a provider. This idea was supported by several," Lovell informed Gates on May 22, "and it is, of itself, an irrefragable argument of the impropriety of distributing America into departments. A commander in chief & commanders of the separate armies is the only distinction which should be known."

In the end, by the extremely close vote of five states to four, with two divided (and two unrepresented), the Board's recommendation was accepted. In a last-minute effort to prevent Schuyler's return to the Northern department, the New England states had pressed to have Schuyler made second in command with the main army under Washington. This move failed, but, in the opinion of Roger Sherman, "would probably have been carried if Rhode Island had been represented."[29] William Duer had to admit that effecting Schuyler's reinstatement had not been easy. "There was never," he confided to Robert R. Livingston on May 26, "a more difficult card to play. General Gates had the address whilst at the place [Congress] to insinuate himself into the good graces of even the honest part of the House." However, "truth assisted with management," as he euphemistically described it, "at length effected all our wishes, and we carried the question upon his being reinstated in his command in the Northern department."

The vote itself was illuminating as to the relative strength of the two major factions in Congress at this point. Voting with New York to return Schuyler to his command were Pennsylvania, Maryland, Virginia, North Carolina and South Carolina. The opposition was composed of the New England states—with the exception of Rhode Island, which was not represented—and New Jersey and Georgia divided on the question. Had the states been fully represented, Schuyler's opponents would have carried the day. The two absent members of the New Jersey delegation were Abraham Clark and Jonathan Sargeant, "whose political line of conduct," reported Duer, "lies to the eastward of Birams' River [i.e., with New England, Byram's River being the boundary between New York and Connecticut]." In addition, Richard Henry Lee had voted with New England on this, as he did on most other questions, but (this time), his was a minority position. The unexpected support of the majority of the Virginia delegation assured victory for the Schuyler-faction.

No one, least of all his friends, ever seriously expected that Gates would remain with the army and serve under Schuyler. "General Gates will most assuredly not take the post of hazard both to his life and reputation, to be under the absolute direction of a man 35 leagues off," James Lovell opined. "I daily expect to hear of confusion from that department."[30] William Gordon, the historian, also feared that Gates would resign rather than serve in a subordinate capacity, and he exhorted him not to do so. On June 7 Gordon appealed to Gates's patriotism and reminded him of the high objectives for which he had taken up arms. Reluctantly, however, Gordon was forced to admit that while Gates might be willing to disregard his personal feelings in the interest of the cause, Schuyler would not. "I am afraid I shall never have it to record of him," he informed Gates, "that like a general in old times he said to his fellow general, we have been quarrelling between ourselves, now we have the common enemy to engage, we will lay aside our own private disputes till we have beaten the enemy, and then if you have a mind to it we will take them up again."

However, before Gates received Gordon's letter, he had requested from Schuyler and been granted permission to leave the Northern department. As Jonathan Trumbull, Jr., reported, "he thinks himself extremely ill-used, & is not insensible to the injury." He also was well aware of whom he had to thank for that injury. "Major General Gates a few days since arrived in this city greatly chagrined," wrote the New York delegates on June 19, "and enraged against your delegates to whom he ascribes what without solid reason, he is pleased to call his disgrace. As in this enquiry justice has been our view, and truth our guide," they smugly concluded, "we feel ourselves very indifferent about his resentment."[31]

In fact, Gates found it impossible to shake the self-righteousness of the New York delegates even though he took the extraordinary and inexpedient step of accusing them on the floor of Congress. On June 18, at the request of Roger Sherman, Gates was admitted to the House, ostensibly to communicate intelligence of some importance. After a few general remarks concerning affairs in the Northern department, he got to the real reason for his presence. He claimed that he had been appointed to the command of the Northern department in May and that "a few days since without having given any cause of offence, without accusation, without trial, without hearing, without notice, he had received a resolution by which he was in a most disgraceful manner superseded in his command."

Up to this point he had remained calm, but now, losing his temper, he accused the New York delegation of being the authors of his disgrace and singled out James Duane as the principal culprit. An undignified shouting match ensued, with the New Yorkers demanding Gates's ejection and the New Englanders contending that he should be heard. The New Yorkers finally carried the day and Gates departed. William Duer bragged to Schuyler of his part in the proceedings. "You will perhaps think it was improper for me to second the motion that he should be ordered to withdraw," he wrote, "but I plainly saw that he was brought in with an intention to brow beat the New York members, whom he considers as his mortal enemies, and I was determined to let him see that it was indifferent to me whether I offended him or not."[32]

Gates made a serious mistake in abusing the privileges of the House, and much of the esteem he hitherto had enjoyed dissipated as he delivered his diatribe. Friends who persuaded him to follow this course had done so with little regard to the effect it might have upon his reputation. Instead, they were probably motivated by a desire to embarrass the delegates from New York. As such, it entailed far more than the problem of command in the Northern department. For the New York delegation had, in a few short months, initiated and carried through a program disadvantageous to New England.

In February of 1777 not a single delegate sat in Congress from New York. By mid-April, six delegates were there and appeared to the critical eye of John Adams "as determined as any men ever were or could be." Four of these were singled out by Adams for special praise: William Duer, Philip Livingston, James Duane, and John Jay. With regard to the latter two, Adams commented that they "had arrived at the honor of being ranked with the two Adamses. I hope they will be duly sensible of the illustrious distinction and be sure to act in a manner becoming of it."[33]

In terms of initiative, ingenuity, and political shrewdness, the New

Yorkers more than lived up to this distinction. The fact that they were nearly all related by marriage undoubtedly added to the cohesion and effectiveness of the group. Philip Livingston's uncle, Robert Livingston, Jr., was James Duane's father-in-law, while Philip's uncle William had John Jay for a son-in-law. All, in turn, were related to Philip Schuyler through the intermarriage of Livingstons and Schuylers which had occurred frequently over nearly a century of close family alliance. With familial and political interests in common, the delegates planned and executed a bold political program.

Early 1777 had found New York's interests in Congress "at a very low ebb." Many of the New Yorkers' friends were absent—William Hooper, Joseph Hewes, Edward Rutledge, Benjamin Harrison, George Read, Thomas Stone, and Samuel Chase among others—and many seats were "filled by strangers." At Duane's urging, the New York delegates adopted a "cautious and deliberate plan," and "concealing even our feelings," they set about winning the support of the new members. Instrumental to this process was the lavish living style adopted by the New Yorkers, "for it was not a time to consult parsimony."

Duane and his colleagues also decided not to fatigue and irritate Congress with complaints, but rather "to confine our attention to a single point till it was accomplished, keeping every other subject in the deepest reserve." With the assistance of their new-found friends, the New Yorkers scored one success after another. They rescued their kinsman Schuyler from nearly certain disgrace and returned him triumphantly to command the Northern department. And while this was their first, and most important object, a maneuvre affecting the Northern commissary gave nearly as much satisfaction.

Still smarting at Walter Livingston's forced resignation as deputy commissary, the New Yorkers were determined that Joseph Trumbull's victory should be a hollow one. They first convinced Congress that the purchasing commissary for the Northern department should be a New Yorker, since the markets he would draw from would be within that state. Having won this point, they then succeeded in having their friend, Jacob Cuyler, appointed to that post.[34]

While Duane had reason to be pleased with what he had accomplished in so short a time, he did not delude himself by thinking it was any more than a temporary victory. Gates, soon after his disastrous appearance in Congress, was informed by some candid members that it had never been intended that he should command the Northern department—that in this matter his supposed friends had treacherously misled him. He "ought to feel more pain and resentment from this circumstance than from anything that fell from me," Duane confided to Schuyler, and

"I am apt to think he does." Apparently convinced that he had been made a fool of, Gates sent no further protests to Congress, nor did he resign as many had believed he would. In part, Duane believed this was due to Gates's expectation that Schuyler would soon be elected governor of New York, "and that then he will be reinstated in the possession of what he has much at heart, the command of the Northern department."[35]

With a powerful British army massing in Canada for the invasion of New York, it was not the most opportune time for the commander of the Northern department to become involved in a gubernatorial campaign. Although neither Schuyler, nor his rival, General George Clinton, could spare time for active campaigning they were not unconcerned with the course of the election campaign. During the late spring of 1777, they exchanged numerous letters with their respective supporters and speculated on the political future of New York, and at the same time attempted to halt the British advance from Canada. However, to the disappointment of both Schuyler and Gates, the governorship was won by George Clinton and General John Burgoyne captured Ticonderoga.

Saratoga

DESTINED to witness the most extensive military operations of the war, the campaign season of 1777 began uneventfully. As spring turned to summer, General Howe massed 16,445 officers and men at New York preparatory to launching a new offensive. Across the bay in New Jersey, the American army prepared to meet the expected British thrust toward Philadelphia. With a hard core of 9,000 Continentals plus assorted militia detachments, Washington awaited Howe's move with some confidence. It proved to be a long wait, for the British commander appeared loath to leave the comforts of the city.

In Canada, Sir John Burgoyne readied an army of invasion which he optimistically believed would crush the American army in northern New York and triumphantly occupy Albany before the close of the season. The greatest obstacle in Burgoyne's way seemed to be Ticonderoga, and since the British mistakenly believed that the fort was garrisoned by as many as 12,000 men (when in fact it had 2,500 at most), they proceeded cautiously to gather a force capable of prosecuting a long siege. In their final form, British plans called for Burgoyne to proceed against Ticonderoga with 7,173 men, while Lt. Col. Barry St. Leger with 675 regulars and an unspecified number of Canadians and Indians attempted to flank the Americans via Lake Ontario and the Mohawk River. General Carleton was to remain in Canada with 3,770 men.

Burgoyne's timetable called for the capture of Ticonderoga in the early summer, and then a leisurely march to Albany either by way of Lake George or, if the enemy was too strong in that direction, via the lower end of Lake Champlain through Skenesboro. Burgoyne did not expect Howe to meet him in Albany, nor was it ever intimated to Howe that he should. Everyone concerned believed that Burgoyne would have little difficulty in handling whatever opposition the Americans offered, as long as Howe tied down Washington and the main army. Howe, as it turned out, had every expectation of keeping Washington fully occupied. He planned a campaign that would either force Washington to fight a decisive engagement or sacrifice Philadelphia—either way, he felt the outcome would be highly satisfactory.

Howe's second in command, General Sir Henry Clinton, had other thoughts on the subject. Convinced that Howe was mistaken in his belief that the Americans would risk a decisive engagement to protect Philadelphia, Clinton further asserted that no advantage could be gained by capturing that city. Howe's proposed campaign would squander the offensive might of the British army in the pursuit of unattainable or useless objectives. On the other hand, if a strong British force reduced the American fortifications in the Hudson Highlands and secured the river between its mouth and Albany, a junction with Burgoyne could be effected and a major strategic victory won. The State of New York would be effectively taken out of the war, and the rebelling colonies divided, with New England isolated from the rest. In addition, the real attraction of such a plan, from Clinton's point of view, was that it was just the vital threat that Washington could not afford to ignore. He would have to risk his army in a decisive battle and the British would then have their opportunity to crush it, and with it the American rebellion.

In the end, Howe agreed to provide a force sufficient to reduce the Highland fortifications after Burgoyne reached Albany. But the advance from Canada to Albany would be entirely Burgoyne's responsibility. Indeed, Howe believed that advance to be essential for the success of his own operations against Philadelphia, since it would prevent the Americans from concentrating sufficient forces to protect their capital. It would appear that neither the ministry nor Burgoyne expected Howe to do more in the way of supporting the northern expedition.[1]

Since the Americans intended to act defensively, they could adopt no fixed plan. Assuming, however, that the British would attempt to gain the objectives they had failed to reach the previous year—Howe, Philadelphia and Burgoyne, Albany—a general strategy evolved. Washington would block any move against Philadelphia, and, if favorable conditions developed, he would attempt to deal Howe a crippling blow. In the north, the fortifications of Ticonderoga were strengthened and the New England militia called forth to augment the Continental regiments deployed to oppose Burgoyne's advance.

There was a serious question whether Ticonderoga was actually as defensible as the British and Congress thought it was. Every general officer concerned with holding the post—including Schuyler, Gates, St. Clair, and Arnold—at one time or another had serious reservations concerning its defensibility. The main works of the fort were partially destroyed by the French when they evacuated it in 1759, and the British, and later the Americans, had made rather ineffective attempts to repair the damage. Consequently, Schuyler, Gates, and St. Clair urged the erection of new fortifications on the higher ground to the east of the old fort. The western lines, they recommended, should be either abandoned altogether or only lightly defended.

The new works on Mount Independence, begun during the fall of 1776, were still not complete in the spring of 1777. Nevertheless, many in Congress and the army felt that they were stronger than the old fortifications. Those who took this view proposed a congressional resolution directing the abandonment of the old works and the concentration of the American forces on Mount Independence. However, the best Congress would do was to leave the responsibility up to the commander on the spot. In early May, this meant Gates, and James Lovell strongly urged him on May 1 not to attempt foolishly to hold the western lines and thus lose his army, the stores, and his reputation.

The New York Convention took quite another view of the problem. One week after Lovell's letter, Gouverneur Morris wrote Gates that the Convention was protesting the congressional resolve empowering him to abandon Ticonderoga. Morris said that he was convinced that the British would concentrate on a major push against Philadelphia, and that no offensive operation would be mounted against the United States from Canada. In addition, he pointed out, if the British did strike up the lakes, the abandonment of Ticonderoga would allow them to bypass the garrison at Mount Independence and cross from Lake Champlain to Lake George without opposition.

Obviously, whatever other attributes Morris may have had, a talent for grand strategy was not one of them. According to Alexander Hamilton, who was by this time one of Washington's aides, the general officers of the army were agreed that the enemy would attempt the conquest of the State of New York, which endeavor had been frustrated the year before. Also, no general would dream of leaving a strong body of enemy troops in his rear to threaten lines of communication and supply. Thus, Gates quite justifiably ignored Morris' advice and the complaints of the New York Convention. Indeed, Schuyler concurred with Gates in this instance, and, soon after resuming command in the north, reported to Congress that he had directed General St. Clair to take command at Ticonderoga and concentrate upon making Mount Independence defensible. For, as he put it, the western lines could not be held even if all of the men in the department were committed to their defense.[2]

An acute manpower shortage added to the mounting concern felt by the northern commanders. The expiration of enlistments, desertion, and sickness had reduced the effective strength of the garrison at Ticonderoga far below the congressional estimate of 2,500 men. And the New England militia seemed reluctant to turn out and supply the requested reinforcements. In large part this was due to a rather farcical mixup in the manpower recruitment procedures followed in the western counties of Massachusetts. Hampshire County, for example, was supposed to send 1,500 men to the northern post. However, as Timothy Danielson, a county official, explained, few were likely to go. The county had gone to great expense to hire substitutes to meet the county's quota for the Continental army. Now, Danielson complained, "the very men that have paid large sums of money to hire Continental soldiers to enlist are now drafted to march to Ticonderoga, while the men they hired are rioting at home on their money, unconcerned about the fate of this country. While the one is quitting his family, his farm and husbandry, to reinforce at Ticonderoga, the other is sporting from house to house, and from tavern to tavern, spending the money the honest farmer has earned with the sweat of his face. . . . Unless some effectual measure is taken to send off the Continental soldier," he concluded, "it may be depended on, the militia will not march to any advanced posts."[3]

Faced with a manpower crisis, Schuyler despaired of holding the northern posts. On the first of July he informed General Heath—who, as commander of the Eastern department was charged with the responsibility of forwarding reinforcements to the Northern army—that while he had no doubt Ticonderoga could be held if properly garrisoned, unless the New England militia arrived soon, the posts would be lost and the army driven south in defeat. Time was indeed running out. The most recent reports received from St. Clair placed Burgoyne's main force only 15 miles away at Crown Point.[4]

The long awaited offensive began on July 2 when Burgoyne launched a two-pronged thrust designed to cut Ticonderoga's communications to the south. To the west of the fort, General William Phillips, commanding the advance of General Fraser's corps, drove in the American outposts and occupied the small prominence, Mt. Hope, which effectively commanded the road between Ticonderoga and the head of Lake George. At the same time, Baron von Riedesel landed on the east bank opposite Ticonderoga and struck at Mount Independence, threatening the envelopment of the American position from the east. Although they met no effective resistance, the British refrained from attacking the main works. Instead, the overly cautious Burgoyne took steps to bring the stronghold under siege. The key to this operation was a high, steep hill called Sugar Loaf. The Americans had made no effort to defend the hill because the high command had decided that cannon could never be hauled up its rugged slope. General Phillips took a different view, commenting "where a goat can go, a man can go, and where a man can go he can drag a gun." Putting this philosophy to the test, the British had two 12-pounders in place atop the hill on July 5. Enjoying an unobstructed field of fire, the guns commanded Ticonderoga at 1,400 yards and Mount Independence at 1,500.

Up to this point, the American garrison's morale seems to have been good. "Our numbers are few but in high spirit, and seem determined to conquer or die," an officer reported from the beleagured post on July 3. Nonetheless, at three o'clock on the afternoon of the 5th, St. Clair made the decision to remove the garrison and supplies during the night and retreat to Skenesboro. St. Clair's reason for ordering a retreat was that while the garrison could give a good account of itself against a British assault, it could not withstand a siege. The latter could only result in the loss of the fort, the garrison, and all public stores. Thus, St. Clair believed that he would serve his country best by extracting his army from the surrounding British army and maintaining a force between the enemy and the relatively undefended portions of New York to the southward.[5]

Although St. Clair's decision was sound—and eventually would be acclaimed by his fellow officers—the immediate effect of the evacuation of Ticonderoga was to bring a storm of criticism down upon himself and Schuyler. The strength of this reaction was due both to the psychological unpreparedness of the civil authorities to accept defeat in that quarter and to the deep hostilities previously aroused by the Schuyler–Gates rivalry.

As late as July 4, Gouverneur Morris wrote complacently to Hamilton that he was convinced the British were only making a feint in the north to prevent an attack upon Howe's army. Indeed, Congress assured St. Clair when he was given his command that it expected no determined attack from Canada, and St. Clair therefore took his 11-year-old son with him to Ticonderoga. The news of the abandonment of that post was received with shocked disbelief.

Even General Washington failed to realize the extent of the threat in the north until it was too late to save the post. Not until a few days before its abandonment did Washington order a redisposition of his forces to support the Northern army. Abandoning the position he had taken at Middlebrook, New Jersey, to block a move by Howe against Philadelphia, Washington marched with the main body of his army north to Morristown and placed one division under General Sullivan even further north at Pompton, New Jersey. At the same time a force under Brigadier General Samuel Holden Parsons was detached to relieve Brigadier General John Nixon's brigade at Peekskill on the Hudson, to enable the latter officer to hurry northward with his men to join Schuyler's army. But it was too late to save Ticonderoga. Before the new troop dispositions were effected, news arrived of the loss of the fort and the headlong retreat of the Northern army.

Schuyler's enemies in Congress were quick to make political capital of the loss of the northern stronghold. Ignoring the warnings of Schuyler and St. Clair concerning the weakness of Ticonderoga's defenses, much was now made of General Gates's prediction that the fort was ill-prepared to meet the British offensive which was certain to come. At the same time, some men attached to the Northern army intimated that the post could have been held if the army's commanders had had greater courage. One such, Jonathan Trumbull, Jr., could find no convincing reason why the garrison, well supplied with provisions, small arms, cannon, and ammunition, should have abandoned the fortifications "at the *appearance* only of not more than twice their number, I say the *appearance* only, because I don't yet learn that a gun had been fired, save by scouting parties."

Trumbull further observed that General Schuyler had only "the little handfull of fugitives from Ty, & the small body of militia already collected," with which to contest Burgoyne's triumphant advance. "Without speedy and effectual support they will not be able to maintain themselves," he warned, "& if *running* comes in vogue I know not where they may stop." In addition, St. Clair had already become a scapegoat in the eyes of the people, and it was doubtful if the militia would consent to serve under him. Trumbull apparently concurred in this opinion, for he confided that the accusations of cowardice and treachery leveled at St. Clair were "not without too much & too great reason."[6]

A similarly harsh view of St. Clair's actions emanated from Washington's headquarters. "The stroke at Ticonderoga is heavy, unexpected and unaccountable," Hamilton confided to John Jay on July 13. "If the place was untenable why not discovered to be so before the Continent had been put to such an amazing expence, [sic] in furnishing it with the means of defence? [sic]. If it was tenable, what, in the name of common sense could have induced the evacuation? I would wish to suspend my judgment on the matter; but certainly present appearances speak either of the most abandoned cowardice, or treachery." To add to Washington's consternation, Howe embarked his troops aboard transports and it was generally assumed that he would sail up the Hudson and effect a juncture with Burgoyne. Thus, Washington hurriedly put the main army in motion toward Peekskill in hopes of placing it athwart the Hudson and checking Howe's advance.

Congress, in the meantime, responded to the disaster by directing General Benedict Arnold to collect New York and New England militia "and check the progress of Gen. Burgoyne, as very disagreeable consequences may be apprehended, if the most vigerous [sic] measures are not taken to oppose him." Apparently, Congress no longer had faith in Schuyler's ability to accomplish this task, and the orders were sent directly to his subordinate.[7]

Unofficially, certain members of Congress were a good deal more blunt in their estimation of Schuyler's talents and his responsibility for the situation in the north. "We have letters from General Schuyler in the Northern department giving us an account of the untoward situation of our affairs in that quarter," Samuel Adams wrote Richard Henry Lee, "and I confess it is no more than I expected, when he was again intrusted with the command there." From his letters, it appeared that Schuyler did not even know the whereabouts of his army. "Gates is the man of my choice," Adams rather needlessly informed Lee, "he is *honest* and *true,* and has an art of *gaining the love of his soldiers* principally because he is *always present* with them in *fatigue and danger.* But Gates has been disgusted!" Other congressmen were even more pointed in their observations, and blamed the "shameful business" upon placing the New England troops under the command of "Scotch officers [i.e., St. Clair] and others in whom even less confidence is to be placed." New England was now laid open to attack, and not more than a third of the militia even had arms. However, a New Hampshire congressman wrathfully declared, "we can do better with oak saplings under officers in whom we can confide than with the best arms when commanded by cowards and traitors."[8]

Schuyler, for his part, was quick to shift the blame to New England. If that section had seen fit to fill the regiments in the Northern army as they had been requested to do, he asserted, the post might never have been lost. Schuyler conveniently forgot that in March, General Washington had diverted most of the New England troops destined for Ticonderoga to Peekskill or the main army in New Jersey, and had duly informed Schuyler of the change. In addition, of those men who were sent as replacements, Schuyler now claimed that one-third had been Negroes and little boys. "I will however go on smilllng [sic] with contempt on the malice of my enemies," he assured Washington on July 18, "and attempt to deserve your esteem, which will console me for the abuse which thousands may unjustly throw out against me."[9] Typically, Schuyler, having won back the command of the Northern department, refused any share of the responsibility for the failures of the Northern army.

The New England delegates in Congress, of course, realized the tack Schuyler would take in attempting to shift the blame for the defeat. "An attempt will be made to throw the whole blame in the Northern department upon the New England states," James Lovell predicted on July 21, and he was not one to sit idly by and let it happen. "I called a hornet's nest about my ears by *soberly* asserting that Schuyler was beloved by the Eastern States, especially by the officers from thence," he gleefully informed William Whipple, "that he was the key to the militia of Albany County, and that the Indians called him father. I asserted that I was told so six weeks ago by a gentleman of intelligence, veracity and honor [i.e., James Duane, when he was arguing for the reinstatement of Schuyler]. The ungrateful curs said I was *satirizing* and Middleton joined them."

While Lovell reported upon events in Congress, Whipple sent back information from New Hampshire designed to absolve the state of any blame for the recent debacle. He contested the veracity of St. Clair's statement that he had barely 3,000 men at Ticonderoga. "I have taken pains to inform myself of the number from this state and am very confident there was at least 2000 and if the other states had as many in proportion there must have been at least 6 or 8000." He also discovered that the New Hampshire men received not one article of clothing after they reached Ticonderoga and were now in a naked condition despite the fact that large quantities of clothing purchased by the New England states had been taken by the clothier general. In Whipple's opinion, the clothing had been sent southward "while the troops belonging to the states who have most exerted themselves to procure necessaries for their men are left naked. If such infamous partiality as this, is to be shown and no notice taken of it by those who ought to be the guardians of all America, I think it's high time for every state to take care of itself."[10]

Despite claims to the contrary by the New England States, Schuyler continued to complain that the militia reinforcements for his army were not materializing. As of the third week in July he estimated his total force at no more than 3,000 Continentals and 1,500 militia. He conceded that more New England citizen soldiers had at various times been with the army, but, as he put it, "they come in, stay a few days, and then leave again." Fearing that Ticonderoga would prove only the first in a long run of defeats for which he would be held responsible, Schuyler once again asked Congress to direct a formal inquiry into his conduct.[11]

With perhaps greater reason, St. Clair also felt an inquiry was necessary to clear his name. But instead of making a political issue of it, as Schuyler had, he requested Washington to convene a court martial. The only favor he asked was that Arnold should not be a party to the inquiry. The outspoken Arnold had publicly condemned the abandonment of Ticonderoga and "declared that some person must be sacrificed to an injured country." Seeing himself surrounded by officers "with little knowledge and very narrow minds," St. Clair begged the commander in chief to select an officer who was unprejudiced and knew something of the military profession to conduct the court martial.[12]

With Burgoyne advancing from the north, and Howe and his army disappearing out to sea to an unkown destination instead of sailing up the Hudson, Washington had little time for conducting inquiries. Also, he confided to Governor Trumbull on July 31, he had doubts whether he could properly initiate an inquiry in the Northern department. It apparently was considered a separate command by Congress and it was therefore Congress' responsibility to order the inquiry. Congress agreed that an investigation was necessary, but also believed that first priority should be given to stopping Burgoyne. Consequently, on July 26 a motion was introduced by New Jersey Congressman Jonathan Sargeant to recall both St. Clair and Schuyler and send Gates to command in the Northern department.

In the course of the debate, supporters of the motion maintained that while Schuyler had long been unpopular with the soldiers from New England, both he and St. Clair now lacked the confidence of *all* the troops in the Northern army. In addition, Burgoyne could only be stopped by a heavy turnout of the New England militia, and the militia would not serve under Schuyler and St. Clair but it would under Gates. Schuyler himself offered confirmation. "The people, especially in the Eastern States, are industriously propogating that the general officers that were at Ticonderoga, and myself, are all a pack of traitors. This doctrine has been preached in the army by many of the people that have come up from New England," he informed Washington, "and by some from this state [i.e., New York], which greatly prejudices the service, as it tends to destroy that confidence which troops ought to have in their officers."[13]

On the other hand, those who opposed the motion claimed that conditions were to blame, not individuals. According to this group, no one could have effectively opposed Burgoyne. Also, while this group was willing to have St. Clair recalled and have his conduct investigated, it was felt that Schuyler should be recalled only if the first investigation definitely implicated him.

Each report from the northward weakened the position of Schuyler's friends, but by a valiant effort they managed to continue the debate and put off a vote on the motion. James Duane, leader of this rearguard action, urged Congress not to be stampeded into any rash measure. The attack upon Schuyler, he asserted, was the work of a combination of the New England states and arose from resentment and "private views." William Williams of Connecticut denied the charge, but acknowledged that those states did not have confidence in the generals and some regard should be paid to their joint desire to see them removed. Sargeant, and Daniel Roberdeau of Pennsylvania (who respectively introduced and seconded the motion to recall Schuyler and St. Clair), hotly denied belonging to any combination or being activated by anything other than a desire to discover the truth.[14]

To the growing frustration and apprehension of the New England delegates, Congress still delayed. "Will you believe [that] that same obstinacy which withstood the sending of Schuyler to Headquarters in the Jersies 7 weeks ago, now also withstands calling him hither to give an account of our affairs in the Northern department and of the causes of the relinquishment of Independence, to say nothing of the western part," queried Lovell. "He writes that the Tories will all join Burgoyne and the timid Whigs and Six Nations of Indians and that the Eastern militia will not stay with him: yet we are not to send a more popular fighting general in his place. . . . If the Eastern States do not muster all possible proofs that they have done as well at least as others," he warned, "a number in Congress with the Northern council of war and Schuyler, and more than one of the Jersies, will cry out 'New England *alone* is to blame.' "[15]

Lovell would have felt much better had he known that on the same day that he wrote, July 29, William Duer admitted to Schuyler that he should not be surprised if he were shortly recalled to give account for the loss of Ticonderoga. In addition, the New York delegates were beginning to doubt the wisdom of blocking Schuyler's recall. As they pointed out to the New York Council of Safety, if they should succeed and Schuyler continued in the Northern department, and if the New England states withheld their militia, "the calamities of the country in that quarter [would] increase." It was therefore questionable if either Schuyler's or the state's best interest would be served by pursuing their present course.[16]

With the opposition weakening, the New Englanders managed to push through a resolution on July 29 calling for a full inquiry into the evacuation of Ticonderoga and Mount Independence, "and into the conduct of the general officers who were in the Northern department at the time of the evacuation." Thus, the resolve was intentionally worded so as to include Schuyler—who was not at Ticonderoga. In addition, a committee was assigned to recommend a mode of conducting the inquiry, and it contained members who could not be considered friends of Schuyler. Indeed, three of the five were New Englanders—John Adams, Eliphalet Dyer, and Nathaniel Folsom—and one of the remaining two, Daniel Roberdeau, had actively supported the motion to recall St. Clair and Schuyler. "I doubt not that Gates will be sent," Lovell reported on August 1, "and I hope the militia of New England will do justice to our labors, by turning out and behaving well. The unpopularity of the Northern commander has been declared a bar to our hopes— therefore the change."[17]

However, although Congress finally decided to recall St. Clair and Schuyler, and Gates was the logical choice to succeed the latter, it attempted to shift the burden of that choice to the commander in chief. Washington's response on August 3 represents the true measure of his tact and his grasp of the political overtones of such a move. "At the same time that I express my thanks for the high mark of confidence which Congress have been pleased to repost in me by their resolution authorizing me to send an officer to command the Northern army," he wrote President Hancock, "I should wish to be excused from making the appointment. . . . The Northern department in a great measure, has been considered as separate, and more peculiarly under their [Congress'] direction, and the officers commanding there always of their nomination. I have never interfered, further than merely to advise, and to give such aids as were in my power, on the requisitions of those officers. The present situation of that department is delicate and critical," he concluded, "and the choice of an officer to the command may involve very interesting and important consequences." Neither the commander in chief nor anyone else had any idea how "interesting and important" some of those consequences were to be.

According to James Lovell, the New York delegates were responsible for asking Washington to name Schuyler's successor since they hoped he would name someone other than Gates. This failing, Congress voted 11 states to 1 to appoint Gates to the command, "which is far from five to four, and two divided."[18] The last being a reference to the vote by which Schuyler had been restored to his command in May.

Men who had hitherto supported Schuyler's pretensions to command, and viewed criticism of him as merely the product of partisanship and envy, now were forced to reevaluate his qualities as a leader. By August 1, even Alexander Hamilton candidly admitted he had made a mistake concerning the man who in a few years would be his father-in-law. "I have always been a very partial judge of General Schuyler's conduct," he admitted in a confidential letter to Robert R. Livingston, "but I am at last forced to suppose him inadequate to the important command with which he has been intrusted. There seems to be a want of firmness in all his actions, and this last instance in my opinion is too unequivocal to be doubted." As to Schuyler's excuses that the reverses in the north were due to panic on the part of the soldiers, Hamilton observed that during the last campaign, when affairs with the main army were at their lowest ebb, he never saw anything like panic among the troops. "They appeared in the worst of times as resolute & spirited as in the best. What could be the reason for this but that their commanders always set them an example by putting on the face of fortitude and resolution amidst all the causes of dejection they experienced; and what can be the reason that the contrary is the case with respect to the Northern army at this time but that their commanders observe different conduct."

Certainly the conduct of the Northern commanders had been uninspiring. Time and again the army had deployed to make a stand, only to be ordered to continue its retreat—often when the enemy was still miles away. A strong position was finally selected by Schuyler at Stillwater, and on August 4 the army began constructing fortifications. But on August 15 Schuyler again ordered the army to continue its retreat toward Albany, and by the 18th most of the army was encamped only nine miles from that city.

Schuyler justified his refusal to give battle by claiming that the few thousand dispirited men in his command could not hope to check a British force which he estimated at 10,000 men. This estimate was grossly inaccurate. When Burgoyne reached Fort Edward on August 4 he had with him 6,640 officers, men, and servants. While Burgoyne's force was steadily dwindling as units were detached for garrison and guard duty to protect his ever lengthening line of supply, Schuyler's command was growing as reinforcements arrived from Washington's army. Nixon's, Poor's, Learned's, Glover's, and Paterson's brigades of Continentals gave the Northern army a hard core of over 5,000 veteran troops. In addition, thousands of militia had joined or were on their way to swell the ranks of Schuyler's force. So it was Burgoyne, not Schuyler, who faced a numerically superior force.[19]

The Northern commander conveniently discounted the Continental troops sent him as nothing but "boys, or rather children, and Negroes that disgrace our arms," and further complained that the Connecticut and Massachusetts militia would not turn out since they refused to serve under his command.[20]

The army's continued retreat lowered morale and increased criticism of Schuyler's generalship. "It seems odd," wrote one officer, "that our retreating is so rapid that we can hardly keep within hearing of the enemy, or even know where they are." Faith in the Northern army and its commander reached its lowest point on August 18, 1777, when Poor's brigade crossed to the south side of the Mohawk at Loudon's Ferry and the remainder of the army encamped at the point where that river joins the Hudson, only nine miles from Albany. *"This town* is falling;" Jonathan Trumbull, Jr., announced from Albany, "if the army makes one more move toward it all is lost. . . . The next *move* of the retreating army will bring them around if into town."[21]

On August 10, a few days before the army fell back to the Mohawk, Philip Schuyler was informed by President Hancock that he had been removed from command and ordered to Washington's headquarters for an inquiry into his conduct as commander of the Northern department. He protested to Hancock the "indignity" of being removed from command when his army was about to engage the enemy. Perhaps when he wrote this letter Schuyler did think a battle was imminent; however, two days later he ordered the retreat to the Mohawk, surrendering the last defensible position north of Albany.[22]

Just when all seemed lost, the prospects of the Northern army suddenly brightened. On August 19 Horatio Gates assumed its command. He was warmly welcomed by the Continental officers and men. Upon his arrival, "gladness appeared in every countenance. Joy circulated through the camp." "General Gates takes command of the Northern army this day," noted a Continental field officer, "which I think will put a new face upon our affairs."[23] An added boost to the army's morale came the next day with news of the American victory at Bennington. Ironically, it was New England militiamen, of whom Schuyler had complained so bitterly, who gave General Burgoyne his first serious setback.

In order to replenish his dwindling supplies and secure horses for his dismounted dragoons, Burgoyne had sent a detachment of 650 men under Lieutenant Colonel Baum toward the American supply depot at Bennington. Several miles short of his objective, on August 16, Baum was met by militia General John Stark and Colonel Seth Warner with some 1,200 New Hampshire, Vermont, and Massachusetts militia. In the battle which ensued, the American militia successfully carried out a frontal assault against entrenched regulars, mortally wounded Baum, and nearly wiped out his detachment.

The battle was still far from over, however, for a second detachment of 642 German mercenaries under Lieutenant Colonel Breymann had been ordered to Baum's support and arrived on the 17th. Although the American force was considerably scattered and disorganized after the previous day's victory, it was able to meet and repulse the German attack, to counterattack, and finally rout the enemy. In the end, the militia captured most of the equipment brought forward by Baum and Breymann (including four field pieces), killed 207 of the German troops, and captured about 700 more. Thus, the militia which Schuyler ridiculed inflicted nearly 1,000 casualties upon Burgoyne and denied him vital supplies—both important steps toward his ultimate defeat.

After weeks of despair, Bennington had a tonic-like effect on the Northern army and a grateful Congress made John Stark a Continental brigadier general. At the same time that he learned of the action at Bennington, Gates received good news from the western Mohawk Valley.

British plans for their Northern campaign in 1777 called for an invasion of the Mohawk Valley by way of Lake Ontario and a thrust at Albany from the west. This move would not only destroy grain in the valley, upon which the American army was heavily dependent, but also cause the weakening of the Northern army opposing Burgoyne as troops were shifted to meet the threat from the west. And at first it appeared that the plan was working.

Meeting no opposition, the mixed force of British regulars, Loyalists, and Indians commanded by Lt. Colonel Barry St. Leger reached the Mohawk in July and invested Ft. Stanwix (or Ft. Schuyler, as the Patriots now called it). Beyond this fort, the valley stretched virtually defenseless east to Albany some 100 miles away. To meet this danger, Schuyler detached 950 volunteers under the command of General Arnold to relieve Stanwix. The departure of this force on August 8 was undoubtedly a consideration in the decision arrived at a few days later to abandon the strong defensive position at Stillwater.

Two days before Arnold's force left Stillwater, a force of New York militia under General Nicholas Herkimer was ambushed at Oriskany while attempting to reach the beleaguered garrison. Although badly mauled, and forced to turn back, the militia inflicted heavy casualties on St. Leger's Indian auxilliaries and definitely damped their enthusiasm. When, shortly thereafter, an Indian friendly to the American cause, accompanied by a half-witted white boy, brought news that Arnold was approaching with a vast army, the Indians promptly decamped, and St. Leger was forced to abandon the siege and follow his erstwhile allies back to Canada. Consequently, Arnold returned on August 31 and a reunited Northern army could then turn to face Burgoyne.

The significance of these victories was not lost on the new commander of the Northern department. Not only would they "retard the impetuosity of his [Burgoyne's] further approach," but Gates also believed they would result in his army being reinforced by "large bodies of militia from all quarters." Additional Continental reinforcements also reached the Northern army in late August—the 2nd and 4th New York Regiments and Colonel Daniel Morgan's corps of 400 riflemen. The time had come to seek out Burgoyne's army.

Gates was quick to recognize the impossible situation of the Northern army which he found "encamped on different islands" at the mouth of the Mohawk, and he pledged "not [to] wait to be attacked, but to endeavour to turn the tables on my antagonist." Thus, on September 6 the army was placed under orders to march "at a minutes warning" and on the 8th it began to retrace its steps northward, reaching and occupying its old lines at Stillwater the following day. Then on the 13th, the army advanced another four miles to a stronger position at Bemis Heights, and with Morgan's riflemen and a newly formed corps of light infantry under Henry Dearborn deployed to give early warning of the enemy's approach, the stage was set for the long-deferred encounter with Burgoyne.[24]

Schuyler was at first reluctant to leave the army. He apparently thought his services were necessary in bringing in the New York militia.[25] He also may have wished to share in any victory which might now be forthcoming. Remarking on this possibility, James Lovell observed that if Schuyler "is not a valient [sic] man, he certainly knows how to use the world; he is far from a foolish man." Whipple disagreed with Lovell. With a major battle in the offing, he did not believe Schuyler's wisdom would stand in the way of his cowardice. "I hope that wont happen till a certain letter writer gets to a place of safety," he observed sardonically, "for I think it would be a pity he should be discomposed least he should be seized with a fit of rheumatism or a certain eruptive disorder that the gentleman is subject to on certain occasions. This would produce such a fit of letter writing that much paper would be wasted as well as much precious time in a certain room reading those precious performances."[26] Whipple need not have worried. Before any clash occurred with the enemy Schuyler had left the army. He thus retained intact the unique record of being the only high-ranking American officer in the Revolution who was not present at a single battle!

When Schuyler departed, he left behind a divisive force in the form of General Arnold and two former aides, Henry B. Livingston and Richard Varick, who now became members of Arnold's staff. Arnold was never a good subordinate under the best of conditions, and by late August he was in a particularly mutinous mood. When Congress promoted a number of brigadiers in February, Arnold was not one of them. He felt aggrieved since he was senior to the men promoted over him, and he had served with distinction in the Canadian campaign. The only reason given for passing over him was that Connecticut already had more than her share of general officers based upon the number of troops she had contributed.

Many in Congress had felt that Arnold deserved promotion, and when he again distinguished himself in the repulse of the British at Danbury, he was made a major general on May 3. Arnold was not satisfied, however, and requested that Congress predate his commission to give him his proper place in the line ahead of those appointed in February. After a lengthy debate, and a close vote, Congress denied his request. Some believed that Congress refused Arnold's request because it was offended by what bordered upon a demand for preferment.[27]

Feeling his honor insulted, Arnold promptly requested leave from Schuyler to quit the Northern army. Schuyler finally prevailed upon him to remain, arguing that his departure at that time (August 1) would have left Schuyler with no general officer capable of commanding the army. So Arnold stayed, but he did so reluctantly and his pride still smarted over Congress's refusal to grant him his requested preferment.[28] Gates was apparently unaware of this explosive situation when he assumed command of the Northern department.

Later, on October 5, James Lovell was to warn Gates that he might expect trouble from Arnold. "I fear that sprightly gentleman [Arnold] will be duped, by an artful senior now disgraced [Schuyler], so as to become a tool for base purposes. I will do my best neither one nor the other shall detract from your reputation here, if they should basely attempt it. You ought not to suffer yourself to be embarrassed there a moment after discovery of plain intention in any man to do it." Lovell's warning would have been more helpful if it had come a few weeks earlier.

Schuyler's former aides, Varick and Livingston, were just the sort of men Lovell had in mind. Both were fanatic in their loyalty to Schuyler and made no secret of their hatred for Gates. Varick had additional reason to bear a grudge against Gates. During the previous winter one of the officers at Ticonderoga had attempted to murder Varick and Gates had not, in Varick's opinion, been active enough in the apprehension and punishment of the villain.[29] The degree of Livingston's attachment is indicated by his assertion that he was "chagrined to the soul" when he thought of Gates reaping the fruits of Schuyler's labors!

Evidence of Varick's malice is found in his letter to Schuyler of September 12 in which he reported with obvious relish "that a little spirit happened on Wednesday evening between Gates and Arnold. *Intra nos.*"

The cause of the dispute referred to by Varick is uncertain. It may have concerned the transfer of the New York militia from Poor's brigade (in Arnold's division) to Glover's brigade in another division. In any event, it was not of major importance. The serious split between Gates and Arnold did not occur until after the battle at Freeman's Farm (Saratoga) on September 19.

Burgoyne made contact with the American defenses on September 17, and two days later attempted to turn the American left and possess himself of some high ground which would compromise the American lines. Gates received news of this movement and immediately ordered Morgan's riflemen and Dearborn's light infantry to engage the enemy. Both sides fed in additional troops and a heavy engagement raged through the afternoon. With the arrival of more British reinforcements and a train of artillery, the Americans retired to their lines. The battle was anything but a British victory, however, since Burgoyne had not only been prevented from reaching his objective but had suffered nearly 600 casualties (as compared to Gates's 320) in the process.

Gates, in his report to Congress, referred to the American units involved as simply a detachment of the army, not specifying that most of them were from Arnold's division nor mentioning that officer's laudable conduct on the field of battle. In view of their previous disagreement, it is quite possible that this omission was an intentional slight on Gates's part. In any event, Arnold interpreted it as such. He also protested to Gates on September 22 the decision to detach Morgan's corps from Arnold's division and use it as an independent force responsible directly to headquarters. No matter how well-founded his other grievances were, Arnold had no ground to stand on in objecting to that order. It was a militarily sound decision which resulted in the employment of the riflemen in their proper capacity as scouts and pickets who would immediately detect and report directly to American headquarters any movement by Burgoyne.

Both Varick and Livingston were delighted with the growing discord between Gates and Arnold. "Matters between Genl. Gates and Arnold are got to such a pitch," Varick confidently informed Schuyler on September 25, "that I have the fullest assurances Arnold will quit the department in a day or two." Indeed, Arnold had that very evening (September 22) requested leave to go to Philadelphia.

According to Varick, Gates had withheld reinforcements on the day of the battle which would have resulted in an unqualified American victory. He went even further and declared that Gates had had absolutely nothing to do with the battle from first to last, and that Gates's sole motivation in halting the retreat of the American army at the Mohawk and returning it to Stillwater was "to cast an odium on your [Schuyler's] reputation, in hopes that Burgoyne would be frightened by his movement."

The latter contention is so far-fetched that historians have ignored it in writing of the Battle of Saratoga. However, those same historians have obligingly accepted the first part of Varick's tale as an accurate analysis of the battle. It is significant that Arnold himself did not think to complain of this when he wrote to Gates on September 22 and 23. Had there been even a bit of truth in Varick's contention, then it seems that depriving Arnold of a smashing victory would most certainly have headed the list of his grievances.

Many of Gates's contemporaries, as well as more recent historians, have allowed personal prejudice and bias to obscure the realities of the military situation at Saratoga. Gates occupied an extremely strong position which could not be stormed successfully by the enemy. Furthermore, with the American right flank secured by the Hudson, Gates could, and upon two occasions did, bring sufficient force to bear to counter Burgoyne's attempt to turn the American left.

The British commander's position was far less enviable. With slightly more than 6,500 officers and men he had somehow to break through the American army and reach Albany before dwindling supplies and the onset of winter forced a retreat to Canada. The strength of the American position further limited Burgoyne's actions—if he was to get through to Albany it had to be around the American left flank.

Gates, fully aware of his adversary's predicament, posted Morgan's riflemen and Dearborn's light infantry in advance of and to the left of the American lines, and detachments from these units constantly probed the British right flank and rear, bringing in prisoners every day. With the possibility of surprise reduced to practically zero, Gates took the further precaution of placing his ablest subordinate—Arnold—in command of the American left. In this way he checked successfully Burgoyne's flanking manoeuvres on September 19 and October 7 while committing only a fraction of the men under his command. If Burgoyne wished to fritter away his command in such engagements, so much the better. But Gates was not about to take the unnecessary risk of committing his entire force—nearly two-thirds of which were green militia—to a general engagement. Time was on Gates's side; he knew it, and he used it to his best advantage.

Although Arnold received Gates's permission to leave for Philadelphia, and therefore no longer held any command, he remained in camp. Gates was content for him to do so, and was willing to let bygones be bygones. However, he warned Arnold that Livingston and Varick were untrustworthy, and for their own ends were poisoning his mind and creating prejudice and suspicion. Arnold refused to believe him.[30]

After more than two weeks of stalemate, Burgoyne sent a reconnaissance force to probe again the American left. He had been forced to put his army on half-rations on October 3, and his situation was rapidly becoming desperate. As soon as the enemy's activity was noted, Gates assumed personal command of the American left wing and engaged the British advance guard. Again, as on September 19, both sides committed more and more men until an engagement of major proportions had materialized. Although Gates maintained the overall command and direction of the battle, Arnold, as a volunteer, played an important role on the field of battle itself. The decisive action of the day occurred between three and four o'clock in the afternoon when the 1st, 2nd, and 3rd New Hampshire regiments struck the enemy right and Morgan's riflemen enveloped the British right flank and rear. As the British units on the extreme right attempted to change front to meet Morgan's men, they were struck by Dearborn's light infantry and driven back in disorder. In the end, Burgoyne's force was thrown back with heavy losses. Arnold, at the very close of the battle, while storming a German redoubt which guarded the right flank of the British camp, fell severely wounded in the same leg that had been hit at Quebec. Gates, upon this occasion, paid ample tribute to the "gallant General Arnold" in his official report to Congress.

Although the original plans of Burgoyne's campaign had not called for any assistance on the part of either General Howe or General Clinton, Burgoyne, after the reverses at Oriskany and Bennington, requested Clinton to make a strong diversion up the Hudson—possibly as far as Albany—which would force Gates to divide his army and meet the threat to his rear. However, although Clinton succeeded in capturing the American forts in the Highlands and proceeding as far north as Kingston, he failed to go far enough soon enough to do Burgoyne any good. Despairing of help, Burgoyne commenced a retreat on the night of October 8, leaving behind some 500 sick and wounded. Gates, however, was too quick for him. Having previously sent General John Fellows and some 1,300 Massachusetts militia to block Burgoyne's escape route, he sent the riflemen and light infantry after the fleeing enemy and on the 10th followed with the bulk of his army. By the 13th, Paterson's and Poor's brigades were in position on Burgoyne's western flank while the riflemen and light infantry had reinforced the militia on the north. With the Hudson to the east and the remainder of Gates's army south of him, Burgoyne had no other choice but to surrender.

Just at the last, Burgoyne received some assistance from Clinton. News of the latter's activity below Albany reached Gates while he was awaiting Burgoyne's answer to his demand for an unconditional surrender. Fearing for his rear, and wishing to move as soon as possible to protect Albany from this new threat, Gates accepted terms which would allow the British troops to be sent back to England on condition that they would not serve again during the war with America. The threat from Clinton proved an empty one. After burning Kingston on October 16, he retired to New York City. Eventually, as a result of well-founded suspicions that the British did not mean to honor the terms of the surrender agreement, Burgoyne's troops, or the Convention army as they came to be known, were not allowed to return to England. Instead they were interned in various prisoner-of-war camps for the duration of the war.

Although some criticism was leveled at Gates for accepting anything short of unconditional surrender, that did not materially affect the significance of the victory he had won, nor detract from its glory. Although France had given secret support to the United States since 1776, a major American military victory was necessary to bring her into a formal alliance with the new nation. Saratoga provided such a victory, made possible the American-French alliance, and turned England's struggle with her colonies into a world war involving, in the end, most of the European powers. Of more immediate importance, however, was the effect the victory had in lifting American morale, which had plummeted a few weeks before when Howe defeated Washington's army and captured Philadelphia. Unfortunately, it also invited invidious comparisons between the victorious Gates and the often defeated Washington. This in turn precipitated a series of events which divided the army and Congress in a manner unrivaled before or after the winter of 1777–78.

Congressional Criticism
Shifts to Washington

W HILE General Gates exceeded the hopes of even the most optimistic by defeating and capturing Burgoyne's army, General Washington confirmed the predictions of the pessimistic by failing to prevent Howe from capturing Philadelphia. It is not surprising that some concluded that Washington was not the best man for the supreme command.

Before the campaign of 1777 began, it appeared that Washington was in a good position to thwart any attempt by Howe to capture Philadelphia, and, indeed, win a decisive victory which might bring the war to an end. These were Washington's views when he outlined the situation for Schuyler on March 12. His main point was that it was essential to keep most of the American army concentrated near the center of the theater of war. Then, operating upon interior lines, it could be hurled with devastating effect against a divided enemy. This was a sound military axiom, and had Washington actually followed it, he might have enjoyed an outstanding success in the ensuing campaign.

Washington's reason for informing Schuyler of this maxim was to justify his decision not to send heavy reinforcements to the Northern army, and, indeed, to divert to Peekskill eight Massachusetts regiments originally intended to reinforce Ticonderoga. The principal British objective in the coming campaign, Washington contended, would be Philadelphia. He believed that reports of British troops being sent to Canada were a ruse by the enemy, and that those troops would eventually be sent to reinforce Howe for the drive on Philadelphia. The same view was expressed by Washington's aide, Alexander Hamilton, on April 5. No serious effort would be made in the Northern department, he confidently asserted. "Philadelphia is an object calculated to strike and attract their attention. It has all along been the main source of supplies towards the war and the getting it into their possession would deprive us of a wheel we could very badly spare in the great political and military machine."

Congress was understandably concerned with the fate of Philadelphia, and in April it requested Washington to establish a strong camp on the western bank of the Delaware. In this manner the city could be more certainly protected, and should developments in the north demand it, men could be sent from Philadelphia to Peekskill as easily as they could from the present camp at Morristown, New Jersey. "In the whole of this business, Congress mean not in any manner to interfere with the designs, or to counteract the judgment of your Excellency," Washington was informed, "but wish you freely to call up to headquarters, all, or any part of the troops encampt here as you shall please." There was one situation, however, which Congress was willing to admit would preclude the action they recommended. "Should the enemy propose to remain in Jersey to attack your army, or should your Excellency mean to make a decisive impression on them when your numbers are sufficient, in either of these suppositions, the troops ought not to be here."[1]

To allay congressional fears and ascertain Howe's intentions, Washington moved the main camp of the army south from Morristown to Middlebrook, New Jersey, in May. This move placed the American army in a better position to meet General Howe should he attempt to advance against Philadelphia. Nevertheless, it appeared that Washington's plans for the coming campaign had undergone certain changes since he wrote Schuyler in March. While he still placed an exaggerated value on holding Philadelphia—and would risk a general engagement to save it— the commander in chief no longer contemplated forcing a decisive battle on Howe; a decision which, considering the disparity in numbers and quality between the two armies, must be considered a wise one. So, when Howe made a few halfhearted attempts in June to draw the American army out to do battle, Washington declined the offer.

Hamilton correctly predicted to Robert R. Livingston on June 28, that such "Fabian conduct" would be criticised by some who would attribute it to "cowardice or weakness." But such critics could be ignored, and Hamilton firmly believed that it was sound policy not to risk everything in one general engagement, for if it were lost, might not the American cause be lost with it? Only if the situation of the army were truly desperate, or, alternatively, if numbers and other factors assured it success, should the Continental army risk a pitched battle with Howe's regulars. On the other hand, not as impressed with the value of Philadelphia as his chief, Hamilton concluded that Howe's only chance for victory in the coming campaign "lies in fighting us and giving a general defeat at one blow."

Given the situation existing in the Jerseys in June, Washington's strategy was undoubtedly correct. However, in early June the situation was suddenly and drastically changed, and Washington's response to this change left something to be desired. A few days after the fall of Ticonderoga, Howe suddenly pulled his troops out of New Jersey and placed a force of some 17,000 men aboard transports in New York Harbor—and there they remained for nearly three weeks.

At first, most of the American officers, Washington included, believed that Howe was preparing a strike up the Hudson to effect a junction with Burgoyne. Consequently, Washington shifted his camp northward to Morristown once again, detached units to reinforce the Northern army, and prepared to send even more men as soon as Howe made his move. Then, on July 23, Howe's force put to sea and disappeared to the southward.

With Burgoyne pressing toward Albany, the Northern army apparently in a state of panic, and Howe headed for an unknown destination, Washington was in a quandary. To add to the confusion, a message from Howe to Burgoyne was intercepted which informed the latter that an expedition against Boston would take the place of the one planned up the Hudson. "I am making demonstration to the Southward," Howe concluded, "which I think will have the full effect in carrying out our plan into execution—success attend you."[2]

This message was almost certainly bogus. Howe had never planned to make a move up the Hudson—at least not until Philadelphia should fall—and he certainly had no intention of returning to Boston. Based upon his last experiences in that city, it was the last place on the continent he would be likely to go. However, although Washington was skeptical—and failed to rush men to New England as a result—there were others who believed the report. Nathaniel Folsom, congressman from New Hampshire, reported that it was generally thought in Congress that Howe's objective was somewhere in New England.[3]

Washington, however, saw through Howe's ruse. On July 24, one day after Howe's departure, correctly assuming that the British objective was still Philadelphia, Washington left Smith's Clove on the Hudson and with the main army set off toward the Delaware. It is difficult not to speculate about the possible consequences had Washington acted differently. If instead he had turned northward and joined forces with the Northern army, he might have forced Burgoyne into an unconditional surrender by mid-August. Then, returning to Pennsylvania with the united armies, flushed with victory and outnumbering Howe, he could have dealt the second, and perhaps decisive, blow against the British.

To be sure, Howe might have occupied Philadelphia in the meantime, but, as Hamilton realized and reported to Gouverneur Morris on September 1, "Should he [Howe] be satisfied with the splendor of his acquisition and shut himself up in Philadelphia, we can ruin him by confinement. Should he leave a garrison there and go forward, we can either fall upon that or his main body diminished as it will be by such a measure with our whole force." Washington, along with Howe, still placed an unrealistic value upon Philadelphia.

The New England delegates objected to Washington's move toward Philadelphia for a different reason. They were still convinced that Howe would assist Burgoyne either by invading New England or by an operation up the Hudson. Nathaniel Folsom repeated this fear as late as August 5, although Howe's fleet had finally been spotted off the Delaware Capes.[4] James Lovell also expressed his conviction that Washington's move would "give Howe and Burgoyne full swing in New England and New York," although Gates, too, had assured him that Philadelphia was Howe's objective. "I do not know whether I tell his story right," he added, for once questioning the military wisdom of Gates, "for I did not believe what he said enough to fix it in my memory." Lovell's fears were soon dispelled by the sighting of Howe's fleet at the entrance to Chesapeake Bay. "We have found Howe again," he reported; "I thought he was lost in the Gulph Stream."[5]

On August 25, 1777, Howe landed his army at the head of Chesapeake Bay. With provisions for only three weeks, Howe had kept men and horses aboard ship for six weeks, and his army was somewhat unsteady when it finally came ashore. Some American observers speculated that the British army would be unable to move for some weeks while it recouped its strength and found horses to replace those which had died at sea. General Howe, showing uncharacteristic vigor, surprised everyone by immediately setting his army on the road to Philadelphia.

Washington now paid the price for ignoring his own maxim, which he had expressed to Schuyler some months before, against dividing his force in the face of the enemy. He was forced into a general engagement, seriously weakened by the absence of 3,000 Continentals he had sent to the Northern army. To compensate, Washington chose what he thought to be a strong defensive position with Brandywine Creek in his front.

General Greene's division, strengthened by two extra brigades, held the center of the line astride the Philadelphia road where it crossed the stream at Chadd's Ford, and the left was secured by General John Armstrong and 1,000 Pennsylvania militia. The right wing, consisting of three divisions, was under the command of General Sullivan. Howe's plan was simple enough. While General Wilhelm von Knyphausen, commanding one wing of the army, made a feint at Cadd's Ford, Lord Charles Cornwallis with the other wing would secretly cross the Brandywine some 12 miles upstream, and fall upon Sullivan's right and rear. Howe assumed that Washington would be careless enough not to post pickets at the higher fords. He assumed correctly. On the afternoon of September 11 the British attack was carried through as planned, and Washington came very near to losing his entire command.

The American army was saved from certain destruction by the tenacious fighting of Stirling's and Stephen's divisions which, with the Delaware regiment and Hazen's "Canadian regiment," held fast on the American right when the rest of Sullivan's command fled. Facing Howe's best troops, and outnumbered two to one, the Americans repeatedly repulsed determined attacks. Five times they were driven from their positions, and five times they counterattacked and regained the ground they had lost. Under overwhelming pressure, the American right finally gave way, but by that time Green had shifted two brigades to meet Cornwallis' men and cover the army's retreat. When darkness fell, the British and Germans were too exhausted to follow.

Although Washington had only 11,000 men as opposed to Howe's estimated 13,000, numbers in this battle did not make the difference. Washington was simply out-generaled. When Washington finally received news of Cornwallis' flanking column closing on his right, instead of being alarmed and taking immediate steps to meet it, he jubilantly informed Greene that Howe had made a terrible blunder by dividing his force, and the Americans could now press forward to victory. Subsequent events amply testify to the commander in chief's lack of perspicacity at that crucial moment.

Although most of the American army escaped, it sustained more than 600 casualties, at least half of whom were killed, and it could no longer form an effective shield for Philadelphia. Washington soon withdrew his army across the Schuylkill, leaving Wayne's division of 1,500 men to harrass the enemy. Wayne was spoiling for a fight, and on the night of September 19 reported that he was in position opposite Howe's exposed right flank. If Maxwell's division could be moved up to cover the enemy's left flank, and Washington circle to take Howe's center in the rear, then they would "complete Mr. Howe's business."

Wayne seriously overrated the ability of the American army to resume the offensive, and more seriously underestimated the intelligence and ability of his opponents. "I believe he [Howe] knows nothing of my situation," he confidently reported to Washington, "as I have taken every precaution to prevent any intelligence getting to him." On the very next night, at one o'clock in the morning, three brigades of British infantry, flints removed to prevent an accidental firing, fell with fixed bayonets upon Wayne's camp at Paoli, Pennsylvania. The surprise was complete, and without firing a shot, the British killed or wounded some 300 Americans and took nearly 100 prisoners.[6]

Through a series of skillful maneuvres, Howe managed to force Washington further to the westward, leaving Philadelphia unprotected. Informed that the city could no longer be defended, Congress fled to York, and the British entered the city without resistance on September 26. Washington, in one last desperate effort to recoup his losses, launched a massive attack against the British lines at Germantown on October 4. With the advantage of numbers (11,000 against 9,000) and a partial surprise, the battle at first seemed to be going in Washington's favor. However, the entire plan was far too complicated to have much chance of success under ideal conditions, and the presence of a heavy ground fog materially reduced those chances. Most of the 3,000 militia never came in contact with the enemy, while General Adam Stephen, apparently under the influence of strong spirits, led his brigade in a devastating attack against the rear of Wayne's division, which resulted in a general rout. Finally, after two and a half hours of intense fighting, the Americans were thrown back with casualties exceeding 1,000. The British, on the other hand, lost only half this number. In a few short weeks in September and October, with an army only slightly smaller than Howe's, the commander in chief had lost every engagement; sustained casualties in excess of 2,000 killed, wounded, and captured; and lost Philadelphia to the enemy. Little wonder that some in the army, and more in Congress, began to question his abilities as supreme commander.

Not that Washington had escaped criticism in the past. The loss of Fort Washington and the retreat through New Jersey the previous fall had led some to question his fitness to command. His fatal indecision over whether Fort Washington should be abandoned or held had been lamented by Col. Joseph Reed, then adjutant general. "Oh! General— an indecisive mind is one of the greatest misfortunes that can befall an army," he wrote Charles Lee on November 21, 1776. "How often have I lamented it this campaign." Indeed, Reed then looked upon Lee as the one man who could save the army from total destruction. Lee, of course, had been flattered by Reed's remarks, and inclined to agree with him. "Accident may put a decisive blunderer in the right," he had observed to Reed on Nov. 24, "but eternal defeat and miscarriage must attend the man of best parts if cursed with indecision." He then informed Reed that he was making haste to join the main army, "for to confess a truth," he immodestly remarked, "I really think our Chief will do better with me than without me."

Lee had been even more outspokenly critical of the commander in chief in a letter to Horatio Gates on December 13, 1776. "The ingenious manoeuver at Fort Washington has unhinged a goodly fabrick we had been building," he bitterly noted; "there never was so damned a stroke— entre nous, a certain great man is most damnably deficient." When Lee was captured by the British a few minutes after this letter was written, a figure around whom an anti-Washington faction could have collected was removed from contention.

With the successes at Trenton in December of 1776, and Princeton in January of 1777, criticism of Washington within the army had subsided. However, there were still occasional complaints by members of Congress who regretted the extensive powers they bestowed upon Washington before their panicky evacuation of Philadelphia in mid-December, 1776. According to one member, the New England states along with a few of the delegates from New Jersey [probably Jonathan Sergeant and Abraham Clark] were the most critical of the commander in chief. It was even felt by some that Congress wished to assume direction of the army. John Adams pooh-poohed suggestions of this sort, and explicitly denied that Congress had in any way interfered with Washington's control of the army. "Such a collection of lies," he observed to his wife, "would be a curiosity for posterity."[7]

The reverses suffered by Washington in the fall of 1777, however, once again brought forth criticism of his generalship. His losses that fall were the worst so far suffered by the American army—and, in contrast, the success of Gates at Saratoga was the outstanding victory of the war. Comparisons unfavorable to Washington were inevitable, as were speculations whether Gates could have coped with Howe more successfully.

In congratulating Gates on the outcome of the battle at Freeman's Farm, Governor Trumbull added that he had just been informed "of General Howe's having outgeneraled us, and stole a march for Philadelphia. . . . 'Tis strange," he concluded bitterly, "that such an army must continually retire without once daring to fight an enemy who at the same time they affect to consider as their inferiors." John Adams was more kind when he observed that "all the apology that can be made for this part of the world is, that Mr. Howe's march from [Head of] Elk to Philadelphia, was through the very regions of passive obedience. The whole country through which he passed is inhabited by Quakers." Thus, unlike Gates, Washington had not been heavily reinforced by militia.[8]

James Lovell, as usual, was far less charitable in his assessment, and informed Gates on October 5 that he and his army were being favorably contrasted to Washington and his. He also rather maliciously suggested that if Gates "would give Burgoyne a little leisure to exercise his talent at farce-writing which he discovered in the Boston blockade, he would furnish the work with a winter evening's entertainment at the expense of Congress and General Washington." Even Henry Laurens— not ordinarily one of Washington's critics—expressed his growing doubts to his son, John, who served on Washington's staff. "You know I abhor telltales but sounds hurt me exceedingly. I know the effects of loose tongues, I know the cruelty of tongues speaking the feelings of designing hearts, nevertheless I am afraid there may be some ground for some of these remarks."[9]

Open criticism of Washington was forestalled initially by an attempt to make General John Sullivan the scapegoat for the recent defeats. This tactic had a number of advantages for the New Yorkers and their allies in Congress. On the one hand they could blacken the reputation of a New Englander, and on the other, protect Washington from an unfavorable comparison with Gates, whom they loathed.

The key figure in attributing the American defeat to Sullivan was Thomas Burke, the North Carolina congressman, who was at Brandywine and observed some of the events of that bloody day. According to Burke, Sullivan was informed at 2 P.M. that a large body of the enemy was approaching his right flank, and accordingly began to make dispositions to receive the blow. "Soon after this," Burke reported, "General Sullivan was informed by a countryman, a major of militia, that he had come along the road which immediately led to that ford [where Cornwallis was crossing], and had seen no enemy, whereupon he dispatched information to General Washington that he was convinced from the countryman's intelligence that no enemy was upon that rout, and the General [Sullivan] in consequence thereof halted the troops destined to resist them." From this ill-considered move flowed all of the misfortune of the day. "These miscarriages snatched from my hopes the glory of a complete victory, which was certainly in our power, if Sullivan had not by his folly and misconduct ruined the fortune of the day. . . . This unfortunate general has ever been the Marplot of our army," Burke concluded, "and his miscarriages are I am persuaded owing to a total want of military genius."[10]

Despite the fact that all of the high-ranking officers involved in the battle testified that Sullivan was not in any way to blame for the defeat, "the Maryland officers in his division, the delegates of that state, the great Burke, the friends of St. Clair and connexions of Schuyler accomplished to cast such reflections upon his want of capacity . . . that a majority . . . affected the resolve to recall Sullivan till his conduct should be enquired into." When this move was blocked by a special request from Washington that the recall be suspended until a more opportune time, Samuel Chase of Maryland attempted to have the Maryland troops removed from Sullivan's division. This, as James Lovell observed, "would have been in effect throwing out S[ulliva]n, for the soldiers of other divisions would be unwilling to serve under a man discarded by the Marylanders." With some difficulty, this attempt to dispose of Sullivan was also defeated.[11]

Sullivan reacted passionately against attempts to place the odium of defeat on him. "I was . . . astonished to find that upon the vague report of a single person who pretends to know all about the late battle of Brandywine (though I am confident he saw but little of it) Congress should pass a resolve to suspend me from the service. . . . If the reputation of general officers is thus to be sported with upon every vague & [?] report," he informed President Hancock, "those who set less by their reputation than myself must continue in the service." Thus, after giving a detailed account of his action on the day of battle, he announced his intention to resign.[12]

The arrival of Sullivan's letter provided an opportunity for Henry Laurens to discover exactly what was behind the attack on Sullivan. "We yesterday [October 9] received a long chatechistical letter from Gen. Sullivan," he wrote to his son, "the sequel of which is a desire to withdraw himself from the army, which gave me an opportunity of turning to a gentleman, 'did not I tell you this would be the effect of stigmatizing an officer upon the vague opinion and report of a member of Congress.' What do you think [al]though a very sensible man was his answer, [']Why did they then use my friend Schuyler so?['] The cases are by no means parallel but admit they are, would you complete the ruin of the 13 United States because a man in a party opposite to yours has done them an injury?"[13]

Laurens' opinion concerning the reasons for making Sullivan a scapegoat was borne out by Eliphalet Dyer. "Sch—ler and St—C—r were continually brot [sic] on the stage, and no one but a N E—d man could satisfye their resentments, and to have taken one of a low carracter, would not answer their purpose. Wherefore," he commiserated with Sullivan, "as they [Schuyler and St. Clair] were to be brot to a Court of Enquiry so must you, as they must be recalled till an enquiry could be had, so must you or our conduct must be deemed partial." Nonetheless, Dyer was optimistic concerning the future. The resolution recalling Sullivan had been forced upon the majority by a determined few at just the right moment, when spirits were at low ebb in Congress. Now, after calm consideration, and after Washington's letter, many regretted their hasty action. Indeed, by October 23 Dyer trimphantly reported to Sullivan that "you have obtained a complete victory and conquest over your enemies in Congress (and those who have attacked you without) they now wear long faces, they hang their heads, they are mute, you will hear no further from them; every attack which has been made upon you is now despised."[14]

With the failure to make Sullivan the scapegoat for the reverses suffered by the main army, the spotlight was again turned upon Washington by a group of congressmen led by James Lovell, Joseph Reed (now a Pennsylvania congressman), and Jonathan Sergeant. On November 17 Lovell wrote a letter to Gates which was so lavishly flattering that it should have embarrassed the general. However, the flattery was only an opening so that Lovell could broach the extremely delicate subject of having Gates replace Washington as commander in chief. "Repeated slights and unjustifiable arrogance combined with other causes to drive from the army those who would not worship the Image & pay an undeserved tribute of praise and flattery to the great and powerful," he bitterly informed the northern commander. "We have had a noble army melted down by ill judged marches—marches that disgrace their authors & directors—& which have occasioned the severest & most just sarcasm & contempt of our enemies." But the indignation of the public was being aroused, he assured Gates, and soon it would be "so great & so general that nothing inferior to a commander-in-chief will be able to resist the mighty torrent of public clamor & public vengeance." Having carefully baited his hook, Lovell enticingly wiggled it in front of Gates. "In short," he concluded, "this army is to be totally lost unless you come down & collect the virtuous band, who wish to fight under your banner, & with their aid save the southern hemisphere. Prepare yourself for a jaunt to this place—Congress must send for you—I have ten thousand things to tell."

If possible, Sergeant was more blunt in his opinion of Washington. "Things look gloomy below," he wrote. "We want a general; thousands of lives and millions of property are yearly sacrificed to the insufficiency of our Commander-in-Chief. Two battles he has lost for us by two such blunders as might have disgraced a soldier of three months standing,— and yet [we] are so attached to this man that I fear we shall rather sink with him than throw him off our shoulders. And sink we must under his management. . . . In short, I am quite a convert to Abraham Clarke's opinion: that we may talk of the enemy's cruelty as we will, but we have no greater cruelty to complain of than the management of our army."[15]

True to Lovell's prediction, Congress did eventually send for Gates—but not to assume the supreme command. Instead, as part of a general overhaul of the administrative organization of the army, a new Board of War was appointed with Gates as its president, and Timothy Pickering, Thomas Mifflin, Joseph Trumbull, and Richard Peters as the other members. Although he urged Gates to accept this position, Lovell lamented on November 27 that he could not take command of the army. "Good God! what a situation we are in! How different from what might have been justly expected! You will be astonished when you come to know accurately what numbers have at one time or another been collected near Phila. to wear out stockings shoes breeches. Depend upon it for every ten soldiers placed under the command of our Fabius 5 recruits will be wanted annually during the war. . . . I expect you will judge me to be in a very sour humor. I am so," he admitted. "For if it was not for the defeat of Burgoyne and the strong appearances of an European war, our affairs are Fabiused into a very disagreeable posture."

While his ears were being filled with flattery—both false and sincere—and criticism of Washington's abilities as commander in chief, Gates clashed with Alexander Hamilton over the number of troops that should be sent from Northern army to what Lovell sarcastically reported "the inconsiderate called the *grand* army." Washington still had hopes of defeating Howe and delivering Philadelphia. Despite the two serious defeats he had suffered, he believed that Howe was in a trap. Obstructions sunk in the Delaware River prevented the British fleet from reaching Philadelphia, and with a few more men the commander in chief felt he could force Howe to surrender. Howe seemed unaware of his danger, and instead of trying to escape, spent most of the autumn chasing Washington and the "grand army" through the hills northwest of Philadelphia. Washington, although he had a force nearly equal in size to the enemy, avoided a major clash.

On October 30 Washington directed Hamilton to go to Gates, explain the situation in Pennsylvania, "and to point out to him the many happy consequences that will accrue from an immediate reinforcement being sent from the Northern army." Hamilton was to have a good deal of discretion in how he chose to handle the business, but "what you are chiefly to attend to," Washington stressed, "is to point out in the clearest and fullest manner to Gen. Gates the absolute necessity that there is for his detaching a very considerable part of the army at present under his command to the reinforcement of this."

When Hamilton reached Fishkill, a few miles north of Newburgh, New York, he found that General Gates had anticipated Washington's needs. One week after Burgoyne surrendered, Morgan's riflemen and

Poor's brigade of Continentals were on their way south, and Hamilton met them at Fishkill. In addition, Learned's and Warner's brigades along with the New York militia were on the march to join the main army. If further reinforcements were necessary, Paterson's and Glover's brigades were posted at Coeymans, 13 miles south of Albany. Hamilton was not satisfied with Gates's efforts to support the main army, and further feared that General Putnam, commanding in the Highlands, might attempt to detain many of the troops sent from Albany to guard against another sortie by the British from New York City. He concluded that at most Washington could expect 4,000 reinforcements and he did not believe this was sufficient.[16]

Pressing on to Albany, Hamilton found that Gates had decided to detach one of his three remaining brigades—Paterson's—to join the rest of the troops already moving to reinforce the main army. On November 5, Hamilton expressed his displeasure to Gates for choosing the weakest of his remaining brigades for this purpose, and flatly stated that he could not "consider it either compatible with the good of the service or my instructions from his Excellency General Washington, to consent, that the brigade be selected from the three, to go to him." But that was not all. "I am under the necessity of requiring, by virtue of my orders from him," he brashly told Gates, "that one of the others be substituted instead of this; either General Nixon's or General Glover's, and that you will be pleased to give immediate orders for its embarkation."

Hamilton was being a little too officious. He had no authority to *order* General Gates to do anything. He was supposed to *convince* him of the need to send "a very considerable part of his army" to Washington, but since he was sending four of his six brigades, as well as Morgan's corps, Gates had complied with Washington's wishes before Hamilton even arrived in Albany. In addition, Hamilton's instructions specifically forbade him to interfere in any plans Gates might already have made for the disposition of his troops in a manner which might better serve the common cause. Indeed, only if Gates merely intended to put his army in winter quarters was the army to be stripped to aid Washington.

Gates, to be sure, had a number of plans for his troops of which he fully informed Hamilton. Some of them were to be maintained in the Highlands and in Albany to prevent another excursion by Clinton, which Gates feared might well happen. Another portion was to be used against Ticonderoga, which he believed could be secured before winter set in. This latter plan had been singled out by Washington in his instructions to Hamilton, and he had been specifically ordered not to interfere with it. Hamilton, however, chose to ignore his instructions and airily brushed aside Gates's plans as of no consequence. Actually, although he continued to badger Gates for more men, Hamilton had more than fulfilled his mission. By his own count some 5,000 Continentals, 2,500 New England militia, and 700 Jersey militia were on the march to the main army.

Since Hamilton represented his demands as those of General Washington, Gates agreed to send Glover's brigade as well. He did inform Washington that he had hoped that the 5,000 men he had ordered to the main army before Hamilton's arrival would have sufficed. Since this was apparently not the case, in compliance with orders, he was sending Paterson's and Glover's brigades—an additional 3,500 men. He warned that it was against his better judgment to do so, since it would be impossible to defend the Hudson Valley without those troops.[17]

It is important to emphasize the fact that Gates, while he may have had reservations concerning the wisdom of stripping the Northern army, never hesitated in sending virtually his entire command to reinforce Washington. His enemies—and future historians—would claim differently, but the evidence speaks for itself. The only block to that reinforcement was General Putnam, and he proved merely a temporary one. When the men began to pour into the Highlands from Albany enroute to Washington, Putnam toyed with the idea of holding them long enough to attack Clinton in New York. Thus, Hamilton, much to his dismay, found many of the Northern troops still at New Windsor when he returned there on November 9. He immediately berated Putnam for disobeying orders, and the next day wrote a furious letter to Washington denouncing the commander in the Highlands as a blunderer and an obstructionist and recommending his immediate removal from command. After cooling off a bit, he found that Poor's brigade had been detained because it was "under an operation for the itch," and Putnam, having given up his plan to attack Clinton, had ordered the other brigades forward. Characteristically, Hamilton never apologized for his abusive attack on Putnam—indeed he still insisted he was an incompetent and should be removed.

Apparently Washington and Congress agreed with Hamilton, for Putnam was shortly ordered to the main army and Gates's Northern command was enlarged to include the Highlands. Consequently, Gates, with the handful of men left in his department, had to secure both the northern and southern extremes of the Hudson River, and somehow execute his new duties as president of the Board of War.

Washington, in the meantime, having received his desired reinforcements, occupied a strong defensive position at Whitemarsh. Contrary to expectations, he did not show any inclination to make another attempt to defeat Howe. This quite naturally added to the growing discontent within and without the army. "What can be the cause of their lingering inactivity?" queried Jonathan Trumbull, Jr., from Albany. "They have before this [December 1] had large reinforcements from this army. If nothing can be done with the whole united Continental force, will there not be reason for complaint?"[18]

Congress was also dissatisfied, and unanimously opposed the desire of some of the officers to take the army into winter quarters. It wanted at least one more determined blow at the enemy and sent a committee to camp to expedite such a plan. Elbridge Gerry, one of the committeemen, reported that the army was stronger than it had been the entire campaign and hoped that Washington would agree to a winter campaign. However, the commander in chief soon revealed his disinclination to do so. On December 4, Howe with 12,500 men marched out of Philadelphia and, parading his men before the American position, attempted to entice Washington to attack him. Washington refused to be drawn, and Howe, declining to attack the strong American position, finally retired to Philadelphia. Within a few days, Washington ordered the army to begin its march to winter quarters at Valley Forge.[19]

The Conway Cabal

IN DECEMBER of 1777, amid rising criticism of General Washington's direction of the fall campaign, rumors spread of a junto of prominent civil and military leaders which intended to drive Washington from the army and make Horatio Gates commander in chief. Many officers and congressmen who spoke disparagingly of the main army's performance against General Howe found themselves stigmatized as members of an "anti-Washington party." As such they were attacked by Washington's defenders and ultimately silenced. George Washington emerged from the controversy as something of a demigod, henceforth immune to all criticism, while his rival, Horatio Gates, found himself shunted to an unimportant command and Thomas Conway—an Irish-French volunteer and the most outspoken critic of the commander in chief—was forced to resign his general's commission and return to France.

While certain facts were mustered to prove the existence of a cabal against Washington, there appears to be strong evidence that there was no such plot. Rather, the allegations and recriminations that swept Congress and the army during the winter of 1777–78 were the product of disappointment combined with the bitter factionalism which marked the Gates–Schuyler controversy. And that controversy was still very much alive. Schuyler partisans were convinced that Gates, by assuming command of the Northern army when he did, had won the laurels of victory which rightfully belonged to Philip Schuyler, and they grasped eagerly at any opportunity to discredit the victor of Saratoga.

On the other hand, Gates's supporters, in their elation over Burgoyne's defeat sometimes made unjust comparisons between the Northern success and Washington's repeated failures. This did not mean they felt Horatio Gates should be commander in chief—at the most three or four expressed opinions that could be so construed—but they did make clear their belief that Gates's presence with the main army would provide the spirited leadership necessary to drive Howe from Philadelphia. Given these circumstances, very little was needed to start rumors that men were conspiring in Gates's favor against Washington. And that little something extra was provided by the driving, often tactless ambition of Thomas Conway.

Born in County Kerry, Ireland, Conway emigrated to France when he was 14 and received a commission as lieutenant of dragoons in the French army. By the time the American rebellion erupted, Conway had taken part in several campaigns on the Continent, distinguished himself on the field of battle, and, at the age of 39 held the rank of colonel and commanded the Regiment d'Anjou.[1] Undoubtedly motivated by a desire to advance himself to higher rank in the French army, Conway obtained leave and offered his services to the United States. Noting his impressive credentials, Congress did not hesitate to grant him a commission as brigadier general on May 13, 1777. In doing so, many congressmen entertained the hope that Conway, fluent in both French and English, could render valuable services as an intermediary between Washington and other high-ranking American officers and the growing number of French volunteers seeking positions in the Continental army.

In the course of the ensuing campaign, Conway proved himself to be the competent professional soldier his credentials had portrayed. Commanding the 3rd Pennsylvania brigade, he and his men distinguished themselves in the battles of Brandywine and Germantown, and were singled out for special praise by General Washington. At the same time, certain facets of Conway's personality made it impossible for him to act as a liaison between his superiors and the French volunteers. Instead, he increasingly became a source of contention within the army.

The principal cause of Conway's growing unpopularity was his inability—or disinclination—to disguise his contempt for most of the amateur soldiers who composed the American army. Dismayed by the unmilitary deportment of the men in his brigade, he rigorously drilled them until they achieved some resemblance to soldiers. This may well have accounted for their outstanding performance in battle, but it certainly made Conway unpopular with his men. Also, his fellow officers viewed the drilling as implied criticism of their failure to do the same.[2]

Far more serious was the growing rift between Conway and Washington. Conway's immediate superior, Lord Sterling, complained constantly of Conway's refusal to obey any order he did not personally approve of, and so the commander in chief was prepared to find the

Irishman insubordinate. He was not disappointed. Most irritating of all to Washington was Conway's contemptuous silence at councils of war and free criticism afterwards of the measures adopted. As a result, the animosity between the two men was soon common knowledge in the army.[3]

Despite the growing enmity between Conway and Washington, the former's performance during the campaign prompted Congress to recommend his promotion to major general. At the same time, two other brigadiers were similarly recommended—Robert Howe and Alexander McDougall. The three names were then sent to Washington for approval. The Marquis de Lafayette wrote the new president of Congress, Henry Laurens, that he "heard with pleasure of the promotions of Congress, and I hope they will be confirmed; cannway [Conway] deserves such a distinction for his fighting so well this campaign."[4] Others, including Washington, were less enthusiastic.

Richard Henry Lee was the only remaining member of the Virginia delegation whom Washington knew well. It was to him on October 7, 1777, that the commander in chief communicated his opposition to Conway's promotion. Conway, he asserted, did not possess the "conspicuous merit" that would justify his advancement over the other brigadiers—all of whom were his senior. Lee promptly assured Washington that Congress would not make any appointment or promotion of which he disapproved. He also reported that it was generally believed that Conway would resign if he was not promoted. Some congressmen, however, believed that Conway would resign *when* he was promoted, since his sole object in coming to America was to "carry from this country home with him, a rank that will raise him in France."[5]

Richard Henry Lee was apparently unaware that Conway had another, perhaps more compelling reason for seeking promotion. In September, Congress had granted "Baron" Johann de Kalb a commission as major general, and at his insistence predated it to July 31 to give him equal rank with the Marquis de Lafayette. The "baron" was a Bavarian soldier of fortune named Johann or Hans Kalb. He had added the "de" when he joined the French army and the "baron" when he sought a commission from the Continental Congress. He had come to America with the backing of his protector, the powerful Comte de Broglie, to promote de Broglie's aspirations to displace Washington as commander in chief. Apparently realizing the impracticality of this scheme, Kalb decided to remain and accept a commission as major general.[6]

Conway bitterly complained that Kalb was his junior in the French army and that Congress, by making him his superior in the Continental army, "must injure my character very much." He therefore demanded immediate promotion and warned Congress that if this were not done he would be forced to give up his commission and return to France. Kalb categorically denied Conway's assertions, claiming that Conway "hardly was a sublieutenant" when he, Kalb, was already the major of a regiment. As a result of uncertainty concerning the respective ranks Conway and Kalb bore in the French army, and Washington's apparent hostility towards Conway, Congress decided to defer action on his request for promotion.[7]

This was the situation on November 3, 1777, when Washington received from Lord Stirling the startling and dramatic letter which precipitated the "Conway Cabal." "The enclosed was communicated by Col. Wilkinson to Major McWilliams," Stirling reported; "such wicked duplicity of conduct I shall always think it my duty to detect." The enclosure read: "In a letter from General Conway to General Gates he says—'Heaven has been determined to save your country, or a weak general and bad councellors would have ruined it.' "[8]

Washington immediately informed Conway that he had heard of the contemptuous remarks made by him in his letter to Gates, and quoted the excerpt Stirling had transmitted to him. Conway replied on November 9 that he was not certain those were the exact words he had used since he had not kept a copy of his letter to General Gates. But he readily admitted that he had been critical of Washington's handling of the late campaign.[9] In fact, the quotation was bogus. When Conway had a chance to examine his letter to Gates he discovered that it did not contain the offending words. Doubt was also cast upon the identity of the man who gave the false information to Major McWilliams. Wilkinson vehemently denied he did so, and hinted that it could have been another of Gates's aides—Major Robert Troup, a close friend of Alexander Hamilton, who might have confided in the latter when he was in Albany to gather reinforcements for Washington's army.[10]

Despite the vagueness of the accusation against Conway, Washington apparently never questioned its authenticity. Equally surprising was his extreme reaction to Conway's alleged criticism. Considering the personal enmity between the two men, Washington could hardly have expected more flattering remarks from Conway. Furthermore, Washington must have been aware that many of the other French officers were disillusioned with his leadership and often more outspoken in their criticism than Conway. Only a few weeks before the Conway incident, Kalb, in assessing Washington's capacity as a general, decided that "il est trop lent même indolent, beaucoup trop faible et ne laisse pas d'avoir sa dose de vanité et de présomption. Mon opinion est que s'il fait quelqu'action d'éclat il la devra toujours plus à la fortune ou aux fautes de son adversaire qu'à sa capacité" (he is too slow, even lazy, much too weak, and not without his dose of vanity and presumption. My opinion is that if he does anything sensational he will owe it more to his good luck or to his adversary's mistakes than to his own ability).[11] One can only speculate concerning Washington's reaction had he seen the contents of *that* letter!

Gates first heard about the affair from Thomas Mifflin. "An extract from General Conway's letter to you has been procured, and sent to headquarters. The extract was a collection of just sentiments," he concluded, "yet such as should not have been entrusted to any of your family." This letter arrived on December 3, a month after Stirling had written to inform his chief of the "wicked duplicity." And, when the messenger arrived with Mifflin's letter, Gates was just concluding a letter to Conway in which he attempted to dissuade the brigadier from resigning as a result of his not being promoted. Since Mifflin reported that Washington had sent the incriminating excerpt to Conway, Gates added a postscript asking from which of his letters the extract was copied so that he might detect "the person, who has been guilty of that act of infidelity."

Although Washington had not informed Gates of the incident, the latter felt obliged to write to the commander in chief on December 8. He did not at this time contest the content of the excerpt since he did not yet know what it was, but he did call for a full investigation to discover who had betrayed his private correspondence with General Conway. To expedite such an investigation, he asked Washington to disclose the name of the person who had supplied the information, "and it being unknown to me, whether the letter came to you from a member of Congress, or from an officer," he concluded, "I shall have the honor of transmitting a copy of this to the President, that the Congress may in concert with your Excellency, obtain, as soon as possible, a discovery, which so deeply effects the safety of the States."

More than a month was to pass before Washington replied to this letter, and in the meantime matters were complicated by Conway's renewed efforts to attain higher rank. Although Conway informed Gates on November 9, 1777, that he had sent his resignation to Congress, he also indicated that he would be willing to serve "the cause in which General Mifflin is engaged" if he could do so with propriety. Conway here refers to the interest he had in common with Mifflin in seeing better discipline instilled in the Continental army, and indicates that despite his blustering he was not yet ready to resign his commission.

Indeed, two days later, Conway wrote Mifflin (a member of the

Board of War) and expounded upon his knowledge of the various European methods of training and disciplining troops. He then mentioned that at a recent council held at headquarters it was decided that the army needed an inspector general to perform just such duties for the Continental army. Although he did not come right out and ask for the appointment, it was clear that he wanted it. And, despite the fact that Richard Henry Lee reported to Washington on November 20 that "Gen. Conway has not lately been mentioned in Congress," he was promoted to major general and made inspector general of the army with little opposition on December 13, 1777.[12]

Knowing that Washington would not be pleased by his promotion and new appointment, Conway wrote to him explaining that he had only the interest of the United States at heart in filling the post of inspector general and that the rank of major general was "absolutely requisite for this office." With something less than complete candor he also declared that he had "neither apply'd nor solicited for this place." However, he informed the commander in chief, if his appointment was in any way "productive of any inconvenience or in any ways disagreeable" he was ready to resign immediately and return to France.[13]

Washington informed Conway on December 30 that his "appointment of Inspector General to the army, I believe has not given the least uneasiness to any officer in it." But he added that Conway's promotion to major general would raise objections among the brigadiers. "By consulting your own feelings upon the appointment of the Baron de Kalb," he observed, "you may judge what must be the sensations of those brigadiers, who by your promotion are superceded." In fact, General Sullivan had informed Washington that very day that several of the general officers intended to lodge a formal protest against the promotion with both the commander in chief and Congress.

Although Washington's reply was cold and formal, it was not openly hostile. The fact that Conway chose to interpret it as such indicates that he probably never intended to act as inspector general, and, as had earlier been hinted, he merely wanted the rank of major general so that he could return to France and gain promotion in that army. This seems to be the only reasonable interpretation of his quick reply in which he revealed his open contempt for Washington by sarcastically comparing him to Frederick the Great. "What you are pleased to call an extraordinary promotion is a very plain one," he rather immodestly informed Washington. "There is nothing extraordinary in it, only that such a place was not thought of sooner. The general and universal merit, which you wish every promoted officer might be endowed with, is a rare gift. We see but few men of merit so generally acknowledged. We know but the great Frederick in Europe, and the great Washington in this continent. I certainly was never so rash as to pretend to such a prodigious height."[13]

His insult to Washington was intentional, but its full consequences could not have been suspected by Conway. He surely did not wish to offend Lafayette, but through his actions he succeeded in making that influential gentleman his enemy. The Marquis de Lafayette, because of his connections with the French court, had been granted a commission as a major general in the Continental army. For the same reason he became the leader of the French officers who had also obtained Continental commissions. As such he had at first advanced Conway's pretensions and considered him a brave and capable officer. However, Conway's criticism of Washington, his subsequent promotion and appointment as inspector general, and the open contempt he now evinced for the commander in chief turned Lafayette against him.

Although he still thought Conway "a very brave and very good officer," Lafayette realized that he was also an opportunist. Conway "calls himself my soldier," Lafayette advised Washington, "and the reason of such behavior for me is that he wishes to be well spoken of at the French court, and his protector, the Marquis de Castries is an intimate acquaintance of mine."[14]

There were others who concurred with this estimate of Conway's character. Major John Laurens, one of Washington's aides, informed his father, Henry Laurens, that "When General Conway went from camp he gave out that he meant to return to France, his countrymen understood that manoeuvre; it has succeeded to his wish, and I believe now he is exceedingly indifferent whether he acts inspr. genl. or no. I am rather inclined to think that he prefers returning with his splendid titles to France, where he hopes to obtain a lucrative and peaceful office."[15] This assessment of Conway assumed additional importance due to the fact that Henry Laurens was the new president of Congress, having succeeded Hancock in November of 1777.

While both Lafayette and John Laurens appear to have assessed Conway's character accurately, they were mistaken about his plans for an early return to France. In a letter to General Gates of January 4, 1778, Conway revealed no inclination to leave the army—although he did make it clear that Washington's hostility might make it impossible for him to perform his duties as inspector general. His principal reason in writing, however, was to inform Gates that he had discovered the culprit of the excerpted letter episode. In a private conversation with General Sullivan that officer had told him the whole story. While Wilkinson was on his way to Congress with the news of Burgoyne's surrender, he had stopped at Reading and given Lord Stirling, in writing, the extract allegedly from Conway's letter. Lord Stirling had then transmitted the extract to Washington. Further, Sullivan asserted "that he had heard Lord Stirling mention this in public company before several general officers." Conway had thereupon sought out Wilkinson and asked for an explanation. "He assured me that he had read my letter to you several times, and that the paragraph attributed to me in that letter, and transmitted to General Washington, was not in it. Whether, General Wilkinson[16] has been guilty of indiscretion," Conway concluded, "or Lord Stirling of something worse, I cannot determine. But I think no body is injured in this more than you and I."

On the same day that Conway was writing to the victor of Saratoga, Washington answered Gates's letter of December 8, 1777, which he had just received. He too informed Gates that it was Wilkinson who had given the incriminating excerpt to Lord Stirling. However, he had an interesting interpretation of that incident. At the time, Washington declared, "I considered the information as coming from yourself, & given with a friendly view to forwarn, & consequently forearm against a secret enemy, or, in other words, a dangerous incendiary, in which character, sooner or later, this country will know Gen. Conway, But— in this, as in other matters of late, I have found myself mistaken."

Washington was displeased that Gates had seen fit to send a copy of his letter of December 8 to Congress. "But, as some end doubtless was intended to be answered by it, I am laid under the disagreeable necessity of returning my answer through the same channel."[17] In this Washington was being a trifle hypocritical, for he had already laid his exchanges with Conway before Congress. Thus, he unjustly berated Gates for involving Congress in the Conway affair. Also, aside from the fact that Washington had himself already brought Congress into the picture with regard to Conway, the Conway–Gates letter was no secret in either military or civil circles. Understandably, Gates felt the need for an investigation to save his reputation in the eyes of both his fellow officers and the members of Congress.

Washington's dislike for Conway is easily understood. He was by all accounts self-seeking, conceited, and critical of his superiors to the point of insubordination. However, the reasons for Washington's quick condemnation of Gates are not as clear. It appears that as late as the previous spring the two men had still been on very friendly terms with one another. In part, perhaps, the campaign of 1777 and the differing fortunes of the two altered their attitudes toward one another. Washington, always conscious of his own shortcomings, probably blamed himself for his failure to stop Howe. However, when others joined in this criticism, and when his failure was contrasted with Gates's success, a tinge of jealousy may have colored his feelings toward his former friend. Gates, for his part, allowed his head to be turned by flattery, and in his new role as public hero was much too inclined to listen to criticism of the commander in chief. Thus, the ingredients for misunderstanding and suspicion were present by January of 1778.

Another important factor in the growing rift between Washington and Gates was the failure of the two to meet and make clear their respective positions in the affair. For a number of reasons, the letters they exchanged served only to complicate matters and create further misunderstandings. The best example of this is found in Washington's letter to Gates of February 9, 1778. At that late date, Washington still did not understand certain important facts concerning Gates's response to the Conway letter affair. "It is not unreasonable to presume," he wrote, "that your first information of my having notice of General Conway's letter came from himself, there were very few in the secret, and it is natural to suppose, that he being immediately concerned, would be most interested to convey the intelligence to you. It is also far from improbable, that he acquainted you with the substance of the passage communicated to me; one would expect this, if he believed it to be spurious, in order to ascertain the imposition and evince his innocence. . . . If he neglected doing it, the omission cannot easily be interpreted into anything else, than a consciousness of the reality of the extract, if not literally at least substantially. If he did not neglect it, it must appear somewhat strange that the forgery remained so long undetected; and that your first letter to come to me from Albany of the 8th of Decmr. should tacitly recognize the genuineness of the paragraph in question."

This string of suppositions and probabilities, which in Washington's mind convicted Gates of deception at the very least, was based upon a false premise. Gates heard of the affair from General Mifflin, not Conway, and Mifflin did not know or did not tell what the excerpt contained. Contrary to Washington's assertion, then, Gates had no knowledge of the contents of the excerpt when he wrote his letter of December 8. Indeed, it appears that Gates did not have this information until he received Washington's letter of January 4!

Gates, on the other hand, further aroused Washington's suspicion by not showing Washington Conway's letter when he discovered that the excerpt was a forgery. Instead he gave it back to Conway who claimed he did not have a copy of it. Conway then proceeded to show the original to a number of congressmen and even suggested to President Laurens that it be published. Laurens quickly scotched this idea, and although Conway did not show him the letter, Daniel Roberdeau did. Thus he could report on January 27 that "it is true General Washington was misinformed, the letter does not contain the words which had been reported to him, but ten times worse in every view."[18] Apparently the real letter was a damning critique of the conduct of Washington's campaign the previous fall, and Gates concluded that it was up to Conway to decide whether or not Washington should be informed of its true content. It was a difficult decision for a man of honor to make. However, in view of the fact that it was a confidential letter, Gates believed he acted correctly in returning it to the sender. It is surprising that Washington expected him to do otherwise.

Another complicating element in the Conway Cabal was the existence of a faction in Congress critical of Washington's leadership. Indeed, it is *the* factor which tended to make the cabal appear far more serious than it actually was. There had always been those in Congress who refused to view the commander in chief as a demigod, and this group was naturally enlarged as a result of the military reverses of 1777. The hard core of Washington's critics in Congress consisted of Benjamin Rush and Joseph Reed of Pennsylvania, Jonathan Sergeant and Abraham Clark of New Jersey, and James Lovell of Massachusetts. After the reverses at Brandywine and Germantown, James Duane of New York may have joined the group.[19] In addition, there were many more who were now convinced that Washington was something less than infallible.

The division between Washington's defenders and his critics was made even more bitter because it was superimposed upon the factionalism associated with the Gates–Schuyler rivalry. Schuyler, although removed from command, still had his champions who wished to see him restored to that command as soon as he was cleared of any blame for the loss of Ticonderoga. In general, the champions of Gates were associated with the critics of Washington, while Schuyler's supporters defended the commander in chief. Of course, James Duane is a notable exception, and there were some who had favored placing Gates in the Northern command who were not critical of Washington's leadership. For the most part, however, the factions were nearly identical.

This development should not have surprised anyone—nor alarmed them. Those who had extolled Gates's military prowess were naturally gratified by the verification of their opinion provided by the victory at Saratoga. It was also to be expected that some would conclude that Gates had greater ability than the unsuccessful Washington. The thing which is really surprising is that only a very few members of Congress ever seriously thought of removing Washington from the chief command. Nevertheless, the extent of the cabal was greatly exaggerated by those who confused the critics of Washington with those who sought his removal.

George Washington himself was partially responsible for this confusion. The mere fact that he took notice of the criticism leveled at him and sought to justify his actions—when he had never deigned to do so before—seemed to indicate the existence of a serious plot to depose him. His increasing sensitivity to criticism of his conduct of the last campaign and the unfavorable comparisons which were made between the fortunes of the Northern army and those of the Grand army were in part responsible for the intensity of his reaction. However, the commander in chief's suspicions were further inflamed by those who were closest to him—the Marquis de Lafayette, Nathanael Greene, and John Laurens, in particular.

In December the Marquis took it upon himself to inform Washington of his enemies in Congress. "There are open dissensions in Congress," he reported; "parties who hate one another as much as the common enemy, stupid men who without knowing a single word about war undertake to judge you, to make ridiculous comparisons; they are infatuated with Gates without thinking of the different circumstances, and believe that attacking is the only thing necessary to conquer. Those ideas are entertained in their minds by some jealous men and perhaps secret friends to the British government who want to push you in a moment of ill humor to some rash enterprise upon the lines or against a much stronger army."[20] It was indicative of Lafayette's impetuosity that he did now allow his ignorance of American politics to prevent him from thus analyzing actions by members of the Continental Congress. Some of the suggestions—particularly those which imputed treason to some of the delegates—were too fantastic for Washington to heed, but the rest he may well have been inclined to believe.

John Laurens reflected the views of Washington's official family when he wrote his father, President of Congress Henry Laurens, that "a certain party, formed against the present commander in chief" were supporting General Conway. At the head of this party, he reported, was General Thomas Mifflin. "I hope some virtuous and patriotic men," he concluded, "will form a countermine to blow up the pernicious junto spoken of above."[21] Laurens' opinion was of particular significance.

In early January of 1778, Lafayette apparently expressed the opinion of those close to Washington as to the nature of congressional factionalism when he wrote President Laurens that "it is perfectly clear to every body that Congress is divided in three parts—the first and I wish it can be more numerous, those virtuous citizens, who desire truly

happiness success and freedom to the whole continent, without any base self-interest . . .—the second part is what is called the southern party, or Gates's faction, or Mifflin's forces . . . ,—the third party is the northern faction—those two last were since a long time silently working one against another, but now ready to break up in open dissensions— let us consider what has been done since some days. General Gates's success have turned all the heads and raised his party to the highest degree—some have been audacious, ungrateful, and foolish enough as to hope it would reflect on General Washington's reputation and honor— men indeed to be pitied as well as despised!—they erect themselves abso- lute judges without having the least idea not only of military knowledge, but even of common sense." As final proof of a scheme to lessen Washington's authority and prestige, Lafayette pointed to the fact that Congress made "a distinction between his [Washington's] army and this of General Gates—the Northern department the commander in chief of the northern troops and so on."[22] He overlooked or was ignorant of the fact that Washington himself had recognized the Northern department as a separate command the previous year when he declined Congress' invitation to name Schuyler's successor.

Dr. James Craik, an old friend of Washington, further fed grow- ing fears of a junto. After visiting the camp, he wrote his friend, "I was informed by a gentleman whom I believe to be a true friend of yours, that a strong faction was forming against you in the new Board of War and in Congress." He had not informed Washington of this while at the camp because he wished to verify the report on his way south through Pennsylvania and Maryland. "All the way down I heard it and I believe it is pretty general over the country. . . . It was said that some of the Eastern and Southern members were at the bottom of it. Particu- larly," he warned, "one who has been said to be our enemy before, but denied it, R.H.L. [i.e., Richard Henry Lee] and that G-C M——n [i.e., Mifflin] in the new Board of War was a very active person. This last I am afraid is too true." Craik was wrong about Lee's involvement in the cabal. Both he and Washington had been warned against Lee by Benjamin Harrison, Lee's foremost political enemy.[23]

With the exception of his erroneous accusation of Richard Henry Lee, Craik's letter merely confirmed what Washington already sus- pected concerning the machinations of Mifflin. Far more shocking in- formation came from Patrick Henry, who was now governor of Virginia. Henry had received an unsigned letter from York which deplored the present condition of the army and offered as a solution the removal of Washington and his replacement by either General Gates, Lee, or Conway. The shock, for Washington, was that Henry identified the author as Dr. Benjamin Rush, a man whom Washington until then had counted a close friend. By now it must have seemed to the commander in chief that no one was above suspicion.[24]

The most direct and violent attack upon the commander in chief was saved until last, however. On January 26 a member of Congress delivered to Henry Laurens a sealed document which had been discovered on the stairs of the building in which Congress was meeting. After quickly perusing the contents, Laurens immediately dispatched the incendiary missive to Washington. Entitled "Thoughts of a Freeman," it was a detailed condemnation of Washington's leadership with special attention to the failures of his campaign of the previous fall. "The proper method of attacking, beating, and conquering the enemy has never yet been adopted by the commander-in-chief," the anonymous author charged. Also, "the late success to the northward was owing to a change of commanders;" and "that the southern army would have been alike successful, had a similar change taken place." And, finally, the most damning accusation, "that the people of America have been guilty of idolatry, by making a man their god; and the God of heaven and earth will convince them by woeful experience, that he is only a man; that no good may be expected from the standing army, until Baal and his worshipers are banished from the camp."[25]

Small wonder that Washington and his close associates feared that a powerful cabal was forming to force a change in the chief command. However, while there was some basis for their fears, most of the Conway Cabal was a product of the suspicious imagination of a few of Washington's friends, which at times bordered upon hysteria. Henry Laurens, after nearly giving way to his son's mounting fears, was finally able to view the situation calmly and assess its true proportions. "I think the friends of our brave and virtuous General," he wrote his son on January 12, "may rest assured that he is out of the reach of his enemies, if he has an enemy, a fact of which I am in doubt of. I believe that I hear most that is said and know the outlines of almost all that has been attempted, but the whole amounts to little more than tittle tattle, which would be too much honored by repeating it."

Laurens, as president of Congress, and with a long-standing reputation of avoiding attachment to any faction, was in a particularly good position to analyze the true nature of the cabal as far as Congress was concerned. He testified that he had never heard Washington's virtue, bravery, or military abilities questioned by a member of Congress. There had been the inevitable comparisons between Gates's success in the North and Washington's lack of it in Pennsylvania, but, he observed, "Answers are easily given to such silly remarks, when one is disposed to reply." Finally, he attempted to dispel any remaining fears with the following observations:

> I am not insensible that Gen. Washington has been in several instances extremely ill used by the neglect of those [i.e., Congress] who ought to be his grand support and to prevent every cause of complaint on his part, but if I were with him half an hour and would persuade myself he wanted information, it would be very easy to convince him there has not been anything *designedly* done or omitted to affront him— I speak of so large a majority as 9 in 10.
>
> The General very well knows that we are, and will continue to make suitable allowances for all defects seeming or real. We are in a state of infancy, yet thank God, we are not quite so foolish nor so wicked as our parent. Men whisper and very harmless things too about Gen. Washington. Loud bellowing scandal appears in every newspaper upon the name of his antagonist Sir William—but I will dwell no longer upon this matter.[26]

Henry Lauren's letter, which John showed to Washington, had the desired effect. The Conway cabal was now recognized for what it was— the product of a handful of malcontents of whom only Thomas Mifflin and Thomas Conway showed any real malice toward Washington. After the receipt of Laurens' letter, no more was heard from Washington's official family concerning plots or cabals.

Having dispelled the hysteria associated with the cabal, Laurens turned his efforts to patching up the differences between Gates and Washington. "In conversation with Gen. Gates without speaking on my side," Laurens wrote his son, "I discovered an inclination in him to be upon friendly terms with our great and good General." Gates also indicated to the president that he disapproved of the sentiments expressed by Conway in his now infamous letter, and further, upon being informed of Conway's letter to Washington in which the latter was compared to Frederick the Great, Gates agreed with Laurens that Conway had been "guilty of the blackest hypocricy—if not, he is chargeable with the guilt of an unprovoked sarcasm, and is unpardonable." In fact, Gates convinced Laurens that he had never consciously been involved in any cabal against the commander in chief. Conway, Laurens was convinced, was the solitary villain of the piece. "Shall such a man separate friends or keep them assunder?" he queried. "It must not be."[27]

John Laurens could soon report the happy effect his father's letter had had on the commander in chief. "He seems sensible that the gentleman who you mention to have conversed with you upon certain matters, is only the instrument of more dangerous and inveterate personages," John Laurens informed his father.[28] Obviously, Washington was not fully convinced of Gates's innocence, but he was willing to give him the benefit of the doubt and, rather unflatteringly and unfairly, assume that he was the dupe of more ambitious men.

Nevertheless, while Gates and Washington never resumed their once cordial relationship, they slowly recovered a mutual respect which made it possible for them to continue to work together until the conclusion of the war—Washington as commander in chief and Gates, eventually, as second in command of the army.

Thus ended the Conway Cabal—a French concoction which, like soufflé, was mostly air. For their part in the affair, both Conway and Mifflin found they had no future in the army and eventually resigned. As for Congress, by the spring of 1778 no one would admit that he had been a party to the criticism directed at the commander in chief. Washington eventually benefited the most from the cabal. Henceforth he was to be virtually immune from criticism of his conduct of the war—past or present.

To Yorktown and Beyond

THE WAR was far from over in the spring of 1778. Yorktown was still three and a half years away and a treaty of peace some five years. Nevertheless, a major turning point had been reached and passed. Factionalism was on the decline in both Congress and the army, and, as a result, civil–military relations steadily improved from the nadir they had reached during the winter of 1777–78. There were a number of reasons for these developments. For one thing, the agreement on a final draft for the Articles of Confederation in November 1777 had removed one of the primary causes of factionalism in Congress. Although differences remained concerning the nature of the central government, these differences were no longer a matter of immediate and pressing urgency of the kind which produced serious division in Congress.

Equally important, however, was the change in the nature of the war itself. With the signing of the alliance with France, the American rebellion was submerged in a world war which was little more than an extension of the great war for the empire of mid-century. Consequently, Great Britain could no longer devote the attention and effort to the war in America that she had before 1778. Following the British withdrawal from Philadelphia to New York in the late spring of 1778, General Clinton, who relieved Howe as commander in chief on May 8, refrained from mounting a major offensive until the opening of the southern campaign in 1780.

From a war of motion, ranging from one end of the colonies to the other, the war became relatively static, and was limited to a few restricted spheres of operations—the largest and most active encompassing New York City and its environs. Limiting the scope and importance of military operations imposed limitations on ambition and, consequently, personal rivalry among officers in the Continental service declined markedly. Limiting the scope of military operations also eased relations between the army and Congress by virtually eliminating a major cause of friction between the two—the losing of major battles.

In addition, the lessening need to appoint or promote general officers was productive of greater harmony between Congress and the Continental army. The appointment of general officers had been one of the most divisive responsibilities of Congress ever since June of 1775. After the spring of 1778, however, because of the inability of Great Britain to increase her military efforts in North America, the American military establishment reached a plateau. Of the 27 major generals appointed by Congress before Yorktown, 25 had been chosen by May of 1778. Similarly, of the 68 brigadier generals commissioned by Congress, 57 received their appointments before December of 1777.

Thus, while internal division within both Congress and the army can be found after 1778, it never again approached the intensity evinced in the Gates–Schuyler controversy or the Conway Cabal. Indeed, much of the lingering factionalism that can be discerned after 1778 was a result of the continued presence in Congress and in the army of some of the key participants of earlier factions and intrigues. Eventually, even these potential sources of discord were eliminated or neutralized.

General Thomas Conway, for example, resigned and returned to France by the end of the year 1778. Before doing so, however, he was involved in one final dispute which also marked the last major controversy touching the Northern department.

With the failure of the Burgoyne campaign of 1777, many in Congress as well as the army began to think in terms of an American counteroffensive in 1778 which might yet secure Canada for the United States.

Such a plan was first put forward by Horatio Gates as president of the Board of War. In view of the weakness of the British garrisons in Canada, he proposed that Brigadier General John Stark should lead a "burn and destroy" expedition into that country, and, if conditions were favorable, occupy Montreal. If successful, this move "would entirely prevent the enemy from annoying us from that quarter for a year or two beside the report of our forming a descent on Canada again would reach the Court in Great Britain and must perplex their consuls in carrying on the war for the ensuing year and would divide their forces as they would undoubtedly send a considerable part to Canada."[1]

Whatever merits the original plan may have possessed, they were soon lost sight of in a dispute over who was to lead the expedition.

As a result of discussions within the Board of War, the size of the proposed expedition steadily increased until, by late January of 1778, it was decided that one and perhaps two major generals, instead of the original lone brigadier, would be required to head the projected "eruption into Canada." At this point Conway was called in to confer with the Board of War, and rumors were rife that he was to be given the Canadian command.

The Marquis de Lafayette passed this news on to Washington and observed, somewhat immodestly, that "they will laugh in France when they'll hear that he [Conway] is chosen upon such a commission out of the same army where I am." He quickly assured the commander in chief that he did not mean that he would consider such a command, for it would take him from the main army and his command of the Virginia division.[2] Nevertheless, when Lafayette learned that it was the Board of War's intention to offer him the command, with Conway as second in command and Stark third, he did not refuse. Rather, he made a concerted but unsuccessful attempt to rid himself of Conway, whom he neither trusted nor liked.

In the end, after months of wrangling and petty bickering the Board cancelled the Canadian expedition. Although they agreed on nothing else, both Lafayette and Conway decided in mid-February, a few days after their arrival in Albany, that "the expedition was quite impossible." Despite the considerable support the plan at first enjoyed in Congress, that support quickly disappeared when it appeared that neither men, supplies, nor transport were available in the Northern department to carry it into execution. Then, as Henry Laurens reported in March, one could "scarcely find a man in Congress . . . who favored it. Except my own," when the expedition was first proposed, "I do not remember three dissenting voices. Now—well 'I never liked that Canada Expedition' is unanimous." Conway expressed disappointment, but Lafayette was mortified. He had written letters to France bragging that he was the commander of an army, and now he feared that he would be laughed at.[3]

Lafayette reassumed his command in the Grand army under Washington, but Conway, after being assigned to McDougall's new command in the Highlands, was ordered by that officer back to Albany where, he complained to Gates on April 2, "I have not . . . as many men as will guard the valuable stores in that place." Protesting against "this unaccountable way of boxing me about," he declared that he was determined to resign and return to France if a more suitable command was not offered him. His resignation was tendered to Congress on April 22 and accepted immediately.

It was soon evident that Conway had not expected Congress to accept his resignation; that he had proffered it with the hope that it would force Congress to give him an active field command. A further embarrassment was Congress' refusal to grant him the customary certificate of honorable discharge. Even Lafayette was moved to protest this slight. "You know my sentiments of some parts of his life, which remain fixed in my mind," he wrote Henry Laurens, "but General Conway is an officer in the French service, a gentleman of bravery and talents, and I can't refuse to my own feelings to beg you would mention to Congress that I have wrote you on his behalf. I do not believe they will deny some lines to him."[4] But, despite repeated pleas by Lafayette and Gates, Congress refused to grant the certificate.

On July 4, 1778, the issue of an honorable discharge was nearly made superfluous when Conway met General Cadwalader on the field of honor and was shot in the head. (Cadwalader was an outspoken supporter of Washington, and the duel was the climax of a dispute between the two officers concerning Conway's role in the cabal.)[5] The wound, though not mortal, forced Conway to delay his return to France until the end of November, when he departed, certificateless, aboard a French frigate.

Horatio Gates suffered far less than Conway as a consequence of supposed association with an anti-Washington junto. Throughout the late winter and early spring of 1778 he ably and energetically fulfilled his duties as president of the Board of War in York, and regularly rode out to Valley Forge to attend Washington's council meetings. While relations between the two men were not warm, there was little or no trace of animosity. Indeed, when Gates wished to take the field once more, the commander in chief warmly recommended him for the command in the Hudson Highlands—a command second only to that of the Grand army. Consequently, on April 15, Congress directed Gates to repair at once to Fishkill, resume his command of the Northern department, and secure the Hudson River and communications between New England and the Middle states.[6]

News of Gates's appointment goaded his old antagonist Schuyler to state bitterly to Richard Varick that it was what he had expected since Gates "has the luck of reaping harvests sown by others." Undoubtedly alluding to his own activities during the summer of 1777, Schuyler's remark represents an overly generous assessment of his own accomplishments. Schuyler's congressional supporters, particularly the New York delegates, may have shared his view but they accepted the appointment with better grace. "[Gates] has sense enough to see that he hath made some wrong steps," Gouverneur Morris informed Robert R. Livingston on May 3, "and tho' I will not promise his amendment as a man, I think

I can venture to say that as a politician he will not differ with the state who may afford him such essential aid or do him so irreparable mis-chief as ours in his present situation." Nevertheless, the New Yorkers had to meet him halfway, for, as Morris put it, "if . . . he doth not work well, remember you my friends are answerable for the consequences."

Since the British had no plans for the Hudson Valley in 1778, Gates's command in the Highlands was uneventful. He therefore wel-comed his reassignment in October to the Eastern department where the enemy's presence in Rhode Island promised some active campaigning. Leaving slightly more than 13,000 men to secure New York City, Clin-ton shifted British, German, and Loyalist regiments to Rhode Island until the total force there approached 6,000 men. Some Americans, in-cluding Gates, believed that the British were preparing to shift major operations in the next campaign to New England.

Despite the apparent promise, the Eastern command also proved a disappointment. Here too the war of motion that had marked the first three years of campaigning gave way to a static holding action that the British were to follow in the north until the end of the war. Fatigued by petty labors and in poor health, Gates requested and, at the end of 1778, received a furlough and spent several months recuperating at his home in Virginia, Traveller's Rest. From this semiretirement, Congress re-called Gates to meet the threat posed by a new British offensive in the South.

In June of 1780, Congress offered him the command of the South-ern army. The military situation in that quarter was critical, and the British were enjoying their greatest success of the war. On May 12, 1780, General Benjamin Lincoln, Gates's predecessor in the Southern command, surrendered Charleston and an American army numbering some 5,446 men to Sir Henry Clinton after offering little more than token resistance. The surrender at Charleston was the greatest single military disaster suffered by the Americans during the war, and it left the Carolinas and Virginia to the none too tender mercies of General Lord Charles Cornwallis and Colonel Banastre Tarleton.

Gates disregarded the warning allegedly made by his friend Charles Lee, "Take care lest your Northern laurels turn to Southern willows," accepted the appointment, and hurried south to check Cornwallis' ad-vance through the Carolinas. Only two days after taking command—with a force of some 3,000 men, two-thirds of whom were militia—he was forced to give battle to the British at Camden. The result was a stunning British victory that swept away the last organized American opposition in South Carolina.

The battle which destroyed Gates's military reputation began and ended in confusion. According to Gates's intelligence, Camden was held by a detachment under Lord Rawdon, while the main British force was some miles away. Consequently, Gates ordered a night march to bring his troops into position for a dawn attack. What he could not know was that Cornwallis, having rushed to the assistance of Rawdon, decided to adopt the same tactic with the result that the two armies collided at two o'clock in the morning of August 16th. The Americans retired in disorder and were reformed only with great difficulty to meet the British attack which came at daybreak. Cornwallis sent his regulars forward in a bayonet charge against the Virginia and North Carolina militia on the American left. The militia promptly threw down their guns and ran, sweeping with them all in their path. The American right, under Baron de Kalb and composed of the Continental veterans of the Delaware Regiment and the 2nd Maryland Brigade, held and even advanced. But with the collapse of the American left, they found themselves surrounded and suffered 650 casualties (including the mortally wounded Kalb) before the remaining 700 could extricate themselves. The British lost 324 men in the attack, but American losses were staggering—between 800 and 900 killed and wounded and about 1,000 captured.[7]

The American defeat was traceable to two causes, neither of which were within Gates's power to alter. His army was composed largely of raw, inexperienced militia, poorly equipped and fed. For the two weeks preceding the battle they had subsisted upon a diet of molasses, fresh meat, and green corn meal—with the result that most of the men were debilitated by dysentery when they faced the naked steel of the British bayonet charge. The second cause was the disposition of the troops which chanced to place the weakened militia opposite Cornwallis' strongest units. Some of Gates's enemies, Hamilton in particular, pointed to this deployment as the key to the disaster and proof of Gates's military incompetence.[8] It should be noted, however, that the deployment was made after the clash with the British advance guard in the early morning darkness, and Gates had no way of knowing what units would be arrayed against him or in what order. Finally, since Cornwallis seized the initiative and launched the attack on the morning of the 16th, the Earl was free to strike at the weakest portion of the line no matter what deployment Gates made.

Gates's disgrace and removal from command of the Southern department did not spring entirely from his defeat at Camden. If losing battles, even major ones, was in itself justification for removing generals, few if any of the American generals would have been in the field by the fall of 1780—including the commander in chief. Rather, Gates's disgrace after Camden was due to the efforts of his enemies in the army and in Congress to blacken his name and force him from the army.

Foremost again among Gates's enemies was his old rival, Philip Schuyler. The former commander of the Northern department was deeply embitterd by what he fancied was unjust treatment by the pro-Gates faction in Congress. Following his removal from command of the Northern army, and his and St. Clair's recall to face a formal inquiry into the loss of Ticonderoga, Schuyler was forced to wait more than a year before court-martial proceedings were initiated. The long delay was occasioned largely by the unsettling effects of Congress' flight to York during the fall of 1777 and the series of crises that followed in Congress and the army. On October 1, 1778, however, the court-martial finally convened at Fredericksburgh, New York, with Major General Lincoln sitting as president.[9]

Only one charge was brought against Schuyler, but it was a serious one: *"Neglect of Duty,* in not being present at Ticonderoga to discharge the functions of his command from the middle of June, 1777, until it was no longer possible to maintain Ticonderoga and Mount Independence . . . ,—under the 5th article of the 18th section of the Rules and Articles of War." More specifically, the indictment charged that "the main army of the Northern department being stationed at those posts, it was General Schuyler's duty to have been at the head of that army, and to have remained there, when he knew the enemy were actually advancing against it." Thus, in addition to neglect of duty, there was also an intimation of cowardice in the charges brought against Schuyler.

Such charges, had they been brought a year earlier, would surely have goaded Schuyler into an angry and sarcastic denunciation of Congress, and the resulting impression made upon the court would not have been a favorable one. However, it was a new, a reformed, Schuyler who presented his defense at Fredericksburgh. Neither by word nor deed did he derogate the wisdom of Congress, and, although he had often in the past complained of Congress' neglect and lack of support, he now produced selected letters illustrating that Congress had always shown the highest confidence in his abilities. Relying almost entirely on the written record—as selected from his letter books— Schuyler maintained that Congress had never intended that he should command at Ticonderoga, but, indeed, it had appointed General St. Clair specifically for that duty in May of 1777. Further, he presented evidence of his industry in collecting men and supplies for Ticonderoga, a task he could not have performed had he been at that post, located as it was in an uninhabited corner of the department under his command.

Schuyler's dignified and restrained demeanor undoubtedly made a good impression on the court and for this he was apparently largely indebted to James Duane, to whom he wrote proudly at the end of the trial that "not a single angry word has escaped me. If I have the happiness of living a little longer with you I shall become the meekest man of the age, and I shall by no means believe that a misfortune; I begin to make comparisons between what I was and what you have made [me]. In proportion as I conquer the unhappy propensity to anger which enslaved me I feel myself a happier and I hope a better man."[10]

Nevertheless, as soon as the court delivered its verdict of not guilty, some of his old peevishness could be detected in his letter to Congress begging that he now be allowed to resume his command in the army or to resign and thus to release him from "a situation of all others the most painful and which indeed I have incessantly experienced every moment of my tedious suspension." On the evening of December 3, 1778, Congress formally confirmed "the sentence of the general court martial acquitting Major General Schuyler, with the highest honor." Schuyler thanked the president of Congress for "the approbation expressed by Congress" of the court's verdict and begged that his resignation now be accepted.[11]

The New England delegates were, as ever, ready to accept his resignation, but New York, with the support of the Southern states, managed to table the request when it was first introduced on January 5, 1779, and finally to reject it on March 18. It soon appeared, however, that Schuyler actually did want to resign—if not at first, then certainly after long months of debate had given ample evidence that Congress did not unanimously approve of his past conduct. On April 19, 1779, on motion made by Samuel Adams, Congress accepted Philip Schuyler's resignation.[12]

Schuyler did not "fade away" into retirement; he soon returned to Congress as a delegate from New York. He played an active part in the reorganization of the army, and, as the head of various committees sent to confer with Washington, he soon established a cordial relationship with the commander in chief. Consequently, he was in an excellent position in 1780 to make sure that Gates paid the same price for defeat that he had been forced to render in 1777.

At the same time that Schuyler's influence in Congress was growing, Gates's was declining. By the fall of 1780 it was apparent to some observers that the "Eastern alliance," or Lee–Adams faction, was broken. This was due partly to the return to state politics of a number of the key members of the faction, but it was also the result of the appearance in Congress of a number of military men—John Sullivan, Ezekiel Cornell, and Theodorick Bland, to mention a few—who acted an independent role in Congress and, as admirers of Washington, had no love for the victor of Saratoga. Gates's position was further threatened by the Southern delegates in Congress. These, embarrassed by the performance of the Southern militia, were anxious to shift the blame, and Governor Nash of North Carolina (whose failure to supply the militia adequately from his state was a factor in the Camden defeat) was rather transparently anxious to make Gates the scapegoat.[13]

Thus, on October 5, nearly two months after the battle of Camden, Congress directed General Washington to order an inquiry into Gates's conduct as commander of the Southern army, and, until the results of such an inquiry could be determined, to appoint an officer to supersede Gates. Washington promptly selected Nathanael Greene to make the inquiry and to replace Gates as the commander in the South.

When Greene arrived at Charlotte, North Carolina to assume his new command, he discovered that circumstances made it inadvisable for him to conduct an inquiry into Gates's conduct. Some of the officers whose testimony would be required were either in Virginia or South Carolina, and there was a pressing need for Greene to find some means of coping effectively with the British who were continuing active operations in the Carolinas. Consequently, Greene regretfully informed Gates on December 6 that an inquiry affording him the opportunity of justifying his actions would have to be postponed until "the state of this army will admit of my convening a court agreeable to the tenor of my instructions."[14]

Nevertheless, Greene quickly discovered that "the battle of Camden here is represented widely different from what it was to the Northward." In particular, he found that "many officers think very favorable of his [Gates] conduct, and that, whenever an inquiry takes place, he will honorably acquit myself [sic]."[15] Indeed, Greene was so moved by Gates's fate that in writing to Hamilton on January 10, 1781, he philosophically observed: "What little incidents either give or destroy reputation. How many long hours a man may labor with an honest zeal in his country's service and be disgraced for the most trifling error either in conduct or opinion. Hume very justly observes no man will have a reputation unless he is useful to society, be his merit or abilities what they may. Therefore it is necessary for a man to be fortunate as well as wise and just."

Unfortunately for Gates, the Southern campaign which brought glory to Greene made it impossible to convene a court of inquiry, and the spring of 1781 found Gates in Philadelphia vainly trying to clear his name. Although many congressmen appeared embarrassed by Gates's situation, they hedged by declaring that "no former resolve of Congress should be construed into a suspension of the general." However, he was informed that more positive action would have to be taken by the commander in chief since it was not for Congress to pass judgment on the merits of military officers.[16]

Washington insisted that he could do nothing for Gates. Gates had been removed and an inquiry into his conduct ordered at the request of Congress. Such an inquiry had been and still was impossible because of the "unsettled state of affairs in that quarter [the South]." Further, no charges had ever been lodged with him concerning Gates's conduct, Washington declared, and "I neither had nor have any to make."[17]

Thus Gates found himself in a predicament. Circumstances barred Washington and Greene from conducting an inquiry in accord with the resolution of October 5, 1780, and Congress refused to change that resolution to meet the realities of the military situation in the South. In October of 1781 Gates again pleaded with the commander in chief to intervene on his behalf. "I view as distressing and lament your situation," Washington replied. "I sincerely wish Congress would direct some mode to give relief. But this is not for me to dictate."[18] At last, on August 14, 1782, Congress repealed the resolution of October 5 which directed a court of inquiry into Gates's conduct as commander of the Southern army. It was the only honorable thing Congress could do, especially as it had received a letter from General Greene stating: "That he had opportunity of viewing the ground where Gen. Gates fought, as well as the disposition and order of battle, from all which he was more fully confirmed in his former sentiments, that General Gates was unfortunate, but not blamable, and that he was confident from all the enquiries he has since made General Gates will acquit himself with honor."[19]

General Gates returned to the army in which he was now the second-ranking officer, and served directly under Washington. The two men apparently resumed that cordiality and mutual regard which had marked their relationship in those uncertain days when the war was young and Gates had been the commander in chief's adjutant general. Now, with many campaigns behind them, they awaited word that the treaty of peace had been signed so they could return to their neighboring plantations in Virginia.

The end of the war was distinctly anticlimactic. This was so not only because of the long months of military inactivity following the Yorktown campaign of 1781, but also because the passions, intrigues, and jealousies within Congress and the army which had marked the earlier, more tumultuous years of the war had generally subsided in 1783. True, the basic division between nationalist and federalist over the nature of the central government still persisted, but with the ratification of the

Articles of Confederation, their differences were cast in a new, more restrictive, constitutional framework from which the Constitution of 1787 would eventually emerge.

By the end of the war, the nature of the army and its relationship to Congress were no longer the divisive topics they had first been. Under the pressures of war, the federalists came to agree with the nationalists that a regular army, subordinate only to Congress, was a necessity. Earlier fears that the creation of such an army would result in a military despotism had proved groundless, and the cherished principle of civilian domination of the military was preserved.

Given the ingrained Anglo-American distrust of the military, this subordination of the army was perhaps not too surprising. Nevertheless, when the prospects for American independence were darkest—most notably during the winters of 1776–77 and 1780–81—the army could have wrested power from the feeble hands of Congress. However, guided by George Washington, the army's leadership shunned such a course.

Of course there were those both in the army and in Congress who leaned in the direction of militarism whenever Congress seemed unable to offer the leadership necessary to meet and survive a crisis. Such was the case when General Howe forced Congress to flee Philadelphia in 1776 and again in 1777. Another example was the Newburgh conspiracy, uncovered in March 1783, in which it was proposed that the Continental officers should take matter into their own hands if Congress failed to make equitable compensation for their past services. Washington nipped this plot in the bud with the same vigor he had consistently used throughout the war to check militaristic tendencies.

Indeed, the credit for maintaining that delicate and essential balance between the civilian and military authority so necessary in time of war was largely due Washington for his restraint in exercising his powers as commander in chief. By remaining aloof (with the notable exception of the Conway Cabal) from rivalries that involved many of his subordinates with factions in Congress, he became invulnerable to partisan politics and, in the course of the war, emerged as one of the few symbols of national unity. It is doubtful whether Charles Lee, Philip Schuyler, or Horatio Gates could have accomplished this feat had one of them succeeded to the chief command. They were too committed to partisan politics to have ever commanded that united respect and support of Congress which Washington eventually won. Nor is it at all certain that any one of them could have exhibited Washington's resolution in resisting the temptation to use the army to force decisions upon Congress.

Although he was referring specifically to the crushing of the Newburgh conspiracy, Washington might well have been reviewing the perilous course of civil–military relations during the preceeding eight years when he declared: "Had this day been wanting, the world had never seen the last stages of perfection, to which human nature is capable of attaining."

Appendix A

The rather bizarre story of the attempt to "murder" Colonel Richard Varick while he was visiting Ticonderoga in his capacity as deputy muster-master general of the Northern department is recounted in the two letters from Varick to Philip Schuyler which follow. Both letters are from the Schuyler Papers in the New York Public Library.

November 18, 1776
[Ticonderoga]

". . . . this morning I came over to this place, where I found every thing in confusion at headquarters. General Gates just heaving off with General Arnold & to my astonishment, was informed that Maxwell had also left the ground. I am sure it was never your intention that this post should be commanded by an officer of less rank than a general.—It is now my dear sir, commanded by a *Col. Wayne.* When I return I shall have an opportunity of saying something to you on this subject.

"You will be astonished at the horrid intention of assassination which was attempted against me this noon & on my arrival at this post.

"Col. White being informed of my arrival here, came down to headquarters. General Gates took me out of the house to speak to me on the subject of my duty, and in our walk, met Col. White but took no notice of him. On our return to the door, Col. White called me aside. As I supposed that he intended to speak to me, for my taking liberty with his character, I freely stepped to the back of the general's house, and no sooner had we got about 5 paces beyond the kitchen than his *small sword* was drawn & pointed and I retreated two paces. I damned him & asked what he meant by it, he bid me draw and defend himself. I retreated & damning him asked what he meant by it, he pursued me so closely that I ran before the general's door, where by the [?] saved myself from a damnable *premeditated* murder.

215

I have reason to thank God for his mercy in not suffering the Devil to put it in his head to make use of his pistols. I applied to General Gates for protection, as it was impossible to do the duties of my office, when my life was in jeopardy, without giving me notice or a chance to defend myself.—The general immediately ordered him to be arrested: And at the request of General Arnold ordered two Continentals at his door. —But sir, he had made his escape & Gen. Gates ordered Major Barber to send parties to take him whether dead or alive. The parties went out accordingly. One of them fell in with him in the woods sitting on a stump with his pistols under him & three swords. The officer advanced to him & Col. White cocked and pointed his pistol swearing by God he would shoot him in case he did not stand off. This repeated, the officer levelled his pair & told him he had orders to take him dead or alive. After pausing he asked by whose orders he was sent—the officer informed that it was by Gen. Gates's. He then said, if so, I must give myself up & he was taken with 4 pair of pistols, two small swords and a cutts du chaise [?]. One of the small swords was the property of this *Col. Wayne* as also was one pair of the pistols. —You will here judge how far Mr. Wayne is concerned. —I wish however my dear general, that nothing may be said or done with respect to Col. Wayne till I am able to give you further information. Col. White has said this day, that he waited in the woods for me, that he expected *Col. Wayne* would tell me of it. —What consummate impudence & folly to think that I value myself at the low price of an *assassin*.

"General Gates issued the enclosed order to Col. Dayton & I discover this evening that he has given *Wayne* leave to withdraw the Continentals from White's door which is done on Wayne's giving his word & honor for my security & White's complying with his close arrest. —I waited of Col. Wayne to know by whose orders & what authority the Continentals were withdrawn & he informed me that he had ordered the Continentals to be withdrawn by General Gates's leave. And I am informed that General Gates has given him power to give White a furlough to go to Brunswick free from arrest. —I am informed & have reason to believe the matter is managed at Wayne's intercession, who I believe has acted a part which I cannot approve & therefore have taken a birth with Major Barber as Col. Dayton is going off.

"As I have the fullest evidence to prove White a 'rascal, & scoundrel, & villain & a man of the blackest heart which God Almighty ever created'— being those expressions I avow to have made use of against him—I am determined to hunt him out of the army, as I cannot with safety to myself suffer a man who has attempted to murder me, to remain on a footing with myself. —I must therefore entreat you my dear general to have him arrested, if he is discharged by Col. Wayne, that he may carry infamy with him, even if he should be permitted to go to New Jersey, and that he may be tried as soon as my duty is executed so as to be able to attend to it.

"Unless he will quit the army & give me the most ample testimonials of his gross abuses—I must try to have him brought before another court-martial where I will solicit my own cause. —However my dear general I refer the matter to you, for the rule of my conduct.

"I was waited of this evening by Capts. Ross and Patterson who solicited for White, as he wished to have matters settled. He acknowledged his imprudent conduct towards me this day & had said that if I would acknowledge that I had [?   ] taken liberties with his character he wished to have it settled; I avowed my conduct & said that White had put it out of my power to treat with him at all.

[PS] "I have a pair of pistols as my guardian angels & am advised by Gates and Arnold not to go unarmed till White is removed.

"NB. I must in justice to Col. Wayne, say that he behaves polite to me & has insisted that I take my quarters with him. I shall consider of it."

November 20, 1776
[Ticonderoga]

"When I consider the many instances of infamous & ungentlemanlike conduct of Lt. Col. White as well with respect to some of my friends as myself, I am but justly fired with the most keen resentment, in as much that I think it my indispensible duty to persecute the scoundrel, till he is dismissed the army, with the disgrace due to his base character. I shall thereupon take up the matter with a doubled ardour I leave no stone unturned (as far as justice & propriety will mark my conduct) to load him with disgrace, till I have the pleasure of thinking that my friends and myself have our columinaitor & intended assassin humbled at our feet. —Then I shall cheerfully quit my pursuit. —In this however my dear gen. you will restrain me, when I exceed the bounds of moderation.—

"You may think me warm, but I assure you, I have severely felt & [hated?] the insults & injuries he has perpetrated.

"I have much to say on the state of matters here, and shall take the liberty to say somethings, hoping that you will not take my freedom amiss.—

"Much is to be done here & at Mount Independence to put the posts in a proper state of defence [?   ] a winter sortie. At least 6,000 pickets are to be cut & fixed in the ground. Not one eighth part between Hinman's redoubt & this garrison is picketed, & one snow will prevent the works going on. —The batteau master pays little or no attention to his duty. The barracks on Independence are not half covered, half planked or chimnies built. The barracks in this garrison want much repairs, much more firewood to be cut and in short matters put in quite a different state from what they are. —Cannon shot laying out, &c. —As to the commissaries branch I have made no inquiry as yet. —But to you, my dear sir, I will venture to declare with submission to General Gates, that tho' Col. Wayne be a brave man, he is not the character suited to carry into execution the many and various kinds of things that are absolutely necessary to be done, he has been more accustomed to good company & leaving others to superintend, than to deliberate & spend his time in the more necessary employment [of superintending?] others. —I have been free; but I should have been blamed perhaps if I had not wrote to you, & you should be uninformed from a more proper quarter.—

"I feel dissatisfied at General Gates's changing his orders respecting

Col. White. It is Wayne who influenced him so much, notwithstanding General Arnold's opposing it. —The last gentleman was informed of some matters by Col. Dayton which convinces him that White had no honor.— Now, my dear sir, as Wayne had leave to send him to Brunswick on parole & as White has no honor, what compliments do I pay myself in permitting him to have this priviledge?—As I have reason to think that some officers do not hold themselves bound by your orders, I wish their views to be disappointed, the haughty to be humbled. —I am determined to mark some characters & treat them with as much indifference as my duty to them & myself can permit. —

. . . . .

"As my brother officer of your family has in my opinion, acted a very strange character in affairs between M. White & myself, I wish that my letters may not fall into his hands, tho' he now avows his enmity to White.

"Can you imagine that White has entreated him to take away his confession at the German Flatts from [Gow^r.?]. This I do assert upon my honor to be a fact.—or the major stands in the gap.—"

Appendix B

Continental General Officers, by date of commission
Major Generals

George Washington, 15 June 1775–23 December 1783

Artemas Ward, 17 June 1775–23 April 1776 (resigned).

Charles Lee, 17 June 1775–18 January 1780 (dismissed).

Philip Schuyler, 19 June 1775–19 April 1779 (resigned).

Israel Putnam, 19 June 1775–3 June 1783 (retired).

Richard Montgomery, 9 December 1775–31 December 1775 (killed in action). Brigadier General 22 June 1775–9 December 1775.

John Thomas, 6 March 1776–2 June 1776 (died of illness). Brigadier General 22 June 1775–6 March 1776.

Horatio Gates, 16 May 1776–3 November 1783. Brigadier General 17 June 1775–16 May 1776.

William Heath, 9 August 1776–3 November 1783. Brigadier General 22 June 1775–9 August 1776.

Joseph Spencer, 9 August 1776–13 January 1778 (resigned). Brigadier General 22 June 1775–9 August 1776.

John Sullivan, 9 August 1776–30 November 1779 (resigned). Brigadier General 22 June 1775–9 August 1776.

Nathanael Greene, 9 August 1776–3 November 1783. Brigadier General 22 June 1775–9 August 1776.

Benedict Arnold, 17 February 1777–25 September 1780 (deserted to the enemy). [originally promoted in May but appointment later set at 17 February to give him seniority rights]. Brigadier General 10 January 1776–17 February 1777.

William Alexander (Lord Stirling), 19 February 1777–15 January 1783 (died of illness). Brigadier General, 1 March 1776–19 February 1777.

219

Thomas Mifflin, 19 February 1777–25 February 1779 (resigned). Brigadier General 16 May 1776–19 February 1777.

Arthur St. Clair, 19 February 1777–3 November 1783. Brigadier General 9 August 1776–19 February 1777.

Adam Stephen, 19 February 1777–20 November 1777 (dismissed). Brigadier General 4 September 1776–19 February 1777.

Benjamin Lincoln, 19 February 1777–29 October 1783.

Marquis de Lafayette, 31 July 1777–3 November 1783.

Philippe DuCoudray, 11 August 1777–15 September 1777 (drowned).

Baron de Kalb, 15 September 1777–19 August 1780 (died of wounds).

Alexander McDougall, 20 October 1777–3 November 1783. Brigadier General 9 August 1776–20 October 1777.

Robert Howe, 20 October 1777–3 November 1783. Brigadier General 1 March 1776–20 October 1777.

Thomas Conway, 13 December 1777–28 April 1778 (resigned). Brigadier General 13 May 1777–13 December 1777.

Friedrich Wilhelm von Steuben, 5 May 1778–15 April 1784.

William Smallwood, 15 September 1780–3 November 1783. Brigadier General 23 October 1776–15 September 1780.

Samuel Holden Parsons, 23 October 1780–22 July 1782 (retired). Brigadier General 9 August 1776–23 October 1780.

Henry Knox, 15 November 1781–20 June 1784. Brigadier General 27 December 1776–15 November 1781.

Chevalier Louis DuPortail, 16 November 1781–10 October 1783. Brigadier General 17 November 1777–16 November 1781.

William Moultrie, 15 October 1782–3 November 1783. Brigadier General 16 September 1776–15 October 1782.

Brigadier Generals

David Wooster, 22 June 1775–2 May 1777 (died of wounds).

Seth Pomeroy, 22 June 1775 (declined appointment and was superseded on 19 July 1775).

Joseph Frye, 10 January 1776–23 April 1776 (resigned).

John Armstrong, 1 March 1776–4 April 1777 (resigned).

William Thompson, 1 March 1776–3 September 1781 (died of illness).

Andrew Lewis, 1 March 1776–15 April 1777 (resigned).

James Moore, 1 March 1776–9 April 1777 (died of illness).

Baron de Woedtke, 16 March 1776–28 July 1776 (died of illness).

John Whetcomb, 5 June 1776 (declined appointment).

Hugh Mercer, 5 June 1776–11 January 1777 (died of wounds).

James Reed, 9 August 1776–[?] September 1776 (resigned).

John Nixon, 9 August 1776–12 September 1780 (resigned).

James Clinton, 9 August 1776–23 October 1783.

Christopher Gadsden, 19 September 1776–2 October 1777 (resigned).

Lachlan McIntosh, 16 September 1776–3 November 1783.

William Maxwell, 23 October 1776–25 July 1780 (resigned).

Chevalier de Roche Fermoy, 5 November 1776–31 January 1778 (resigned).
Chevalier de Borre, 1 December 1776–14 September 1777 (resigned).
Francis Nash, 5 February 1777–17 October 1777 (died of wounds).
John Cadwalader, 21 February 1777 (declined appointment to serve in Pennsylvania militia).
Enoch Poor, 21 February 1777–8 September 1780 (died of illness).
John Glover, 21 February 1777–22 July 1782 (retired).
John Paterson, 21 February 1777–3 November 1783.
Anthony Wayne, 21 February 1777–3 November 1783.
James M. Varnum, 21 February 1777–5 March 1779 (resigned).
John Philip DeHaas, 21 February 1777– ——1783 (retired).
William Woodford, 21 February 1777–13 November 1780 (died of illness).
Peter Muhlenberg, 21 February 1777–3 November 1783.
George Weedon, 21 February 1777–June, 1783 (retired).
George Clinton, 25 March 1777–3 November 1783.
Edward Hand, 1 April 1777–3 November 1783.
Charles Scott, 1 April 1777–3 November 1783.
Ebenezer Learned, 2 April 1777–24 March 1778 (resigned).
Jedediah Huntington, 12 May 1777–3 November 1783.
Joseph Reed, 12 May 1777–9 June 1777 (declined).
Count Pulaski, 15 September 1777–11 October 1779 (died of wounds).
John Stark, 4 October 1777–3 November 1783.
Jethro Sumner, 9 January 1779–3 November 1783.
James Hogun, 9 January 1779–4 January 1781 (died of illness).
Isaac Huger, 9 January 1779–3 November 1783.
Mordecai Gist, 9 January 1779–3 November 1783.
William Irvine, 12 May 1779–3 November 1783.
Daniel Morgan, 13 October 1780–3 November 1783.
Ortho Holland Williams, 9 May 1782–16 January 1783 (retired).
John Greaton, 7 January 1783–3 November 1783.
Rufus Putnam, 7 January 1783–3 November 1783.
Elias Dayton, 7 January 1783–3 November 1783.
Charles Tufin Armand (Marquis de la Rouarie) 26 March 1783–3 November 1783.

(From Lynn Montross, *Rag, Tag and Bobtail: The Story of the Continental Army, 1775–1783*)

Notes to the Chapters

I—Congress Adopts an Army

[1] William H. W. Sabine, ed., *Historical Memoirs from 16 March 1763 to 25 July 1778 of William Smith* . . . (New York: Arno Press, 1969), 221–22.

[2] John Adams Diary, *Journals of the Continental Congress* [JCC], 34 vols. (Washington: Carnegie Institute, 1904–1937), II: 24–41.

[3] Lord Dartmouth to Thomas Gage, 15 April 1775, Clarence E. Carter, ed., *The Correspondence of General Thomas Gage* . . . 2 vols. (New Haven: Yale University Press, 1931–33), II: 190–96.

[4] James Duane, Notes on the State of the Colonies, 24 May, Edmund C. Burnett, ed., *Letters of the Members of the Continental Congress* [LMCC] 8 vols. (Washington: Carnegie Institute, 1921–34), I: 100.

[5] JCC, II: 49–53.

[6] Christopher Ward, *The War of the Revolution,* 2 vols. (New York: Macmillan, 1952), I: 147–48.

[7] JCC, II: 55–56.

[8] 13 April, "The Letter Books of Cadwallader Colden. . . ." 2 vols. (New York: New York Historical Society *Collections,* 1876, 1877), [Colden Letter Books], VII: 410–11.

[9] Gage to Dartmouth, 13 May, *Gage Corresp.,* I: 397.

[10] JCC, II: 56, 69, 74; Connecticut Delegates to William Williams, 31 May, LMCC, I: 104.

[11] Deane to Mrs. Dean, 21 May; Titus Hosmer to Deane, 28 May; Joseph Hewes to Samuel Johnston, 5 June, LMCC, I: 94, including note 2, 113.

[12] JCC, II: 76–78.

[13] Elbridge Gerry to the Massachusetts Delegates, 4 June, Elbridge Gerry Papers (Washington: Library of Congress). Subsequent references to

222

Elbridge Gerry's correspondence are to this collection unless otherwise stated, and will be identified by date in the text.

[14] JCC, II: 76–79, 83–85.

[15] John Adams to Moses Gill, 10 June, LMCC, I: 117–18.

[16] L. H. Butterfield, ed., *The Adams Papers*, Series I; Diary and Autobiography of John Adams, 4 vols. (Cambridge, Mass.: Belknap Press, 1961), III: 321.

[17] William Gordon, *The History of the Rise, Progress, and Establishment of the Independence of the United States of America*, 4 vols. (London: 1788), II: 37–38.

[18] Butterfield, *Adams Papers*, III: 321–23.

[19] 17 June, LMCC, I: 127–29.

[20] Edmund C. Burnett, *The Continental Congress* (New York: Macmillan, 1941), pp. 75–76.

[21] JCC, II: 93–94.

[22] John Adams to James Warren, 20 June, LMCC, I: 137.

[23] Douglas Southall Freeman, *George Washington*, 7 vols. (New York: Scribner's, 1948–57), III: 440–41.

[24] Samuel White Patterson, *Horatio Gates, Defender of American Liberties* (New York: Columbia University Press, 1941), pp. 48, 49–50; Freeman, *Washington*, III: 441.

[25] Charles Lee to Henry Laurens, 13 May 1778, Papers of the Continental Congress [PCC] (Washington: National Archives), 158, I: 113; Freeman, *Washington*, III: 441.

[26] 20 June 1775, LMCC, I: 137.

[27] Ibid., pp. 110–11.

[28] 7 June, *Journals of the Provincial Congress. . . .* [JNYPC], 2 vols. (Albany: 1842), I: 32–33.

[29] JCC, II: 99.

[30] 3 June [1775], Livingston Papers, Bancroft Collection (New York Public Library), p. 31. Subsequent references to Livingston's correspondence are to this collection unless otherwise stated, and will be identified by date in the text.

[31] Eliphalet Dyer to Joseph Trumbull, 20 June, LMCC, I: 137–38.

[32] JCC, II: 99; Ward, I: 57–58.

[33] JCC, II: 92, 100–101.

[34] John Adams to Joseph Warren, 21 June, LMCC, I: 141. Joseph Warren had been killed on June 16.

[35] LMCC, I: 142n; 23 June, ibid., p. 142.

II—Provincial Jealousy vs. Continental Unity

[1] By June 12, General Gage estimated that a force of at least 32,000 would be necessary to subdue the rebellion; Thomas Gage to Lord Dartmouth, 12 June 1775, *Gage Corresp.*, I: 404.

[2] Richard Frothingham, *History of the Siege of Boston* (Boston, 1851),

p. 118n; Allen French, *The First Year of the American Revolution* (Boston: Houghton Mifflin, 1934), p. 86n.

[3] William B. Willcox, ed., *The American Rebellion: Sir Henry Clinton's Narrative of the Campaigns, 1775–1782.* . . . (New Haven: Yale University Press, 1954), pp. 18–20; Frothingham, *Siege,* p. 114n.

[4] Peter Force, ed., *American Archives.* . . . , 4th ser., 6 vols. (Washington, 1837–46), (hereafter cited as Force, 4 Ser.), II: 1354; Frothingham, *Siege,* p. 116.

[5] For a detailed account of the proceedings of this council of war, see Samuel Swett, *History of the Bunker Hill Battle* (Boston, 1827).

[6] French, *First Year,* pp. 213–17; Ward, I: 87.

[7] Willcox, *Rebellion,* p. 19.

[8] 25 June, *Gage Corresp.,* I: 406–407.

[9] Thomas Jones, *History of New York during the Revolutionary War,* 2 vols. (New York, 1879), I: 55–57.

[10] Gordon, *History,* II: 51–52.

[11] Force, 4 Ser., II: 1472–73.

[12] Washington to Philip Schuyler, 28 July, John C. Fitzpatrick, ed., *The Writings of George Washington,* 39 vols. (Washington: GPO, 1931–44). III: 374. Subsequent references to Washington's correspondence are to this collection unless otherwise stated, and will be identified by date in the text.

[13] Lewis Henry Boutell, *Life of Roger Sherman* (Chicago, 1896), p. 88.

[14] Deane to Mrs. Deane, 15 July, 20 July; Dyer to Joseph Trumbull, 21 July, Deane to Trumbull, 21 July; Dyer to Trumbull, 28 July, LMCC, pp. 164, 166–68, 181.

[15] French, *First Year,* pp. 29, 35, 48.

[16] 6 June [July], LMCC, I: 151–52.

[17] 9 July, Samuel Adams Papers (New York Public Library). Subsequent references to the correspondence of Samuel Adams are to this collection unless otherwise stated, and will be identified by date in the text.

[18] John Adams to James Warren, 6 June [July], LMCC, I: 152; 27 June, p. 145.

[19] 23 July, The Lee Papers, 4 vols. (New York: New-York Historical Society *Collections,* 1872–75), I: 197–198. Subsequent references to Lee's correspondence are to this collection unless otherwise stated, and will be identified by date in the text.

[20] 21, 23 July, LMCC, I: 171, 173–74.

[21] 28 July, Force, 4 Ser., II: 1747–48.

[22] *Ibid.,* 1625, 1629; Washington to Massachusetts Legislature and to President of Congress, 10 July, 4 August, Fitzpatrick, *GW,* III: 319, 320n., 391–92, 394–95.

[23] French, *First Year,* pp. 321–22n.

[24] 19, 27, 28 July, JCC, II: 190–91, 211–12; John Adams to James Warren, 27 July, LMCC, I: 178.

[25] 23 July, Worthington C. Ford, "The Warren-Adams Letters," 2 vols.,

nos. 72–73 (Boston: Massachusetts Historical Society *Collections,* 1917–25) (Warren-Adams), I: 86; 26 July, LMCC, I: 177–78.

[26] To Thomas Rodney, LMCC, I: 141.

[27] JCC, II: 60, 100–101; New York Delegates to New York Provincial Congress, 30 May, LMCC, I: 103.

[28] Washington to Reed, 15 December 1775, Fitzpatrick *GW,* IV: 164–65.

[29] 30 September 1776, Charles Francis Adams, ed., *Works of John Adams, Second President of the United States,* 10 vols. (Boston, 1850–56), I: 256.

[30] John Adams to Josiah Quincy, 29 July, LMCC, I, 182–83.

[31] To James Warren, 24 July, *Warren-Adams,* I: 89; Force, 4 Ser., II: 1717–18.

[32] 5 October 1775.

[33] John Adams to James Warren [Charles Lee], 13 October, *Warren-Adams,* I: 136–137. The editor, Mr. Ford, mistakenly thought this letter was addressed to James Warren. From the content, however, it could only have been written to Charles Lee. Adams did write to Warren on this date, and this letter to Lee may have been enclosed in that one, thus leading to the confusion.

[34] Benjamin Harrison to Washington, 21 July 1775, LMCC, I: 170–71.

III—The Creation of a Northern Army

[1] JYNPC, I, 64; Governor Trumbull to Albany Committee, 30 May 1775, and New York Congress to Albany Committee, 1 June, Force, 4 Ser., II: 850, 1269; JCC, II: 74.

[2] Governor Trumbull to Albany Committee, 30 May, Force 4 Ser., II: 850.

[3] Burnett, *Cont. Cong.,* 88–89; Eliphalet Dyer to Governor Trumbull, 16 June, LMCC, I: 127.

[4] 12 June, *Gage Corresp.,* I: 404.

[5] To James Warren, 7 June, LMCC, I: 114.

[6] 12 June, *Gage Corresp.,* II: 684.

[7] Ward, I: 142.

[8] Allen to New York Congress, 2 June, and James Easton to Massachusetts Congress, 6 June, Force, 4 Ser., II: 891–93, 919.

[9] John Adams to James Warren, 7 June, LMCC, I: 113–14.

[10] Orders of Massachusetts Committee of Safety to Benedict Arnold, 3 May; Arnold to Massachusetts Committee of Safety, 23 May; Committee at Ticonderoga to Massachusetts Congress, 10 May; Ethan Allen to Massachusetts Congress, 11 May, and Benedict Arnold to Massachusetts Committee of Safety, 11 May, Force, 4 Ser., II: 485, 750, 693, 556–57; Ward, I: 67; L. E. Chittenden, *The Capture of Ticonderoga* (Rutland, Vt.: 1872), p. 100.

[11] James Easton's report to Massachusetts Congress, 18 May; Massa-

chusetts Congress to Arnold, 1 June; Instructions of the Massachusetts Congress to the committee sent to Ticonderoga, 13 June; "Veritas" to Mr. Holt, 25 June; William Delaplace to ?, 28 July, Force, 4 Ser., 624–25, 1382–83, 1407–1408, 1085–87.

[12] The Massachusetts committee to Arnold, 23 June; Arnold to the Massachusetts committee, 24 June; Walter Spooner to Governor Trumbull, 3 July; Edward Mott to Governor Trumbull, 6 July, Force, 4 Ser., II: 1540–41, 1592–93, 1596–99.

[13] JCC, II: 109–10.

[14] President of Congress to Washington, 28 June, and Richard Henry Lee to Washington, 29 June, LMCC, I: 146–47.

[15] Arnold to President of Congress, 11 July, Force, 4 Ser., II: 1646–47.

[16] 15 July, Jared Sparks, ed., *Correspondence of the American Revolution; Being Letters of Eminent Men to George Washington. . .* (Sparks, *Letters to Washington*), 4 vols. (Boston, 1853), I: 4.

[17] JCC, II: 186; New York Delegates to New York Congress, 17 July, Force, 4 Ser., II: 1674; Theodore Rodenbough and William Haskins, eds., *The Army of the United States; Historical Sketches of Staff and Line. . .* (New York, 1896), p. 1.

[18] 3 June [July?], *Correspondence of Silas Deane. . .* (Hartford, Connecticut Historical Society *Collections,* 1870) (Deane Corresp.), II: 251–52.

[19] 19 July, Schuyler Papers (New York Public Library). Subsequent references to Schuyler's correspondence are to this collection unless otherwise stated, and will be identified by date in the text.

[20] 24, 31 July, 15, 23, 29 August, Force, 4 Ser., III: 139–40, 548, 564; II: 1721, 1762.

[21] 1 July, LMCC, I: 150, 189.

[22] 21 July, Force, 4 Ser., II: 1702.

[23] To Governor Trumbull, 14 August, Sparks, *Letters to Washington,* I: 461–63. A British officer stationed at Quebec corroborates this estimate by Major Brown; see, Thomas Gamble to Gage, 6 September, Force, 4 Ser., III: 962.

[24] Brown to Governor Trumbull, 14 August, Sparks, *Letters to Washington,* I: 462; Colonel Hinman to Governor Trumbull, 14 August, Force, 4 Ser., III: 135; JNYPC, I: 57, 76.

[25] Force, 4 Ser., III: 468; Ward, I: 150.

[26] 25 August, Benson J. Lossing, *The Life and Times of Philip Schuyler,* 2 vols. (New York, 1860), I: 393.

[27] To Washington, 27 August, Sparks, *Letters to Washington,* I: 22–24.

[28] Schuyler to President of Congress, 8 September, 153 PCC, I: 125.

[29] Schuyler to President of Congress, 19 September, Force, 4 Ser., III: 738.

[30] Justin H. Smith, *Our Struggle for the Fourteenth Colony. . .* 2 vols. (New York, 1907), I: 343–44; Extract of a letter from Quebec, 1 October, Force, 4 Ser., III: 925–26.

IV—Discord and Disaster in the North

[1] Richard Smith, Diary, 19, 20 September 1775; President of Congress to Schuyler, 20 September, LMCC, I: 200–203; JCC, II: 254–55.

[2] JCC, II: 255–56.

[3] Force, 4 Ser., II: 1000–1002.

[4] Ibid., 1010, 1025, 1304.

[5] JCC, II: 95; LMCC, I: 127, 138.

[6] Gage to Lord Barrington, 6 June, Gage Corresp., II: 682.

[7] JNYPC, I: 68, 77, 79–82; 10 August, New York Journal.

[8] Force, 4 Ser., III: 263, 460, 734–35.

[9] Schuyler to President of Congress, 14 October, 153 PCC, I: 222. These troops were men of Colonel Hinman's and Colonel Waterbury's regiments whose terms of enlistment had expired.

[10] Gunning Bedford to Philip Schuyler, 15 October, Schuyler Papers.

[11] 153 PCC, I: 222.

[12] Force, 4 Ser., III: 1094–95.

[13] Washington Papers (Library of Congress).

[14] Schuyler to President of Congress, 21 October, 153 PCC, I: 242.

[15] Montgomery to Schuyler, 13 November, Sparks, Letters to Washington, I: 480–81.

[16] Smith, Fourteenth Colony, II: 16, 16n.

[17] 20 August, Force, 4 Ser., II: 214.

[18] For the best description of Arnold's expedition to Quebec, see Kenneth Roberts, ed., March to Quebec: Journals of Members of Arnold's Expedition (New York: Doubleday-Doran, 1938). For an excellent fictional version, the novel Arundel, by the same author, is unsurpassed.

[19] Report of the committee sent to confer with General Schuyler, 23 December, JCC, III: 446–52; Montgomery to Schuyler, 13 November, Sparks, Letters to Washington, I: 480–81.

[20] Montgomery to Wooster, 16 December, Force, 4 Ser., IV: 288–89.

[21] Roberts, March to Quebec, p. 40. The best accounts of the American attempt on Quebec are the journals of Arnold's officers contained in this volume.

[22] Quoted in Schuyler to President of Congress, 18 October, Force, 4 Ser., III: 1093–95.

[23] Lockwood to Deane, 16 October, Deane Corresp., I: 83–84.

[24] Lossing, Schuyler, I: 393.

V—The American Army Becomes Truly Continental

[1] 29 August, Force, 4 Ser., III: 455.

[2] Caractacus, "On Standing Armies" (Philadelphia), 21 August, Force, 4 Ser., III: 219–21. May be Samuel Adams. His remarks to Elbridge Gerry, 29 October, are very similar. H. A. Cushing, ed., The Writings of Samuel Adams, 4 vols. (New York, 1904–1908) (Adams Writings), III: 230.

[3] 26 September, LMCC, I: 207–208.

[4] Lee to Rush, 10 October, Fitzpatrick, *GW,* III: 508n.

[5] Richard Smith, Diary, 29, 30 September, LMCC, I: 210–11; JCC, III: 266, 270–71, 2 October.

[6] The general return for the army at Cambridge on October 17 put the total strength at 19,497. However, the rank and file present for duty numbered only 13,923. Force, 4 Ser., III: 1165–66.

[7] Proceedings of the Committee of Conference, 18, 21, 22 October; Committee of Conference to President of Congress, 24 October, Force, 4 Ser., III: 1155–56, 1158, 1160.

[8] Richard Smith, Diary, 26 September, LMCC, I: 207; Proceedings of Committee of Conference, 21, 23 October, Force, 4 Ser., III: 1158, 1161.

[9] Committee of Conference to President of Congress, 24 October, Proceedings of the Committee of Conference, 25 October, Force 4 Ser., III: 1155–56, 1163.

[10] LMCC, I: 253–54.

[11] JCC, III: 285.

[12] LMCC, I: 222–23.

[13] JCC, III: 287, 10 October.

[14] Butterfield, *Adams Papers,* II: 202, 10 October.

[15] Ward, I: 139, 145, 156–57; Willard M. Wallace, *Appeal to Arms* (New York: Harper, 1951), p. 70.

[16] Butterfield, *Adams Papers,* II: 203–204, 10 October.

[17] Force, 4 Ser., III: 993–94.

[18] 29 October, *Adams Writings,* III: 230.

[19] Samuel Ward, Diary, 11, 16 October; President of Congress to New Jersey Provincial Convention, 25 October, William Livingston to Lord Stirling, 8 November, LMCC, I: 225, 231, 240–41, 250; JCC, III: 305, 335, 370, 416.

[20] Dyer to Joseph Trumbull, 1 January 1776, LMCC, I: 292–93.

[21] 58 PCC, p. 317; Richard Smith, Diary, 3 January, LMCC, I: 295; JCC, IV: 29–30, 4 January, 30, 30n; 59 PCC, p. 319.

[22] JCC, III: 321, 4 November 1775; 322, 352, 13 November 1775: 393, 30 November.

[23] 16 October, 31 December, Greene Papers (Clements Library).

[24] To Henry Ward, 21 November, LMCC, I: 256.

[25] JCC, III: 414, 7 December.

[26] Butterfield, *Adams Papers,* III: 324–25.

[27] JCC, III: 444–45, 22 December; Richard Smith, Diary, LMCC, I: 284; President of Congress to Washington, ibid., p. 286.

VI—Charles Lee

[1] John Richard Alden, *General Charles Lee: Traitor or Patriot?* (Baton Rouge: Louisiana University Press, 1951), p. 88.

[2] Merrill Jensen, ed., *English Historical Documents,* IX. [EHD, IX]

American Colonial Documents to 1776 (London and New York: 1955), pp. 851–52.

3 Alden, *Lee,* pp. 91–92.

4 Patterson, *Gates,* pp. 63–64.

5 Alden, *Lee,* p. 104.

6 Ibid., pp. 94–95.

7 C. F. Adams, *Works,* IX: 370–371.

8 Alden, *Lee,* pp. 96–97.

9 Lee to Washington, 24 January, *Lee Papers,* I: 259–60; Washington to Lee, 23 January, Fitzpatrick, *GW,* IV: 266–67.

10 Thomas Nelson, Jr., to Thomas Jefferson, 4 February; Richard Smith, Diary, 26 January; New York Delegates to New York Committee of Safety, 27 January, LMCC, I: 329–30, 339.

11 Richard Smith, Diary, 8, 10, 17 January; Josiah Bartlett to New Hampshire Committee of Safety, 20 January; President of Congress to Schuyler, 20 January, LMCC, I: 302, 307, 317, 321–22; Silas Deane to Mrs. Deane, 14 January, Deane Corresp., II: 348.

12 Wooster to Schuyler, 11 February, 1776, 153 PCC, I: 556.

13 John Adams to James Warren, 18 February, LMCC, I: 354–55, also 257–58.

14 Congress to Lee, 19 February, *Lee Papers,* I: 310–11; President of Congress to Schuyler, 20 February, LMCC, I: 258.

15 153 PCC, I: 544.

16 JCC, III: 325; Wallace, *Appeal to Arms, A Military History of the Revolution,* p. 91.

17 Richard Smith, Diary, 28 February, LMCC, I: 365–66; JCC, IV: 174.

18 LMCC, pp. 389–90.

19 James Duane to Lord Stirling, 1 March; President of Congress to Lee and Schuyler, 1 & 7 March, LMCC, I: 369–71, 380–81.

20 *Ibid.,* pp. 380–81, 408.

VII—Canada Lost

1 Robert Morris to Gates, 6 April 1776, LMCC, I, 416.

2 Burnett, *Continental Congress,* p. 113.

3 Minutes of the Council of War at De Chambault, 7 May, Washington Papers (LC).

4 Ward, I: 197; J. H. Smith, *Fourteenth Colony,* II: 352; John Thomas to Commissioners in Canada, 20 May, Force 4 Ser., VI: 592.

5 14 May, Washington Papers (LC). There appears to have been some confusion among some American officers concerning place names. The town is called Sorel and the river is the Richelieu.

6 J. H. Smith, *Fourteenth Colony,* II: 354.

7 Washington Papers (LC).

8 New Hampshire Delegates to President of New Hampshire, 28 May,

LMCC, I, 466; Josiah Bartlett to John Langdon, 10 June, Whipple Papers (Library of Congress).

[9] Samuel Chase and Charles Carroll of Carrollton, to Congress, 27 May, Force, 4 Ser., VI: 589.

[10] To John Langdon, 17 June, Whipple Papers (LC).

[11] 161 PCC, II: 313; LMCC, II: 46n.

[12] Force, 4 Ser., VI: 744–45; Bayard Tuckerman, *The Life of General Philip Schuyler, 1733–1804* (New York, 1903), pp. 108–109.

[13] 22 May, Washington Papers (LC); 153 PCC, II: 179.

[14] 27 April, LMCC, I: 433.

[15] Butterfield, Adams Papers, III: 386–87. The Hamilton libel referred to was the *Letters from Alexander Hamilton, Concerning the Public Conduct and Character of John Adams, Esq. . . .* (New York, 1800).

[16] LMCC, I: 480, 486, 493; to John Langdon, 14 June, Whipple Papers (LC).

[17] JCC, V: 448–51; LMCC, I: 497; Force, 5 Ser., I: 21.

[18] 13 June, LMCC, I: 486–87.

[19] 7 June, Force, 4 Ser., VI: 938.

VIII—The Clash of Commands

[1] Memo of a Conversation between Generals Schuyler and Gates, 30 June 1776, enclosed in Schuyler to Washington, 1 July, Washington Papers (LC).

[2] Force, 4 Ser., VI: 1200, 1265.

[3] JCC, V: 526.

[4] Force, 5 Ser., I: 115; LMCC, II: 3.

[5] To Richard Henry Lee, 15 July, LMCC, II: 11.

[6] Gates to Hancock, 16 July; Schuyler to Washington, 17 July, Washington Papers (LC).

[7] John Stark, et. al. to Schuyler, 8 July 1776; Schuyler to John Stark, *et al.,* 9 July, Washington Papers (LC).

[8] 29 July, Washington Papers (LC).

[9] LMCC, II: 16.

[10] John Jay, John Alsop, George Clinton, Lewis Morris to Walter Livingston, 17 April, Jay Papers (New-York Historical Society).

[11] JCC, V: 419, 5 June; 8 June, LMCC, I: 478.

[12] 25 June, *ibid.,* p. 504.

[13] Schuyler to Washington, 1 July; Washington to President of Congress, 4 July, Force, 4 Ser., 1199–200, 1265.

[14] JCC, V: 527.

IX—The Battle for the Northern Commissary

[1] Washington Papers (LC).

[2] 6 August, *ibid.*

[3] 22 July, Whipple Papers (LC).

[4] Colonel Matthias Ogden to Aaron Burr, 26 July, Force 4 Ser., I: 603.

[5] William Williams to Joseph Trumbull, 7 August, LMCC, II: 41.

[6] JCC, V: 627–28, 2 August.

[7] 3 August, 7 August, LMCC, II: 35–36, 41.

[8] Schuyler to President of Congress, 16 August, 153 PCC, II: 271.

[9] Gates Papers (New-York Historical Society). Subsequent references to Gates's correspondence are to this collection unless otherwise stated, and will be identified by date in the text.

[10] JCC, V: 617–18, 30 July.

[11] 16 August, 153 PCC, II: 271.

[12] Washington Papers (LC).

[13] 153 PCC, II: 271.

[14] JCC, V: 753; Elbridge Gerry to Joseph Trumbull, 12 September, LMCC, II: 84.

[15] LMCC, II: 84–85. Burnett says that the "gentleman" referred to is Walter Livingston, but from internal and external evidence it is almost certainly Schuyler. Congress received Livingston's resignation on September 12, and he was therefore eliminated as a source of trouble for Trumbull. Also, there is no letter extant from Livingston to Congress on the subject of supplying the Northern army by contract, but there is such a letter from Philip Schuyler.

[16] 153 PCC, II: 382.

[17] Ibid.

[18] JCC, V: 758.

[19] To Mrs. Gates, 27 August, Gates Papers (NYHS).

[20] To Joseph Trumbull, 26 September, LMCC, II: 103.

[21] William Williams to Joseph Trumbull, 28 September, LMCC, II: 105.

[22] 28 September, ibid., II: 107.

[23] Ibid., II: 106–107; JCC, V: 841.

[24] 153 PCC, II: 449.

[25] Washington Papers (LC).

[26] JCC, V: 822–23, 828.

[27] 16 October, 153 PCC, II: 459.

X—The Politics of Command

[1] 17 February 1777, LMCC, II: 260.

[2] To President of New York Convention, 18 February, ibid., p. 261.

[3] To William Whipple, 26 March, Whipple Papers (LC).

[4] To Samuel Holden Parsons, 19 August 1776, LMCC, II: 57, see also p. 61.

[5] JCC, V: 762–63.

[6] Gerry to Gates, 27 September, Gates Papers (NYHS).

[7] To Governor of Rhode Island (Nicholas Cooke), 5 October, LMCC, II: 115–16.

[8] *Ibid.,* pp. 261–62, 269.

[9] JCC, VII: 133; Burke, Abstract of Debates, 12–19 February, LMCC, I: 262.

[10] Roger Sherman to Governor of Connecticut, 4 March; Abraham Clark to Elias Dayton, 7 March; Rush to Wayne, 29 September 1776, *ibid.,* pp. 288, 291; II: 108; JCC, VII: 141.

[11] Josiah Bartlett to William Whipple, 26 March 1777, Whipple Papers (LC).

[12] JCC, V: 753; John Trumbull to President of Congress, 22 February 1777, "Revolutionary Letters. John Trumbull and James Lovell, 1771 [sic]," *The Historical Magazine* 1 (October 1857) (Boston): 289. The date of the letters in the title of the article should be 1777.

[13] Theodore Sizer, ed., *The Autobiography of John Trumbull* (New Haven: Yale University Press, 1953), p. 44.

[14] *Historical Magazine* 1 (October 1857): 189–90, 292.

[15] 19 March, 174 PCC, I: 147–49.

[16] LMCC, II: 308–309, 311–12.

[17] John Trumbull to Lovell, 30 March, *Historical Magazine* 1 (October 1857): 291–92; James Lovell, memorandum [April ?] 1777, LMCC, II: 309n; also p. 347.

[18] To John Adams, 9 January, LMCC, II: 210.

[19] *Ibid.,* 274; 28 February, 174 PCC, I: 135–36.

[20] 7 March, Washington Papers (LC).

[21] 13 March, *ibid.*

[22] 153 PCC, III: 9. The intercepted letter, allegedly written by Joseph Trumbull to William Williams, was published in Gain's *New York Gazkette,* 9 December 1776.

[23] JCC, VII: 180–81; LMCC, II: 304; Tuckerman, *Life of Schuyler,* p. 156.

[24] JCC, VII: 202, 217; Fitzpatrick, *GW,* VII: 268n; Ward, I: 407.

[25] "Trumbull Papers," *CMHS,* 7 Ser., II: 40; 18 April, LMCC, II: 333.

[26] New York Delegates to President of New York Convention, 21 April, LMCC, II: 337; JCC, VII: 279.

[27] New York Delegates to New York Convention, 9 May, LMCC, pp. 357–58.

[28] JCC, VII: 364.

[29] To Jonathan Trumbull, 26 May, "Trumbull Papers," *CMHS,* 7 Ser., I: 51–52.

[30] To Oliver Wolcott, 7 June, LMCC, II: 379.

[31] Schuyler to President of Congress, 8 June, 153 PCC, III: 144; Jonathan Trumbull, Jr., to Jonathan Trumbull, Sr., 9 June, "Trumbull Papers," *CMHS,* 7 Ser., II: 55; New York Delegates to New York Convention, 19 June, LMCC, II: 380.

[32] 19 June, LMCC, II: 384–86.

[33] To James Warren, 17 February and to Mrs. Adams, 19 April, *ibid.,* pp. 260, 335.

[34] Duane to Robert R. Livingston, 24 June, Bancroft Collection, Livingston Papers (NYPL), I: 431.
[35] 19 June, LMCC, II: 382–83.

XI—Saratoga

[1] Willcox, *American Rebellion*, pp. xxv–vi; Piers Mackesy, *The War for America, 1775–1783* (Cambridge, Mass.: Harvard University Press, 1964), pp. 121–22.
[2] Alexander Hamilton to Gouverneur Morris, 12 May, Harold C. Syrett, ed., *The Papers of Alexander Hamilton* (New York: Columbia University Press, 1961) (Hamilton Papers), I: 251–52. Subsequent references to Hamilton's correspondence are to this source unless otherwise stated, and will be identified by date in the text.
[3] Timothy Danielson to Jeremiah Powell, 14 May, William Heath, "The Heath Papers," Massachusetts Historical Society *Collections,* 7th Series, 2 vols. (Boston, 1904–1905), IV: 95–96.
[4] *Ibid.,* pp. 113–34.
[5] Samuel Brewer to Heath, 3 July, *ibid.,* p. 117; "The Trial of Major General St. Clair, August, 1778," *Collections,* New-York Historical Society (New York, 1881) (St. Clair Trial), 13: 147–51.
[6] Jonathan Trumbull, Jr., to Jonathan Trumbull, Sr., 8 and 11 July, "Trumbull Papers," II: 72–74.
[7] 2 July, LMCC, II: 412.
[8] 15 July, *ibid.,* p. 413; Whipple to Lovell, 15 July, Whipple Papers (LC).
[9] Washington Papers (LC).
[10] 21 and 22 July, Whipple Papers (LC). Arthur Middleton was a delegate from South Carolina. He is singled out for criticism by Lovell presumably because he usually supported the so-called Lee-Adams faction in Congress and in this instance defected.
[11] Schuyler to President of Congress, 24 July, 153 PCC, III: 226. From existing records, Schuyler's estimate of the number of men in the Northern army as of July 24 seems to be correct.
[12] 25 July, Washington Papers (LC).
[13] Charles Thomson, Notes of Debates, 26 July, LMCC, II: 424–26; Washington Papers (LC).
[14] 28 July, LMCC, II: 427–28.
[15] To Whipple, 29 July, Whipple Papers (LC).
[16] LMCC, II: 429–30.
[17] To Whipple, 1 August, Whipple Papers (LC).
[18] To Whipple, 4 August, LMCC, II: 437.
[19] George Stanley, ed., *For Want of a Horse* (Sackville, N. B.: Tribune Press, 1961), pp. 170–73; Governor George Clinton to James Duane, 27 August, Sparks Papers, Harvard College Library.

[20] Schuyler to Jonathan Trumbull, 27 July, "Trumbull Papers," II: 91–92; Schuyler to President of Congress, 8 August, 153 PCC, III: 234.

[21] Jonathan Trumbull, Jr., to Jonathan Trumbull, Sr., 8 and 11 August, "Trumbull Papers," II: 107–12; Floyd A. Brown and Howard H. Peckham, ed., *Revolutionary War Journals of Henry Dearborn 1775–1783* (Chicago: The Caxton Club, 1939), pp. 101–102.

[22] Schuyler to President of Congress, 10 August, 153 PCC, III: 242.

[23] Dearborn's Journals, p. 102.

[24] Gates to John Hancock, 20 August, Washington Papers (LC).

[25] Schuyler intimated this in his letter to President Hancock of 15 August, 153 PCC, III: 246.

[26] To Oliver Wolcott, 22 August, LMCC, II: 460–62; 25 August, Whipple Papers (LC).

[27] Thomas Burke to Governor of North Carolina, 23 May, Henry Laurens to Robert Howe, 7 August, LMCC, II: 371, 443; James Lovell to William Whipple, 8 August, Whipple Papers (LC).

[28] Eventually, Congress did grant Arnold's request and predated his commission as major general to February 17—one day before the objectionable appointment of the other major generals. However, this was not done until after the defeat of Burgoyne.

[29] For the details of this interesting episode, see Appendix A.

[30] Richard Varick to Philip Schuyler, 25 September, Henry B. Livingston to Philip Schuyler, 26 September, Schuyler Papers (NYPL).

XII—Congressional Criticism Shifts to Washington

[1] 10 April, LMCC, II: 322.

[2] Howe to Burgoyne (Jared Sparks Copy), 20 July, Washington Papers (LC).

[3] To President of New Hampshire, 26 July, LMCC, p. 426.

[4] To Josiah Bartlette, *ibid.*, p. 440.

[5] To William Whipple, 7 and 11 August, Whipple Papers (LC).

[6] Wayne to Washington, 19 September, Washington Papers (LC).

[7] John Adams to Mrs. Adams, 6 April 1777, LMCC, II: 317.

[8] 29 September, "Trumbull Papers," II: 150–51; to Mrs. Adams, 30 September, LMCC, II: 504.

[9] 16 October, LMCC, II: 521–522.

[10] Burke to Governor Caswell, 17 September, Walter Clark, ed., *The State Records of North Carolina*, 20 vols. (Raleigh, N. C., 1895–1914), II: 620–23.

[11] To William Whipple, 17 September, Whipple Papers (LC).

[12] To President of Congress, 17 September, 160 PCC, 57.

[13] LMCC, II: 514–15.

[14] 11 and 23 October, *ibid.*, pp. 517–18, 530.

[15] Jonathan Sargeant to James Lovell, Samuel Adams Papers (NYPL).

[16] Dearborn's Journals, pp. 112–14; Minute Books, Glover's Brigade, 26

October, H.B.T. Montgomery Revolutionary Manuscripts (HSP); Gates to Washington, 2 November, Washington Papers (LC); Hamilton to Washington, 2 November, *Hamilton Papers,* I: 349–50.

[17] Gates to Washington, 7 November, Washington Papers (LC); Stanley, p. 170.

[18] 1 December, "Trumbull Papers," II: 200.

[19] Gerry to John Adams, 3 and 8 December, Gerry Papers (LC).

XIII—The Conway Cabal

[1] *Dictionnaire de Biographie Françoise* (Paris, 1961), 9: 550.

[2] Louis Gottschalk, *Lafayette Joins the American Army* (Chicago: University of Chicago Press, 1937), pp. 45, 66; Washington to Hancock, 5 October, 152 PCC.

[3] Lord Stirling to Washington, 1777, William Alexander Papers (New-York Historical Society).

[4] Lafayette to Henry Laurens, 18 October "Letters from the Marquis de Lafayette to Hon. Henry Laurens, 1777–1780," *South Carolina Historical and Genealogical Magazine (SCHGM)*, vols. 7–9 (Charleston, 1906–1908), 7: 6.

[5] 20 October, LMCC, II: 527–28.

[6] Baron de Kalb to Richard Henry Lee, 18 September, Dreer Collection (HSP); JCC, IX: 769; Gottschalk, *Lafayette Joins the American Army,* p. 16.

[7] Conway to President of Congress, 25 September, 159 PCC; Baron de Kalb to [?], 28 September, Vail Collection (New-York Historical Society).

[8] Lord Stirling to Washington, Washington Papers (LC).

[9] Conway to Washington, *ibid.*

[10] Wilkinson's account of private conversation with Gates concerning the Conway letter, 28 March 1778, *ibid.*

[11] Henri Doniol, *Histoire de la participation de la France à l'établissement des Etats-Unis d'Amérique,* 6 vols. (Paris, 1884–92), 3: 226–27; Gottschalk, *Lafayette Joins the American Army,* p. 61.

[12] Conway to Mifflin, 11 November, Gates Papers (NYHS); LMCC, II: 563; JCC, IX: 1023–26.

[13] Conway to Washington, 31 December, Washington Papers (LC).

[14] Lafayette to Washington, 30 December, Louis R. Gottschalk, ed., *The Letters of Lafayette to Washington, 1777–1799* (New York: Privately printed by Helen F. Hubbard, 1944), pp. 13–16.

[15] John Laurens to Henry Laurens, 1 January 1778, *The Army Correspondence of Colonel John Laurens in the Years 1777–8. . . .* (New York, 1867), pp. 100–101.

[16] Congress promoted Wilkinson to the rank of brevet brigadier general on November 6 as a result of his bringing the news of the Saratoga victory.

[17] 174 PCC, I: 320–23.

[18] Henry Laurens to Isaac Motte, 26 January; Henry Laurens to John

Laurens, 28 January; Conway to Washington, 26 January, LMCC, III: 52, 60–61, 60n–61n.

[19] See Nathanael Greene to Alexander McDougall, 16 April 1778, McDougall Papers (NYHS) and Duane to Gates, 16 December 1777, Duane Papers (NYHS).

[20] Lafayette to Washington, 30 December 1777, Gottschalk, *Lafayette Letters*, pp. 13–16.

[21] John Laurens to Henry Laurens, 3 January 1778, *Laurens Army Corresp.*, pp. 101–104.

[22] "Letters from Lafayette to Henry Laurens," *SCHGM*, VII: 63–67.

[23] Dr. James Craik to Washington, 6 January, Washington Papers (LC).

[24] Benjamin Rush to Patrick Henry, 12 January, L. H. Butterfield, *Letters of Benjamin Rush*, 2 vols. (Princeton: Princeton University Press, 1951), I: 182–83; also Appendix I: "Rush and Washington," II: 1197–208. Butterfield makes it quite clear that Rush was not part of any plot to discredit or remove Washington.

[25] "Thoughts of a Freeman," Sparks, *Letters to Washington*, V: 497–99; Laurens to Washington, 27 January, LMCC, III: 56.

[26] Henry Laurens to John Laurens, LMCC, III: 28–31.

[27] 3 February, *ibid.*, 69–70.

[28] John Laurens to Henry Laurens, 9 February, *Laurens Army Corresp.*, pp. 120–21.

XIV—To Yorktown and Beyond

[1] Eliphalet Dyer to William Williams, 17 February 1778, LMCC, III: 88–89.

[2] Lafayette to Washington, 20 January 1778, Gottschalk, *Lafayette Letters*, p. 24.

[3] Laurens to John Rutledge, 11 March, LMCC, III: 124–25; Lafayette to Washington, 19 February, Gottschalk, *Lafayette Letters*, pp. 26–28.

[4] Lafayette to Henry Laurens, 1 June, "Letters from Lafayette," *SCHGM*, VIII: 182.

[5] David Franks to Washington, 4 July, Washington Papers (LC).

[6] Patterson, *Gates*, p. 273; JCC, X: 354. Although Gates's command was still designated as the Northern department and included the northern posts, it was now concentrated on the lower Hudson.

[7] Ward, II: 718–21; Wallace, pp. 212–15. Perhaps the best contemporary account is found in the Robert Honeyman Diary (LC), pp. 428–31.

[8] Alexander Hamilton to James Duane, 6 September 1780, *Hamilton Papers*, II: 420–21.

[9] The complete transcript of Philip Schuyler's court-martial can be found in the *Collections of the New-York Historical Society for the Year 1879* (NYHS), vol. 12.

[10] 4 October 1778, James Duane, "The Duane Letters," *Publications of the Southern History Association*, vols. 7–8 (Washington, 1903–1904).

[11] Schuyler to President of Congress, 6 October, 153 PCC, III: 356; JCC, XII: 1186; Schuyler to Washington, 27 December, Washington Papers (LC).

[12] JCC, XIII: 27–28, 332–35, 473.

[13] Governor Nash to Washington, 6 October 1780, Sparks, *Letters to Washington,* III: 107–11.

[14] Greene to Gates, 6 December, Washington Papers (LC).

[15] Greene to Washington, 7 December 1780, Sparks, *Letters to Washington,* III, 168.

[16] John Armstrong to Mrs. Gates, 2 May 1781, Gates Papers (NYHS).

[17] Gates to Washington, 29 April 1781; Washington to Gates, 12 May, Washington Papers (LC).

[18] Washington to Gates, 1 November 1781, *ibid.*

[19] JCC, XXIII: 465–66; Gates to President of Congress, 24 August 1782, 174 PCC, II: 365.

Bibliography

Manuscripts

William L. Clements Library, University of Michigan
    The Nathanael Greene Papers
Library of Congress
    The Elbridge Gerry Papers
    The Diary of Robert Honeyman
    The Washington Papers
    The William Whipple Papers
Harvard College Library
    The Sparks Papers
Massachusetts Historical Society
    The Papers of Timothy Pickering, Matthew Ridley,
    and Winthrop Sargent
National Archives
    The Papers of the Continental Congress
    The Timothy Pickering Letterbooks
New England Historic and Genealogical Society
    The Henry Knox Papers
New-York Historical Society
    The Horatio Gates Papers
    The John Jay Papers
    The Livingston Papers
    The Vail Collection
    The McDougall Papers
    The Duane Papers
New York Public Library
    The Samuel Adams Papers
    The Robert R. Livingston Papers, Bancroft Collection

The Robert Morris Papers
The Philip Schuyler Papers
Historical Society of Pennsylvania
   Dreer Collection
   Hope B. Tyler Montgomery Revolutionary Manuscripts

Newspapers

Connecticut *Journal,* and New Haven *Post-Boy* (Thomas and Samuel Green)
New York *Gazette,* and *Weekly Mercury* (Hugh Gaine)
New York *Journal;* or *The General Advertiser* (John Holt)
Rivington's New York *Gazetteer* (James Rivington)

Printed Source Materials

Adams, Charles Francis, ed. *Works of John Adams, Second President of The United States.* 10 vols. Boston, 1850–56.

Ballagh, James C., ed. *The Letters of Richard Henry Lee.* 2 vols. New York, 1911.

Bolton, Charles Knowles. *Letters of Hugh Earl Percy from Boston and New York, 1774–1776.* Boston, 1902.

Bowdoin, James. "The Bowdoin and Temple Papers [1756–1782]," Massachusetts Historical Society *Collections,* 6th Series, 9. Boston, 1897.

Brown, Floyd A., and Peckham, Howard H., eds. *Revolutionary War Journals of Henry Dearborn, 1775–1783.* Chicago: The Caxton Club, 1939.

Burnett, Edmund C., ed. *Letters of Members of the Continental Congress,* 8 vols. Washington: Carnegie Institute, 1921–36.

Butterfield, L. H. ed. *The Adams Papers,* Series I: Diaries. Diary and Autobiography of John Adams. 4 vols. Cambridge, Mass.: Belknap Press, 1961.

———. *Letters of Benjamin Rush.* 2 vols. Princeton: Princeton University Press, 1951.

Carter, Clarence E., ed. *The Correspondence of General Thomas Gage with the Secretaries of State, 1763–1775.* 2 vols. New Haven: Yale University Press, 1931–33.

Clark, Walter, ed. *The State Records of North Carolina.* 20 vols. Raleigh, 1895–1914.

Colden, Cadwallader. "The Letter Books of Cadwallader Colden." 2 vols. New York: New-York Historical Society *Collections,* 1876, 1877.

Cushing, Henry A., ed. *Writings of Samuel Adams.* 4 vols. New York, 1904.

Deane, Silas. "Correspondence of Silas Deane, Delegate to the First and Second Congress at Philadelphia, 1774–1776." Connecticut Historical Society *Collections,* vol. 2, Hartford, 1870).

———. "The Deane Papers," New-York Historical Society *Collections,* vols. 19–23. New York, 1887–91.

Dickinson, John. *Letters from a Farmer in Pennsylvania to the Inhabitants of the British Colonies.* New York, 1768.

Duane, James. "The Duane Letters," *Publications* of the Southern History Association. Vols. 7–8. Washington, 1903–1904.

Fitzpatrick, John C., ed. *Calendar of the Correspondence of George Washington Commander in Chief of the Continental Army with the Officers.* 4 vols. Washington: GPO, 1915.

————. *The Writings of George Washington.* 39 vols. Washington: GPO, 1931–44.

Force, Peter, ed. *American Archives.* 4th Series, 6 vols. Washington, 1837–46. 5th Series, 3 vols. Washington, 1848–53.

Ford, Worthington C., ed. *Correspondence and Journals of Samuel B. Webb.* 3 vols. Lancaster, Pa., 1893–94.

————. *Journals of the Continental Congress.* 34 vols. Washington: GPO, 1904–37.

————. "The Warren-Adams Letters." Massachusetts Historical Society *Collections.* 2 vols. Boston, 1917–25.

Gardiner, C. Harvey, ed. *A Study in Dissent: The Warren-Gerry Correspondence, 1776–1792.* Carbondale, Ill.: Southern Illinois University Press, 1968.

Gottschalk, Louis, ed. *Letters of Lafayette to Washington, 1777–1799.* New York: Privately printed by Helen F. Hubbard, 1944.

Hammond, Otis G., ed. *Letters and Papers of Major General John Sullivan, Continental Army.* 3 vols. Concord, N. H.: New Hampshire Historical Society, 1930–39.

Heath, William. "The Heath Papers." Massachusetts Historical Society *Collections.* 7th Series, 2 vols. Boston, 1904–1905.

Hopkins, Stephen. *The Rights of the Colonies Examined.* Providence, R.I., 1765.

Jensen, Merrill, ed. *English Historical Documents.* Vol. IX; *American Colonial Documents to 1776.* New York: Oxford University Press, 1955.

Journals of the Provincial Congress, Provincial Convention, Committee of Safety and Council of Safety of the State of New York, 1775–1776–1777. 2 vols. Albany, 1842.

Lafayette, Marquis de. "Letters from the Marquis de Lafayette to Hon. Henry Laurens, 1777–1780." *South Carolina Historical and Genealogical Magazine.* Vols. 7–9. Charleston, 1906–1908.

Laurens, John. *The Army Correspondence of Colonel John Laurens.* New York, 1867.

————, and Henry. "Letters from Hon. Henry Laurens to his son John, 1773–1776." "Letters from John Laurens to his Father, Hon. Henry Laurens, 1774–1776." *South Carolina Historical and Genealogical Magazine.* Vol. 5. Charleston, 1904.

————. "Correspondence between Hon. Henry Laurens and his son, John, 1777–1780." *South Carolina Historical and Genealogical Magazine.* Vol. 6. Charleston, 1905.

Lee, Charles. "The Lee Papers [1754–1811]." New-York Historical Society *Collections.* 4 vols. New York, 1872–75.

Lee, Richard Henry. *Memoir of the Life of Richard Henry Lee, and his Correspondence.* 2 vols. Philadelphia, 1825.

Moore, Frank, ed. *Correspondence of Henry Laurens, of South Carolina. Materials for History Printed from Original Manuscripts.* First Series. New York, 1861.

Roberts, Kenneth, ed. *March to Quebec: Journals of the Members of Arnold's Expedition.* New York: Doubleday, Doran, 1938.

Sabine, William H. W., ed. *Historical Memoirs from 16 March 1763 to 25 July 1778 of William Smith. . .* New York: Arno Press, 1969.

St. Clair, Major General Arthur. "The Trial of Major General St. Clair, August, 1778." New-York Historical Society *Collections.* Vol. 13. New York, 1881.

Schuyler, Major General Philip. "The Trial of Major General Schuyler, October 1778." New-York Historical Society *Collections.* Vol. 12. New York, 1880.

Sizer, Theodore, ed. *The Autobiography of John Trumbull.* New Haven: Yale University Press, 1953.

Sparks, Jared, ed. *Correspondence of the American Revolution; Being Letters of Eminent Men to George Washington, from the Time of His Taking Command of the Army to the End of his Presidency.* 4 vols. Boston, 1853.

Stanley, George, ed. *For Want of a Horse.* Sackville, New Brunswick: Tribune Press, 1961.

Syrett, Harold C., ed., Cooke, Jacob E., assoc. ed. *The Papers of Alexander Hamilton.* New York: Columbia University Press, 1961.

Trumbull, John, et al. "The Trumbull Papers." Massachusetts Historical Society *Collections.* 7th Series, vol. 2. Boston, 1902.

———, and Lovell, James. "Revolutionary Letters. John Trumbull and James Lovell, 1771 [sic]." *The Historical Magazine* I: 289–92. (October 1857) (Boston). The date should be 1777 for the letters.

Wilkinson, James. *Memoirs of My Own Times.* 3 vols. Philadelphia, 1816.

Willcox, William B., ed. *The American Rebellion: Sir Henry Clinton's Narrative of the Campaigns, 1775–1782.* New Haven: Yale University Press, 1954.

Wilson, James. *Considerations on the Nature and Extent of the Legislative Authority of the British Parliament.* Philadelphia, 1774.

General Works

Adams, Randolph G. *Political Ideas of the American Revolution.* 3rd ed. New York: Barnes & Noble, 1958.

Alden, John R. *General Charles Lee: Traitor or Patriot?* Baton Rouge: Louisiana State University Press, 1951.

———. *A History of the American Revolution.* New York: Knopf, 1969.

Anderson, Troyer S. *The Command of the Howe Brothers during the American Revolution.* London: 1936.

Atkinson, C. T. "British Forces in North America, 1774–1781: Their Distribution and Strength." *Society for Army Historical Research Journal* 16 (London, 1937).

Billias, George A., ed. *George Washington's Generals*. New York: William Morrow, 1964.

Bolton, Charles K. *The Private Soldier Under Washington*. New York, 1902.

Boutell, Lewis H. *Life of Roger Sherman*. Chicago, 1896.

Brown, Gerald S. *The American Secretary; The Colonial Policy of Lord George Germain, 1775–1778*. Ann Arbor: University of Michigan Press, 1963.

Buck, Martin H. *Revolutionary Enigma: A Reappraisal of General Philip Schuyler of New York*. Port Washington, N.Y.: Kennikat Press, 1969.

Burnett, Edmund C. *The Continental Congress*. New York: Macmillan, 1941.

Chittenden, L. E. *The Capture of Ticonderoga*. Rutland, Vt., 1872.

Dangerfield, George. *Chancellor Robert R. Livingston*. New York: Harcourt, Brace, 1960.

Doniol, Henri. *Histoire de la participation de la France à l'établissement des Etats-Unis d'Amérique*. 6 vols. Paris, 1884–92.

Ferguson, E. James. *The Power of the Purse; A History of American Public Finance, 1776–1790* Chapel Hill: University of North Carolina Press, 1961.

Flexner, James T. *George Washington*. Boston: Little, Brown, 1965–72.

Fortescue, Sir John. *A History of the British Army*. 14 vols. London, 1902.

Freeman, Douglas Southall. *George Washington*. 7 vols. New York: Scribner's, 1948–57.

French, Allen. *The First Year of the American Revolution*. Boston: Houghton Mifflin, 1934.

Frothingham, Richard. *History of the Siege of Boston*. Boston, 1851.

Gerlach, Donald R. *Philip Schuyler and the American Revolution in New York, 1733–1777*. Lincoln, Neb.: University of Nebraska Press, 1964.

Gordon, William. *The History of the Rise, Progress and Establishment of the Independence of the United States of America*. 4 vols. London, 1788.

Gottschalk, Louis. *Lafayette Joins the American Army*. Chicago: University of Chicago Press, 1937.

Greene, George W. *The Life of Nathanael Greene, Major-Gen. in the Army of the Revolution*. 3 vols. New York, 1867–71.

Hatch, Louis C. *The Administration of the American Revolutionary Army*. New York, 1904.

Heitman, Francis B. *Historical Register of the Officers of the Revolution*. Washington, 1893.

Higgenbotham, Donald. *The War of American Independence: Military Policies, and Practice, 1763–1789*. New York: Macmillan, 1971.

Jellison, Charles. *Ethan Allen: Frontier Rebel*. Syracuse: Syracuse University Press, 1969.

BIBLIOGRAPHY 243

Jensen, Merrill. *The Articles of Confederation.* Madison: University of Wisconsin Press, 1940.

Johnson, Allen, and Malone, Dumas, eds. *Dictionary of American Biography.* 20 vols. New York: Scribner's, 1928–36.

Johnson, Victor L. "The American Commissariat During the Revolution." Ph.D. thesis, University of Pennsylvania, 1939.

Jones, Thomas, and DeLancy, Edward F., eds. *History of New York during the Revolutionary War.* 2 vols. New York, 1879.

Knollenberg, Bernhard. *Washington and the Revolution: A Reappraisal.* New York: Macmillan, 1940.

Lewis, Berkeley R. *Small Arms and Ammunition in the United States Service.* Washington: Smithsonian Institution, 1956.

Lossing, Benjamin J. *The Life and Times of Philip Schuyler.* 2 vols. New York, 1860.

Mackesy, Piers. *The War for America, 1775–1783.* Cambridge, Mass.: Harvard University Press, 1964.

Main, Jackson Turner. *The Sovereign States, 1775–1783.* New York: New Viewpoints, 1973.

Martin, James Kirby. *Men in Rebellion: Higher Governmental Leaders and the Coming of the American Revolution.* New Brunswick: Rutgers University Press, 1973.

Melish, John. *A Military & Topographical Atlas of the United States.* Philadelphia, 1813.

Mintz, Max M. *Gouverneur Morris and the American Revolution.* Norman, Okla.: University of Oklahoma Press, 1970.

Montross, Lynn. *Rag, Tag, and Bobtail: The Story of the Continental Army, 1775–1783.* New York: Harper & Brothers, 1952.

Patterson, Samuel W. *Horatio Gates, Defender of American Liberties.* New York: Columbia University Press, 1941.

Pickering, Octavius, and Upham, Charles. *The Life of Timothy Pickering.* 4 vols. Boston, 1867–73.

Quarles, Benjamin. *The Negro in the American Revolution.* Chapel Hill: University of North Carolina Press, 1961.

Rodenbough, Theo., and Haskin, William, eds. *The Army of the United States: Historical Sketches of Staff and Line with Portraits of Generals-in-Chief.* New York, 1896.

Ropp, Theodore. *War in the Modern World.* Durham, N.C.: Duke University Press, 1959.

Sanders, Jennings B. *Evolution of Executive Departments of the Continental Congress, 1774–1789.* Chapel Hill: University of North Carolina Press, 1935.

Shy, John. *Toward Lexington: The Role of the British Army in the Coming of the American Revolution.* Princeton: Princeton University Press, 1965.

Smith, Justin H. *Our Struggle for the Fourteenth Colony: Canada, and the American Revolution.* 2 vols. New York, 1907.

Steele, Russell V. "Backwoods Warfare, the Rangers and Light Infantry in North America, 1755–1778." *Bulletin of the Fort Ticonderoga Museum* (July 1947): 24–32.

Swett, Samuel. *History of the Bunker Hill Battle.* Boston, 1827.

Thayer, Theodore. *Nathanael Greene: Strategist of the American Revolution.* New York: Twayne, 1960.

Treacy, M. F. *Prelude to Yorktown: The Southern Campaign of Nathanael Greene, 1780–1781.* Chapel Hill: University of North Carolina Press, 1963.

Trevelyan, Sir George O. *The American Revolution.* 4 vols. London and New York, 1905–12.

Tucker, Glenn. *Mad Anthony Wayne and the New Nation.* Harrisburg, Pa.: Stackpole Books, 1973.

Tuckerman, Bayard. *The Life of General Philip Schuyler, 1733–1804.* New York, 1903.

Valentine, Alan. *Lord North.* 2 vols. Norman, Okla.: University of Oklahoma Press, 1967.

———. *Lord Stirling.* New York: Oxford University Press, 1969.

Wallace, Willard M. *Appeal to Arms: A Military History of the Revolution.* New York: Harper & Brothers, 1951.

Ward, Christopher. *The War of the Revolution.* 2 vols. New York: Macmillan, 1952.

Willcox, William B. "The British Road to Yorktown: A Study in Divided Command." *American Historical Review* 52 (October 1946): 1–35.

———. "British Strategy in America, 1778." *Journal of Modern History* 19 (June 1947): 97–121.

———. *Portrait of a General: Sir Henry Clinton in the War of Independence.* New York: Knopf, 1964.

———. "Too Many Cooks: British Planning Before Saratoga." *Journal of British Studies* 2 (1962): 56–90.

Index

THE POLITICS OF COMMAND
IN THE AMERICAN REVOLUTION

was composed in 10-point Linotype Times Roman, leaded two points,
with display type handset in Times Roman
by Joe Mann Associates, York, Pennsylvania;
printed offset by Wickersham Printing Company, Lancaster, Pennsylvania,
on Perkins and Squier 55-pound Litho;
Smyth-sewn and bound in Columbia Triton Shantung over boards
by Vail-Ballou Press, Binghamton, New York;
and published by

SYRACUSE UNIVERSITY PRESS

Syracuse, New York 13210